Teach Yourself VISUALLY

iPhone® 11, 11 Pro, and 11 Pro Max

by Guy Hart-Davis

Visual

A Wiley Brand

Teach Yourself VISUALLY™ iPhone® 11, 11 Pro, and 11 Pro Max

Published by
John Wiley & Sons, Inc.
9200 Keystone Crossing, Suite 800
Indianapolis, IN 46240

www.wiley.com

Published simultaneously in Canada

Library of Congress Control Number: 2020930144

ISBN: 978-1-119-68388-9

Manufactured in the United States of America

V10017216_012820

Trademark Acknowledgments

Contact Us

For general information on our other products and services please contact our Customer Care Department within the U.S. at 877-762-2974, outside the U.S. at 317-572-3993 or fax 317-572-4002.

For technical support please visit https://hub.wiley.com/community/support.

Sales | Contact Wiley at (877) 762-2974 or fax (317) 572-4002.

About the Author

Guy Hart-Davis is the author of more than 150 computer books, including *Teach Yourself VISUALLY MacBook Pro and MacBook Air, Teach Yourself VISUALLY iPad*, and *Teach Yourself VISUALLY Android Phones and Tablets, 2nd Edition*.

Author's Acknowledgments

My thanks go to the many people who turned my manuscript into the highly graphical book you are holding. In particular, I thank Devon Lewis for asking me to write the book; Lynn Northrup for keeping me on track; Kim Cofer for skillfully editing the text; Doug Holland for reviewing the book for technical accuracy and contributing helpful suggestions; and SPi Global for laying out the book.

How to Use This Book

Who This Book Is For

This book is for the reader who has never used this particular technology or software application. It is also for readers who want to expand their knowledge.

The Conventions in This Book

1 Steps

This book uses a step-by-step format to guide you easily through each task. **Numbered steps** are actions you must do; **bulleted steps** clarify a point, step, or optional feature; and **indented steps** give you the result.

2 Notes

Notes give additional information — special conditions that may occur during an operation, a situation that you want to avoid, or a cross reference to a related area of the book.

3 Icons and Buttons

Icons and buttons show you exactly what you need to click to perform a step.

4 Tips

Tips offer additional information, including warnings and shortcuts.

5 Bold

Bold type shows command names, options, and text or numbers you must type.

6 Italics

Italic type introduces and defines a new term.

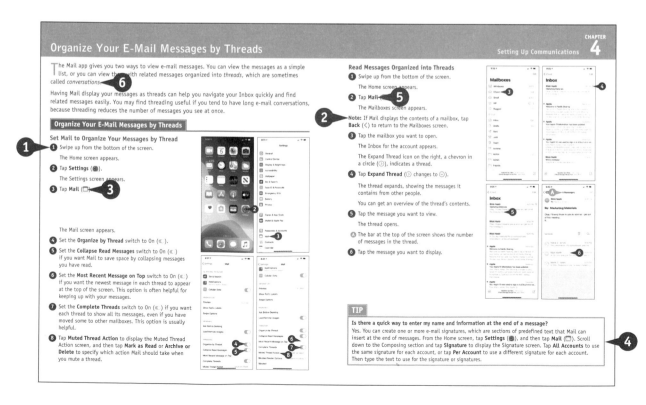

Table of Contents

Chapter 3   Using Voice, Accessibility, and Continuity

Chapter 4   Setting Up Communications

Table of Contents

Table of Contents

Chapter 11   Working with Photos and Video

Chapter 12   Advanced Features and Troubleshooting

CHAPTER 1

Getting Started with Your iPhone

In this chapter, you set up your iPhone to work with your computer or iCloud. You choose items to sync and learn to use the iPhone interface.

Identify and Compare the iPhone Models

The iPhone is a series of hugely popular smartphones designed by Apple. As of this writing, Apple sells six iPhone models that differ in size, power, features, and price. This section explains the six models, their common features, and their differences to enable you to distinguish them and choose among them.

Understanding the Six iPhone Models

As of this writing, Apple sells six iPhone models. Three models are in the iPhone 11 family, which Apple introduced in 2019. The base model in this family is called simply iPhone 11. The other two models are in the Pro line, and have different sizes. The iPhone 11 Pro is the smaller of the two, and the iPhone 11 Pro Max is the larger.

Which iPhone is right for you?

iPhone 11 Pro
Starting at $999

iPhone 11
Starting at $699

iPhone XR
Starting at $599

iPhone 8
Starting at $449

- **iPhone 11 Pro Max.** The Pro Max has the largest screen of the iPhone models — a 6.5-inch OLED screen with 2688×1242-pixel resolution. OLED is the acronym for organic light-emitting diode; these screens are considered top of the range and have a wide viewing angle.

- **iPhone 11 Pro.** The Pro has a 5.8-inch OLED screen with 2436×1125-pixel resolution.

- **iPhone 11.** The iPhone 11 has a 6.1-inch screen with 1792×828-pixel resolution.

These models have a design featuring thin bezels, rounded screen corners, and a "notch" cutout at the middle of the top edge of the screen. The notch contains the front camera and various sensors for features such as Face ID face recognition.

Apple currently continues to sell three iPhones from its previous two generations. The following list explains the models available:

- **iPhone XR.** Introduced in 2018, the iPhone XR has a 6.1-inch screen with 1792×828-pixel resolution. The iPhone XR is similar in size and design to the iPhone 11 — including the thin bezels, round corners, and notch — but contains slightly less powerful hardware and less memory.

- **iPhone 8 and iPhone 8 Plus.** Introduced in 2017, these two models are similar, but the iPhone 8 Plus is physically larger than the iPhone 8. These two iPhones have an older design. There are two primary visual differences between this design and the newer models listed previously. First, these models have thicker bezels and no notch at the top of the screen. Second, below the screen is the Home button, a round button used for navigation and for the Touch ID fingerprint-recognition authentication system.

Understanding the Common Features of the iPhone Models

Each iPhone comes with the Apple EarPods headset, which incorporates a remote control and a microphone, and connects via the Lightning connector at the bottom of the iPhone. None of these iPhone models has a headphone jack; you can connect headphones either wirelessly via Bluetooth or by using an adapter dongle such as Apple's Lightning to 3.5mm Headphone Jack Adapter. Using Apple's headphone adapter prevents you from charging the iPhone via the Lightning port, although you can still charge it wirelessly; you may prefer a third-party adapter that includes a power pass-through.

Each iPhone includes a USB power adapter and a Lightning-to-USB cable. Each iPhone also features wireless charging, which you may find easier and more convenient than using a cable. You will need to get a wireless charger separately.

Each iPhone uses a nano-SIM card to connect to cellular networks but can also use one or more eSIMs, virtual SIM cards that you add electronically.

Each iPhone runs iOS 13, the latest operating system from Apple, which comes with a suite of built-in apps, such as the Safari web browser and the Mail e-mail app. If you buy an older iPhone model, you may need to upgrade it to iOS 13, but this is easy to do.

The iPhone 11 Pro models come in four colors: silver, space gray, gold, and midnight green.

The iPhone 11 models come in six colors: black, white, purple, green, yellow, and (PRODUCT)RED.

The iPhone XR comes in six colors: black, white, blue, coral, yellow, and (PRODUCT)RED.

The iPhone 8 models come in three colors: silver, space gray, and gold.

The iPhone 11 Pro models have triple 12-megapixel cameras on the back and a front-facing 12-megapixel camera with depth-sensing features that enable the Face ID authentication and unlocking system.

The iPhone 11 has dual 12-megapixel cameras on the back. On the front, the iPhone 11 also has a 12-megapixel camera with depth-sensing features for Face ID.

The iPhone XR has a single 12-megapixel camera on the back and a 7-megapixel camera with depth-sensing features on the front.

The iPhone 8 models have a 12-megapixel main camera on the back and a 7-megapixel camera on the front. The iPhone 8 Plus also includes a second camera unit to enable optical zoom and other features. Each iPhone 8 model has a Touch ID fingerprint reader integrated in the Home button.

continued ▶

Apart from physical size and key features, you should consider the storage capacity of the iPhone model you are thinking of buying. Having more storage enables you to install more apps and carry more music, movies, and other files with you. Having plenty of storage is especially important for shooting videos with your iPhone.

Compare the iPhone 11 Models with the Earlier iPhone Models

The iPhone 11 models offer a substantial upgrade over the iPhone XR, the iPhone 8, and the iPhone 8 Plus. The three biggest differences are that the iPhone 11 models have faster processors, better screens, and improved cameras.

On the processor front, the iPhone 11 models have the A13 Bionic chip with third-generation Neural Engine, the iPhone XR has the A12 Bionic chip with second-generation Neural Engine, and the iPhone 8 models have the A11 Bionic chip with Neural Engine. The nomenclature is fair gibberish, but the newer chips and engines are faster and so deliver better performance.

As for screens, the iPhone 11 Pro models have the Super Retina XDR display with HDR and True Tone, the iPhone 11 and iPhone XR have the Liquid Retina HD display with True Tone, and the iPhone 8 models have the Retina HD display with True Tone. Briefly, Super Retina is better than Liquid Retina, which in turn is better than Retina. XDR stands for Extreme Dynamic Range, which gives greater brightness and more natural-looking colors than HDR, which stands for High Dynamic Range. The True Tone feature enables the iPhone to adjust its display colors to match the ambient lighting it detects, making colors appear more consistent in different lighting conditions.

On rear cameras, the iPhone Pro models have triple 12-megapixel cameras: one camera has an ultra–wide-angle lens, the second has a wide-angle lens, and the third has a telephoto lens. The iPhone 11 has dual 12-megapixel cameras, one ultra–wide-angle and the other wide-angle. The iPhone 8 Plus has dual 12-megapixel cameras, one wide-angle and the other telephoto. The iPhone XR and iPhone 8 each have a single 12-megapixel camera.

On front cameras, there is less variation: the iPhone 11 models have a 12-megapixel camera that can shoot video at 4K resolution and 60 frames per second, whereas the iPhone XR and the iPhone 8 models have a 7-megapixel camera that can shoot video at the lower 1080p resolution, also at 60 frames per second.

The iPhone 11 models also have somewhat increased water resistance, but while any improvement is welcome, it may not be relevant to you. In practical terms, the improvements mean the iPhone 8 models should survive 30 minutes in the shallow end of a swimming pool, the iPhone 11 should manage 30-minute immersion in the deep end, and the iPhone 11 Pro models should have no trouble with half an hour in the diving section.

Evaluate iPhone Storage Capacity

The iPhone models are available with different amounts of storage capacity. The following table shows the capacities with sample amounts of contents to give you some idea of what the amounts mean in real terms.

The iPhone 11 Pro models come in 64GB, 256GB, and 512GB capacities.

The iPhone 11 comes in 64GB, 128GB, and 256GB capacities.

The iPhone XR and the iPhone 8 models come in 64GB and 128GB capacities.

Higher capacities command substantially higher prices, so you must decide how much you are prepared to spend. Generally speaking, higher-capacity devices get more use in the long run and are worth the extra cost.

Capacity	Songs	Photos	Video
64GB	5,000	4,000	10 hours
128GB	10,000	8,000	20 hours
256GB	20,000	16,000	40 hours
512GB	40,000	32,000	80 hours

Understanding the Reachability Feature

iOS includes a feature called Reachability to help you use your iPhone with one hand when necessary. With the Reachability feature enabled, swipe down on the bottom edge of the screen to slide the screen down so that you can easily reach the top of it. On the iPhone 8 models, you double-tap **Home** — double-tap rather than double-press — to slide the screen down. After you give a command, the screen slides back up again; if you decide not to give a command, tap **Restore** (▬) to slide the screen back up; on an iPhone 8 model, double-tap **Home** again.

To enable Reachability, first tap **Settings** (⚙), tap **Accessibility** (♿), and then tap **Touch** (✋). Near the top of the Touch screen, set the **Reachability** switch to On (⚪).

Understanding the Live Photos Feature

All of the current iPhone models include a feature called Live Photos that enables you to capture short sections of video before and after a still photo. After capturing the Live Photo, you can make the video segments play by tapping and holding the photo.

You can view your Live Photos on other Apple devices, such as your iPad or your Mac. You can also use a Live Photo as the wallpaper for your iPhone's lock screen.

With the touchscreen used for most actions, the iPhone 11 has only four other hardware controls: the Side button in the middle of the right side; the Ringer On/Off switch at the top of the left side; and the Volume Up button and Volume Down button, below the Ringer On/Off switch. This section illustrates and explains these controls, plus the methods for unlocking the iPhone and locking it again.

Identify the Hardware Controls

The right side of the iPhone has only one control, a button called the Side button. The Side button has multiple functions on its own and in combination with the Volume Up button and the Volume Down button. The remainder of this section explains how to use the Side button.

The left side of the iPhone has three controls:

Volume Down button

Volume Up button   Side button

Ringer On/Off switch

- The Ringer On/Off switch turns the ringer on and off. Move the switch toward the rear of the iPhone, exposing an orange background, to turn the ringer off. Move the switch to the front again to turn the ringer back on.

- The Volume Up button and Volume Down button enable you to control the volume quickly without having to use the touchscreen. These buttons also work in combination with the Side button for other actions.

Turn Your iPhone On and Off

To turn on your iPhone when it is powered off, press and hold **Side** until the Apple logo appears on-screen, then release the Side button. Your iPhone continues to start, and then the lock screen appears.

To turn off your iPhone, press and hold **Side** and either **Volume Up** or **Volume Down** until the Power Off screen appears, then swipe **slide to power off** (⏻) to the right.

Unlock and Lock Your iPhone

To unlock your iPhone, hold it so the front cameras can scan your face. The iPhone unlocks (🔒 changes to 🔓) and the *Swipe up to open* prompt appears at the bottom of the screen. Swipe up from the bottom of the screen. The iPhone unlocks, and you can start using it.

To lock your iPhone and put it to sleep, press **Side** once. Depending on how the iPhone is configured, the iPhone may also go to sleep automatically after a period of inactivity.

Use Sleep and Wake, Siri, App Store, and Apple Pay

When the iPhone is awake, press **Side** once to put it to sleep. When the iPhone is asleep, press **Side** once to wake it.

At any time, press and hold **Side** to activate Siri, which plays a tone and displays a text prompt asking what you want.

When installing an app from the App Store, double-click **Side** to authenticate yourself via Face ID and continue installing the app.

When making a purchase via Apple Pay, double-click **Side** to authenticate yourself via Face ID and confirm the purchase.

Force the iPhone to Restart

If the iPhone becomes unresponsive, a software problem may have occurred. Wait for a minute or two to see if iOS can resolve the problem.

If the iPhone remains unresponsive, you will need to restart it. Press and hold **Side** and **Volume Down** for several seconds. When the screen turns off, release the buttons. The iPhone then restarts, and the Apple logo appears on-screen.

Install and Set Up iTunes on Windows

To sync your iPhone with your Windows PC, you use the iTunes app, which Apple makes available for free. For Windows 10, the current version of Windows, you download iTunes from the Microsoft Store and install it on your PC.

If you do not have a computer, or you do not want to sync your iPhone with your computer, you can set up and sync your iPhone using Apple's iCloud service. See the section "Set Up and Activate Your iPhone," later in this chapter.

Install and Set Up iTunes on Windows

1 Click **Start** (⊞).

The Start menu opens.

2 Click **Microsoft Store** (🖼).

Note: You can also download iTunes from the Apple website, https://www.apple.com/itunes/.

The Microsoft Store app opens.

3 Click **Search** (Q).

The Search pane opens.

4 Type **itunes**.

A list of matching results appears.

5 Click **iTunes** (🎵).

The iTunes screen appears.

6 Click **Get**.

Note: If the Use Across Your Devices dialog box opens, prompting you to sign in with Microsoft and be able to use iTunes on any compatible device, click **Sign In** if you want to do so. Otherwise, click **No Thanks**.

The Microsoft Store app downloads and installs iTunes.

7 Click **Launch**.

Windows launches iTunes.

On first run, the iTunes Software License Agreement dialog box opens.

8 Read the license agreement, or as much as you can bear.

9 Click **Agree** if you want to proceed.

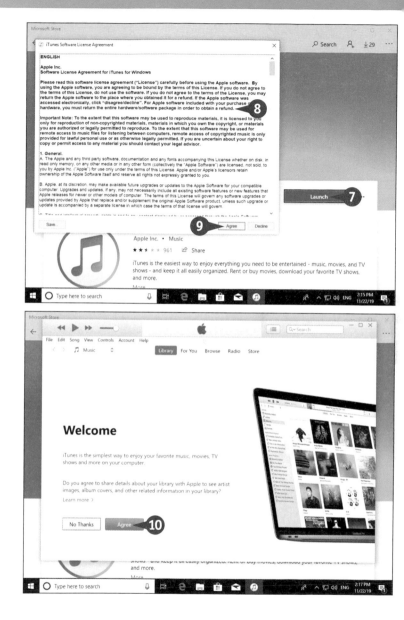

iTunes opens.

Also on first run, the Welcome screen appears, asking if you agree to share details about your library with Apple in order to get artist images, album covers, and other information.

10 Click **Agree** or **No Thanks**, as appropriate.

iTunes opens.

TIP

Can I use other apps to manage my iPhone on my Windows PC?

Yes — various third-party apps are available for managing iPhones, iPads, and the iPod touch on Windows PCs. Some are free apps; others are pay apps.

As a starting point, you might try the iMazing app from www.imazing.com. This app has extensive features for backing up, restoring, and managing iPhones and other devices. Begin with the trial version, which enables you to test the app for free.

Set Up and Activate Your iPhone

Before you can use your iPhone, you must set it up and activate it. First, you choose your language and specify your country or region. You can then either use the Quick Start feature, if you have an iPhone or iPad running iOS 11 or a later version, or continue setup manually. Assuming you continue manually, you connect the iPhone to the Internet through either a Wi-Fi network or the cellular network, choose whether to use Touch ID fingerprint unlocking, and choose a passcode.

Power On Your iPhone

First, power on your iPhone by pressing and holding **Side** — the button on the right side of the iPhone — until the Apple logo appears on-screen. The Hello screen then appears.

Swipe up from the bottom of the screen to start setup. The Language screen appears. Tap the language you want to use, such as **English**.

On the Select Your Country or Region screen that appears, tap your country or region.

Chose Quick Start or Manual Setup, and Connect to Wi-Fi

The Quick Start feature lets you set up your iPhone more quickly by sharing settings from an existing iPhone, iPad, or iPod touch running iOS 11 or a later version. If you have such a device, bring it close to the new iPhone and follow the prompts. If not, tap **Set Up Manually**.

On the Choose a Wi-Fi Network screen, tap the wireless network you want to use; if the Wi-Fi network's name does not appear because the network does not broadcast its name, tap **Choose Another Network**, and then type the network's details. Enter the network password when prompted, and then tap **Join**.

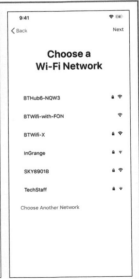

Set Up Face ID

On the Face ID screen, tap **Continue** if you want to set up Face ID now, which is usually the most convenient unlock method; if not, tap **Set Up Later in Settings**. Assuming you proceed, Face ID then walks you through the process of scanning your face twice, either by rotating your head or by moving the iPhone around. If you have difficulty completing Face ID, you can tap **Accessibility Options** at the bottom of the screen, and then tap **Use Partial Circle**.

When Face ID is set up, tap **Continue**.

Create a Passcode

After setting up Face ID, you create a passcode for unlocking your iPhone when Face ID does not work or when iOS requires extra security, such as when the iPhone has restarted. On the Create a Passcode screen, tap the keypad to enter a six-digit numeric passcode, and then re-enter the same passcode when prompted.

If you want to create a different type of passcode, tap **Passcode Options**. In the Passcode Options dialog box, tap **Custom Alphanumeric Code**, **Custom Numeric Code**, or **4-Digit Numeric Code**, as needed. A long custom alphanumeric code is most secure; a long custom numeric code can be highly secure; and a four-digit numeric code is inadvisable.

If you enter an easily guessed passcode, such as *111111* or *abcdef*, iOS warns you and suggests you enter a stronger passcode. Tap **Use Anyway** or **Change Passcode**, as needed.

continued ▶

Set Up and Activate Your iPhone ^(continued)

After setting up Face ID and choosing a passcode, you choose how to complete setting up the iPhone. If you have not used an iOS device before, you can set up the iPhone as a new iPhone. If you have used an iOS device, you can restore an iCloud backup or an iTunes backup of that device to the iPhone. If you have been using an Android device, you can use the Move to iOS app to move data to the iPhone.

Choose How to Set Up Your iPhone

On the Apps & Data screen, you choose between five ways of setting up your iPhone:

- Tap **Restore from iCloud Backup** if you have a backup of your previous iPhone or another iOS device stored in iCloud. Sign in on the iCloud screen that appears, and then continue with the instructions in the next subsection on this page.

- Tap **Restore from Mac or PC** if you have a backup of your previous iPhone or other iOS device on your computer. See the section "Set Up Your iPhone Using Finder or iTunes," later in this chapter, for further details.

- Tap **Transfer Directly from iPhone** if you are upgrading iPhones and have your old iPhone at hand. The Quick Start screen appears, and you can connect the iPhones wirelessly by bringing them close together.

- Tap **Move Data from Android** if you are switching from an Android phone or tablet to the iPhone and you want to transfer data from your old device. You will need to install the Move to iOS app on your Android device. You then run the app, connect the iPhone and Android device by using a pairing code, and choose which data to transfer.

- Tap **Don't Transfer Apps & Data** if you want to set up your iPhone from scratch. Follow the prompts to set up the iPhone manually; see the later subsection, "Set Up Your iPhone Manually," for highlights.

Set Up Your iPhone from an iCloud Backup

Follow the prompts to sign in to iCloud; if you have two-factor authentication enabled, iCloud sends a verification code to your registered device to enable you to authenticate yourself to your new iPhone. On the Terms and Conditions screen, tap **Agree** if you want to proceed.

On the Choose Backup screen, tap the backup you want to use. Then, on the Settings from Your Backup screen, review the settings that you can restore or customize, and tap **Continue** or **Customize Settings**, as appropriate.

Set Up Your iPhone Manually

When you choose to set up your iPhone manually, iOS walks you through a long sequence of configuration screens that enable you to customize how the operating system looks and behaves. The following list explains the key items you configure:

- **Apple Pay.** You can set up Apple's payment system on your iPhone, enabling yourself to make electronic transactions easily, including sending payments to your contacts via the Messages app. If you prefer to set up Apple Pay later, tap **Set Up Later in Wallet**.

- **Siri.** You can set up Apple's voice-driven virtual assistant on your iPhone. Siri enables you to give various commands, such as sending an e-mail message or a text message, and asking for a wide variety of information — for example, getting directions in the Maps app or looking up information on WolframAlpha or on the web. If you prefer not to set up Siri now, tap **Set Up Later in Settings**.

- **Appearance.** iOS gives you the choice between a Light appearance and a Dark appearance. During setup, you choose an appearance on the Appearance screen. The appearance you choose controls how much of the iOS interface appears. Tap **Light** (changes to ✅) or **Dark** (changes to ✅) to see which you prefer, and then tap **Continue**. You can subsequently change appearance by tapping **Settings** (⚙️) on the Home screen, tapping **Display & Brightness** (AA), and then working on the Display & Brightness screen. Here, you can also set the **Automatic** switch to On (◯) and specify the schedule — either **Sunset to Sunrise** or **Custom Schedule** — on which you want iOS to switch appearances automatically.

 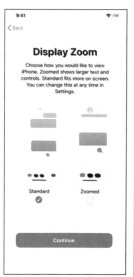

- **Display Zoom.** iOS offers two views, Standard View and Zoomed View. During setup, you choose a view on the Display Zoom screen. Tap **Standard** (changes to ✅) or **Zoomed** (changes to ✅) to compare the two views, and tap **Continue** once you have made your choice. You can subsequently change views by tapping **Settings** (⚙️) on the Home screen, tapping **Display & Brightness** (AA), tapping **View** on the Display & Brightness screen, and using the controls on the Display Zoom screen.

Set Up Your iPhone Using Finder or iTunes

If you want to manage your iPhone from your Mac, you can set it up using Finder on macOS Catalina or iTunes on an earlier version of macOS. If you want to manage your iPhone from your Windows PC, you can set it up using iTunes. You can either restore a backup to the device or set up the iPhone from scratch using Finder or iTunes. This example shows macOS Catalina.

When setting up your iPhone for the first time, you can restore it from a backup of another iPhone — for example, your previous iPhone. If you have already set up this iPhone, you can restore it from its own backup.

Set Up Your iPhone Using Finder or iTunes

1 Begin setup as explained in the section "Set Up and Activate Your iPhone," earlier in this chapter.

2 On the Apps & Data screen, tap **Restore from Mac or PC**.

The Connect to Computer screen appears.

3 Connect your iPhone to your computer via the USB cable.

The Connected to Computer screen appears on your iPhone.

A On macOS Catalina, click **Finder** ( ) on the Dock to open a Finder window if one does not open automatically showing the iPhone's management screens, then click the iPhone.

On your computer, a Finder window opens or iTunes opens or becomes active.

The Welcome to Your New iPhone screen appears.

4 Make sure the **Restore from this backup** radio button is selected (●).

5 Click the pop-up menu button ( ) and select the appropriate iPhone from the menu.

6 Click **Continue**.

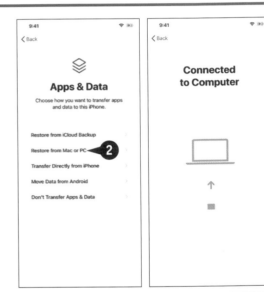

iTunes restores your iPhone from the backup.

When the restore is complete, your iPhone restarts.

The Restore Completed screen appears on the iPhone.

7 Tap **Continue**.

Your iPhone's control screens appear in the Finder window or iTunes window.

You can now choose sync settings for the iPhone as explained in the next section, "Choose Which Items to Sync from Your Computer."

TIP

How do I set up my iPhone from scratch using Finder or iTunes?
On the Apps & Data screen, tap **Restore from Mac or PC**, and then connect your iPhone to your computer via the USB cable. When the Welcome to Your New iPhone screen appears in Finder or iTunes on your computer, click **Set up as new iPhone** (○ changes to ◉). Click **Continue**. On the Sync screen that appears, click **Get Started**. The iPhone's management screens appear, and you can set up synchronization as described in the next section, "Choose Which Items to Sync from Your Computer."

Choose Which Items to Sync from Your Computer

After specifying that you will use Finder or iTunes to sync your iPhone, as explained in the previous section, "Set Up Your iPhone Using Finder or iTunes," you use the iPhone's control screens in Finder or iTunes to choose which items to sync. On the General tab in Finder or the Summary tab in iTunes, you can change your iPhone's name, specify the backup location, and set general options for controlling syncing.

Choose Which Items to Sync from Your Computer

Connect Your iPhone and Choose Options on the General Tab or Summary Tab

1 Connect your iPhone to your computer via the USB cable.

Ⓐ On macOS Catalina, click **Finder** (🙂) on the Dock to open a Finder window if one does not open automatically showing the iPhone's management screens, then click the iPhone.

On macOS Catalina, a Finder window opens. On earlier macOS versions or on Windows, the iTunes window appears.

Note: If your iPhone's control screens do not automatically appear in iTunes, click **iPhone** (📱) on the navigation bar at the top of the screen.

2 On macOS Catalina, click **General**; on earlier macOS or Windows, click **Summary** in the sidebar on the left.

3 To change the iPhone's name, click the existing name, type the new name, and press Enter or Return.

4 Click a radio button (◯ changes to ◉) to specify where to back up your iPhone.

5 If you choose to back up to this computer, click **Encrypt local backup** or **Encrypt iPhone backup** (☐ changes to ✔).

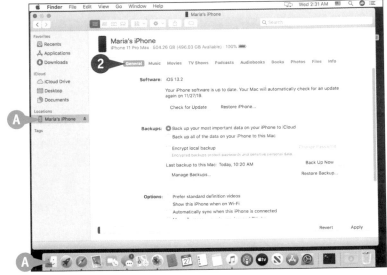

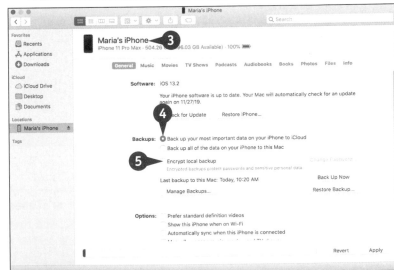

A dialog opens for setting a password.

6 Type a password in the Password box and again in the Verify Password box.

7 On a Mac, click **Remember this password in my keychain** (☐ changes to ☑) if you want to save the password in your keychain.

8 Click **Set Password** to close the dialog.

9 Click **Automatically sync when this iPhone is connected** (☐ changes to ☑) if you want to sync your iPhone automatically when you connect it.

10 Click **Manually manage music, movies, and TV shows** (☐ changes to ☑) if you want to load these items on your iPhone manually rather than using the automated features in Finder or iTunes.

11 Click **Convert higher bit rate songs to AAC** (☐ changes to ☑) if you want to compress larger songs to fit more on your iPhone. In the pop-up menu, choose the bit rate and encoding type, such as **128 Kbps AAC**.

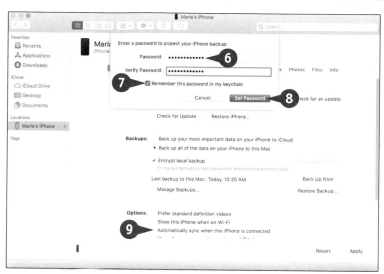

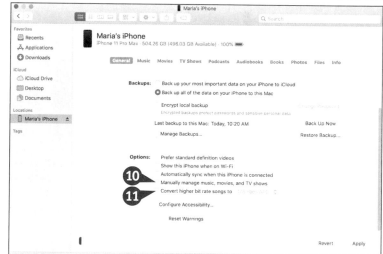

TIP

Should I back up my iPhone to my computer or to iCloud?

If you plan to use your iPhone mostly with your computer, back up the iPhone to the computer. Doing so makes iTunes store a full backup of the iPhone on the computer, so you can restore all the data to your iPhone, or to a replacement iPhone, if necessary. You can also encrypt the backup; doing so enables you to store and restore your passwords. To keep your data safe, you must back up your computer as well. For example, you can use Time Machine to back up a Mac.

Backing up your iPhone to iCloud enables you to access the backups from anywhere via the Internet, but make sure your iCloud account has enough storage to contain the backups. An iCloud backup stores less information than an iTunes backup.

continued ▶

Backing up your iPhone to your computer is convenient but takes up space. You may want to delete old backups manually to reclaim space.

You can easily choose which items to sync to your iPhone. By selecting the iPhone in the sidebar in Finder on macOS Catalina and clicking the appropriate tab, or by selecting the iPhone on the navigation bar in iTunes and then clicking the appropriate item in the Settings area of the Source list, you can specify which music, movies, books, and other items to sync from your computer.

Choose Which Items to Sync from Your Computer (continued)

Manage Your iPhone Backups

1 Click **General** on macOS Catalina or **Summary** on earlier macOS versions or Windows.

2 Click **Manage Backups**.

A dialog opens, showing a list of backups.

3 Click the backup you want to delete.

4 Click **Delete Backup**.

5 Click **OK**.

The dialog closes.

Choose Which Content to Sync

Note: This section uses the Music category to illustrate choosing content to sync. The controls in most of the other categories — such as Movies, TV Shows, and Podcasts — work in the same way, although the specific controls vary.

1 Click the category or tab, such as **Music**.

The contents of the category or tab appear.

2 Click **Sync Music** (☐ changes to ☑).

The remaining controls become enabled.

3 To load a selection of music, click **Selected artists, albums, genres, and playlists** (◯ changes to ●) instead of **Entire music library**.

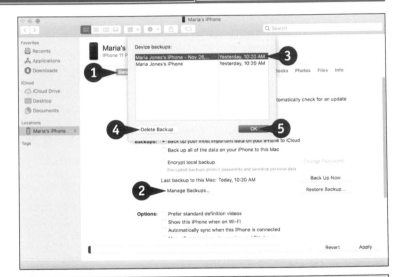

④ Click **Include videos** (☐ changes to ☑)
if you want to include music videos.

⑤ Click **Automatically fill free space with
songs** (☐ changes to ☑) only if you
want to put as much music as possible on
your iPhone.

Note: Filling free space with songs may limit
your ability to shoot photos or videos.

⑥ Click **Artists**, **Albums**, **Genres**, or
Playlists.

That type of content appears.

⑦ Click the check box (☐ changes to ☑)
for each artist, album, genre, or playlist
to include.

Apply Your Changes and Sync

Ⓑ If a content category is being synced
via iCloud, you cannot sync it via Finder
or iTunes. To turn off iCloud sync, tap
Settings (⚙) on the iPhone's Home
screen; tap **Apple ID**, the button bearing
your name; tap **iCloud** (☁); and then use
the controls in the Apps Using iCloud list.

① Click **Apply** or **Sync**, depending on
which button appears.

iTunes syncs the items to your iPhone.

Ⓒ The readout shows you the sync progress.

② When the sync finishes, disconnect your iPhone.

TIP

How can I fit more content on my iPhone?

You cannot install a memory card to increase your iPhone's storage capacity, but you can use the iPhone
Storage feature to remove items you do not need.

Tap **Settings** (⚙) on the Home screen to display the Settings screen, and then tap **General** (⚙). On the
General screen, tap **iPhone Storage** to display the iPhone Storage screen. You can then follow suggestions
in the Recommendations box, such as tapping **Enable** for Optimize Photos or for Offload Unused Apps, or
tap buttons in the lower section to see which apps and files are consuming the most space.

Explore the Interface and Launch Apps

After you set up your iPhone with iCloud or iTunes, you are ready to start using the device. When you wake the iPhone from sleep, it displays the lock screen. You then unlock the iPhone to reach the Home screen, which contains icons for running the apps installed on the iPhone.

You can quickly launch an app by tapping its icon on the Home screen. From the app, you can return to the Home screen by swiping up from the bottom of the screen. You can then launch another app as needed.

Explore the Interface and Launch Apps

1 Tap the screen.

Note: You can also press **Side** to wake the iPhone.

The iPhone's screen lights up.

The lock screen appears.

2 Raise the iPhone, pointing the screen at your face.

Face ID scans your face and attempts to match it to the stored data. If it succeeds, the iPhone unlocks; if it fails, the iPhone prompts you to enter your passcode.

Note: If the iPhone prompts you to enter your passcode, do so.

Ⓐ The iPhone unlocks.

3 Swipe up from the bottom of the screen with one finger.

The Home screen appears.

Ⓑ The iPhone has two or more Home screen pages. The gray dots at the bottom of the Home screen show how many Home screen pages you have. The white dot indicates the current Home screen page.

4 Tap **Notes** (⚊).

The Notes app opens.

Note: If you chose to sync notes with your iPhone, the synced notes appear in the Notes app. Otherwise, the list is empty until you create a note.

5 Tap **New** (✏️).

A new note opens, and the on-screen keyboard appears.

6 Type a short note by tapping the keys.

C If the middle button in the suggestion bar shows the word you want, tap Spacebar to accept it. If one of the other buttons shows the right word, tap that button.

7 Tap **Done**.

The on-screen keyboard closes.

8 Tap **Back** (‹). This button shows the name of the folder, such as All iCloud.

D The Notes list appears, with your note in it.

9 Swipe up from the bottom of the screen.

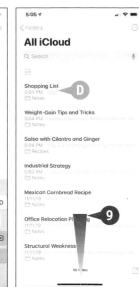

The Home screen appears again.

10 Swipe left to display the second Home screen page.

Note: You can also tap at the right end of the row of dots on the Home screen to move one screen to the right. Tap at the left end to move one screen to the left.

You can now launch another app by tapping its icon.

11 Press the **Side** button.

Your iPhone goes to sleep.

Where do I get more apps to perform other tasks?
You can find an amazingly wide selection of apps on Apple's App Store. Some apps are completely free, whereas other free-to-download apps have "in-app purchases" that make you pay for premium features. Other apps are ones you must pay for, either as a single payment or as a subscription payment. See Chapter 7 for instructions on finding and downloading the apps you need.

Using Cover Sheet and Today View

Your iPhone handles many different types of alerts, such as missed phone calls, text messages, and invitations to events such as meetings. Your iPhone integrates these alerts into Cover Sheet so that you can review them easily.

The iPhone's Today View enables you to view snippets of important and helpful information, such as weather, calendar appointments, and stock updates. You can access Today View either via Cover Sheet or directly from the Home screen.

Using Cover Sheet and Today View

Open Cover Sheet and Deal with Notifications

1 Swipe down from the top of the screen.

Cover Sheet appears.

Note: See the section "Choose Which Apps Can Give Notifications" in Chapter 2 for instructions on customizing the notifications that appear on Cover Sheet.

A You can tap **Clear** (❌) to clear all notifications in a category such as Notification Center.

2 To remove a single notification, swipe it left.

Action buttons for the notification appear.

B You can tap **View** to view the notification in its app.

C You can tap **Manage** to take other actions with the app that gave the notification.

3 Tap **Clear**.

The notification disappears from Cover Sheet.

4 Tap and hold a notification.

The pop-up panel opens, together with action buttons.

5 Tap the action you want to take. For example, for an e-mail message, tap **Mark as Read** to mark the message as read.

Note: To go to the app that raised a notification, tap the notification.

6 When you finish working on Cover Sheet, swipe up from the bottom of the screen.

The Home screen appears.

Open Today View

1 Swipe up from the bottom of the screen.

The Home screen appears.

Note: If the Home screen page that appears is not the first page, press **Home** again or swipe up again to display the first page.

2 Swipe right.

D You can also tap the gray dot at the bottom of the screen.

Today View appears.

Note: You can customize the selection of widgets in Today View. See the section "Customize Today View" in Chapter 2 for details.

3 Swipe up.

Other items appear.

E You can tap a widget to go straight to the related app.

F You can tap an item such as a reminder to mark it as done.

4 Swipe left.

The Home screen appears.

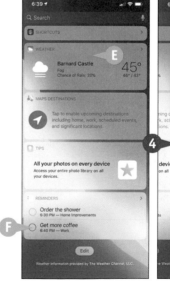

TIP

What happens if I receive a notification when my iPhone is locked?

This depends on the type of notification. For most types of notifications, your iPhone displays an alert on the lock screen to alert you to the notification. Unlocking your iPhone while the alert is showing takes you directly to the notification in whatever app it belongs to — for example, to an instant message in the Messages app.

Using Control Center

Control Center puts your iPhone's most essential controls at your fingertips. From Control Center, you can turn Airplane Mode, Wi-Fi, Bluetooth, Do Not Disturb Mode, and Orientation Lock on or off; control music playback and volume and direct your iPhone's audio and video output to AirPlay devices; change the setting for the AirDrop sharing feature; and quickly access the Flashlight, Clock, Calculator, and Camera apps. Control Center appears as a pane that you open by swiping upward from the bottom of the screen on the Home screen or in most apps.

Using Control Center

Open Control Center

1 Swipe down from the upper-right corner of the screen.

Control Center opens.

A You can drag the **Brightness** slider to control screen brightness. Press the **Brightness** slider to display a larger slider and the Night Shift icon (⬛), which you can tap to turn Night Shift on or off. See the section "Configure Night Shift and Display Zoom" in Chapter 2 for information on Night Shift.

B You can drag the **Volume** slider to control audio volume.

Control Essential Settings

1 Tap **Airplane Mode** (⬛ or ⬛) to turn Airplane Mode on (⬛) or off (⬛).

2 Tap **Wi-Fi** (⬛ or ⬛) to turn Wi-Fi on (⬛) or off (⬛).

3 Tap **Cellular Data** (⬛ or ⬛) to turn Cellular Data on (⬛) or off (⬛).

4 Tap **Bluetooth** (⬛ or ⬛) to turn Bluetooth on (⬛) or off (⬛).

5 Tap **Do Not Disturb** (⬛ or ⬛) to turn Do Not Disturb Mode on (⬛) or off (⬛).

6 Tap **Orientation Lock** (⬛ or ⬛) to turn Orientation Lock on (⬛) or off (⬛).

7 Tap and hold the **Communications** box.

The Communications panel opens.

8 Tap **AirDrop** (⬛) to change the AirDrop setting.

9 Tap **Personal Hotspot** (⬛ or ⬛) to turn Personal Hotspot on (⬛) or off (⬛).

10 Tap outside the Communications panel.

The Communications panel closes.

Choose an AirPlay Device for Audio

C Tap the song information to go to the song in the Music app.

D Tap **Previous** (◄◄) to go back to the start of the song. Tap again to play the previous song.

E Tap **Next** (►►) to play the next song.

F Tap **Pause** (❚❚) to pause playback.

1 Press the Audio box firmly.

The Audio panel opens.

G You can drag the playhead to move through the song.

2 Tap **AirPlay** (◉).

The list of AirPlay devices appears.

3 Tap the audio device to use for output.

The iPhone starts playing audio on that device.

4 Tap the song name.

The Now Playing On panel closes.

5 Tap the screen outside the Audio panel.

The Audio panel closes.

6 Tap at the bottom of the screen.

Control Center closes.

What are the buttons at the bottom of Control Center?

Tap **Flashlight** (🔦) to turn on the Flashlight. Tap and hold **Flashlight** (🔦) to display the Flashlight panel, which lets you choose among four brightnesses. Tap **Timer** (⏱) to display the Timer screen in the Clock app. Tap and hold **Timer** (⏱) to display the Timer panel, which enables you to set timers for preset times from 1 minute up to 2 hours. Tap **Calculator** (🧮) to display the Calculator app; tap and hold **Calculator** (🧮) to get the result of the last calculation. Tap **Camera** (📷) to display the Camera app. Tap and hold **Camera** (📷) to display the Camera panel, which contains commands such as **Take Selfie** and **Record Video**.

CHAPTER 2

Personalizing Your iPhone

To make your iPhone work the way you prefer, you can configure its many settings. In this chapter, you learn how to control iCloud sync, notifications, audio preferences, screen brightness, and other key aspects of the iPhone's behavior.

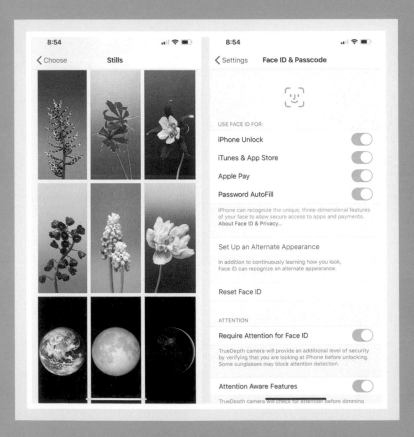

Find the Settings You Need

The iOS operating system includes many settings that enable you to configure your iPhone to work the way you prefer. The central place for manipulating settings is the Settings app, which contains settings for the iPhone's system software, the apps the iPhone includes, and third-party apps you have added. To reach the settings, you first display the Settings screen and then the category of settings you want to configure.

Find the Settings You Need

Display the Settings Screen

1 Swipe up from the bottom of the screen.

The Home screen appears.

2 Tap **Settings** (⚙).

The Settings screen appears.

Ⓐ You can tap **Search** (🔍) and type a setting name or keyword to locate the setting. You may need to drag down the screen to reveal the Search bar.

Ⓑ The Apple ID button, which shows your Apple ID name, gives access to settings for your Apple ID and your accounts for iCloud, iTunes, and the App Store.

Ⓒ The top section of the Settings screen contains settings you are likely to use frequently, such as Airplane Mode, Wi-Fi, and Bluetooth.

3 Tap and drag up to scroll down the screen.

Ⓓ This section contains settings for built-in apps and features developed by Apple.

4 Tap and drag up to scroll farther down the screen. You can also swipe up to move more quickly.

Ⓔ This section contains settings for apps you install. These apps can be either from Apple or from third-party developers.

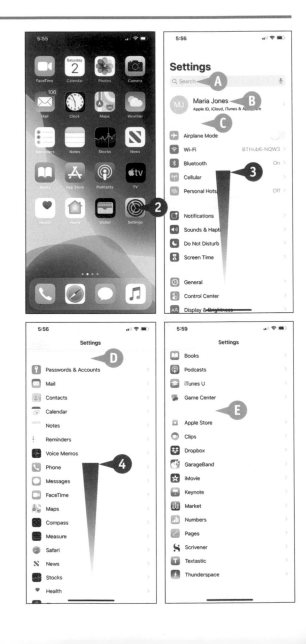

Display a Settings Screen

1 On the Settings screen, tap the button for the settings category you want to display. For example, tap **Sounds & Haptics** (🔊) to display the Sounds and Haptics screen.

2 Tap **Settings** (<) when you are ready to return to the Settings screen.

Note: Tap at the very top of the screen — for example, tap the clock readout or the battery icon — to scroll quickly to the top of the screen. This shortcut action works in most iOS apps.

Display the Settings for an App

1 On the Settings screen, tap the button for the app whose settings you want to display. For example, tap **Safari** (🧭) to display the Safari settings.

2 Tap **Settings** (<) when you are ready to return to the Settings screen.

3 Swipe up from the bottom of the screen.

The Home screen appears again.

Note: When you next open the Settings app, it displays the screen you were last using. For convenience, it is usually best to return to the main Settings screen when you finish choosing settings.

TIP

Where do I find other settings for an app?

As well as the settings that you access by tapping the button bearing the app's name on the Settings screen, some apps include settings that you configure directly within the app. For such apps, look for a Settings icon or menu item.

To configure notifications for an app, tap **Notifications** (🔲) on the Settings screen, and then tap the app's button. To configure Location Services settings for an app, tap **Privacy** (✋) on the Settings screen, tap **Location Services** (➤), and then tap the app's button.

Choose Which iCloud Items to Sync

Apple's iCloud service enables you to sync many types of data — such as your e-mail account details, your contacts, and your calendars and reminders — online so you can access them from any of your devices. You can also use the Find My iPhone feature to locate your iPhone when it goes missing. To use iCloud, you set your iPhone to use your Apple ID, and then choose which features to use.

Choose Which iCloud Items to Sync

1 Swipe up from the bottom of the screen.

The Home screen appears.

2 Tap **Settings** (⚙).

The Settings screen appears.

3 Tap the Apple ID button. This button shows the name you have set for your Apple ID.

4 Tap **iCloud** (☁).

The iCloud screen appears.

5 In the Apps Using iCloud section, set each app's switch to On (⬤) or Off (⬤), as needed.

6 Tap **Photos** (✿).

The Photos screen appears.

7 Set the **iCloud Photos** switch to On (⬤) to store all your photos in iCloud.

8 Tap **Optimize iPhone Storage** to store lower-resolution versions of photos on your iPhone to save space. Tap **Download and Keep Originals** if you prefer to keep original, full-quality photos on your iPhone.

9 Set the **Upload to My Photo Stream** switch to On (⬤) to upload photos to your photo stream.

10 Set the **Shared Albums** switch to On (⬤) to use the Shared Albums feature.

11 Tap **iCloud** (〈).

The iCloud screen appears again.

12 Swipe up to scroll down to the lower part of the screen.

13 Set the **iCloud Drive** switch to On (⬤) to enable iCloud Drive.

14 In the next two sections, set each app's switch to On (⬤) or Off ( ) to control whether the app can use iCloud.

A You can tap **Look Me Up** to control which apps can look you up by your Apple ID.

B You can tap **Mail** to change your name in outgoing iCloud messages or choose advanced settings.

15 Swipe down to scroll up until iCloud Drive appears at the bottom of the screen.

16 Tap **Keychain** (🔑) to display the Keychain screen, set the **iCloud Keychain** switch to On (⬤), and then create a security code if prompted to do so.

17 Tap **Find My iPhone** (◉) to display the Find My iPhone screen, set the **Find My iPhone** switch to On (⬤), and set the **Send Last Location** switch to On (⬤) or Off ( ), as necessary.

18 Tap **iCloud Backup** (◉).

The Backup screen appears.

19 Set the **iCloud Backup** switch to On (⬤).

20 Tap **iCloud** (〈).

The iCloud screen appears again.

TIPS

How much space does iCloud provide?

iCloud provides 5GB of space for a free account. Content and apps you acquire from Apple do not count against this space, nor do your Photo Stream photos or songs included in iTunes Match — but Shared Albums do count. You can buy more space by tapping **Manage Storage**, and then tapping **Buy More Storage** on the iCloud Storage screen that appears.

Should I turn on Find My iPhone?

Yes. Find My iPhone enables you to locate your iPhone when you misplace it or learn where it is when someone takes it. It also prevents someone else from activating your iPhone on his or her own account.

Choose Which Apps Can Give Notifications

S ome iPhone apps can notify you of events that occur, such as messages arriving or updates becoming available. You can choose which notifications an app gives or prevent an app from giving notifications. You can also control notification previews and choose which notifications appear on the lock screen and in Notification Center.

iPhone apps use three types of notifications: badges on app icons, persistent banners, and temporary banners. See the tip for details.

Choose Which Apps Can Give Notifications

1 Swipe up from the bottom of the screen.

The Home screen appears.

2 Tap **Settings** (⚙️).

The Settings screen appears.

3 Tap **Notifications** (▣).

The Notifications screen appears.

A To choose your default setting for notification previews, tap **Show Previews**, and then tap **Always**, **When Unlocked**, or **Never**, as needed.

4 Tap the app for which you want to configure notifications. This example uses **Calendar** (▦).

The screen for configuring the app's notifications appears.

5 Set the **Allow Notifications** switch to On (◯) to enable notifications.

Note: For some apps, all the options appear on the screen for configuring the app's notifications.

6 Tap the button for the notification type you want to configure. This example uses **Upcoming Events**.

The screen for configuring that notification type appears, such as the Upcoming Events screen.

7 In the Alerts section, tap **Lock Screen**, **Notification Center**, and **Banners** to control where alerts appear (✓) or do not appear ( ).

8 Tap **Banner Style** to display the Banner Style screen; tap **Temporary** or **Persistent**, as needed; and then tap **Back** (〈).

9 Tap **Sounds**.

10 Tap the sound you want to use.

Ⓑ You can tap **None** for no sound.

Ⓒ You can tap **Vibration** and choose the vibration pattern for the notification type.

11 Tap the **Back** button (〈), such as **Upcoming Events** (〈) in this example.

12 Set the **Badges** switch to On (⬤) to show badges.

13 To exempt this app from your default preview setting, tap **Show Previews**.

The Show Previews screen appears.

14 Tap **Always**, **When Unlocked**, or **Never**, as needed.

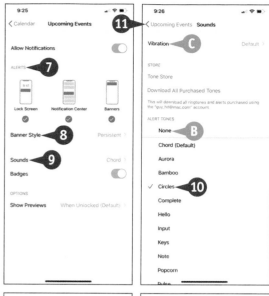

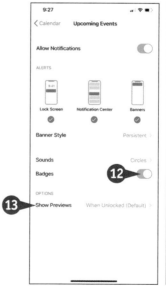

TIP

What are the three kinds of notifications?

A *badge* is a red circle or rounded rectangle that appears on the app's icon on the Home screen and shows a white number indicating how many notifications there are. A *temporary banner* is a pop-up notification that appears briefly at the top of the screen and then disappears automatically after a few seconds. A *persistent banner* is like a temporary banner, but you must dismiss it before you can take other actions on your iPhone. Whichever notification type you choose, you can set the **Sounds** switch to On (⬤) to have your iPhone play a sound to get your attention.

Choose Sounds and Haptics Settings

The Sounds & Haptics screen in Settings enables you to control what audio feedback and vibration feedback your iPhone gives you. You can have the iPhone always vibrate to signal incoming calls, or vibrate only when the ringer is silent. You can set the ringer and alerts volumes, choose your default ringtone and text tone, and choose which items can give you alerts. Your iPhone can play lock sounds to confirm you have locked or unlocked your iPhone. It can also play keyboard clicks to confirm each key press.

Choose Sounds and Haptics Settings

1 Swipe up from the bottom of the screen.

The Home screen appears.

2 Tap **Settings** (⚙).

The Settings screen appears.

3 Tap **Sounds & Haptics** (🔊).

The Sounds & Haptics screen appears.

4 Set the **Vibrate on Ring** switch to On (⬤) or Off ( ), as needed.

5 Set the **Vibrate on Silent** switch to On (⬤) or Off ( ), as needed.

6 Tap and drag the **Ringer and Alerts** slider to set the volume.

A When the **Change with Buttons** switch is On (⬤), you can change the Ringer and Alerts volume by pressing the volume buttons on the side of the iPhone.

7 Tap **Ringtone**.

The Ringtone screen appears.

8 Tap the ringtone you want to hear.

B You can tap **Tone Store** to browse and buy ringtones.

9 Tap **Vibration**.

36

The Vibration screen appears.

10 Tap the vibration pattern you want to feel.

11 If you prefer a custom vibration, tap **Create New Vibration** in the Custom area.

The New Vibration screen appears.

12 Tap a rhythm.

13 Tap **Stop**.

14 Tap **Play** to play back the vibration.

15 Tap **Save**.

The New Vibration dialog opens.

16 Type a name.

17 Tap **Save**.

The Vibration screen appears.

18 Tap **Ringtone** (<).

The Ringtone screen appears.

19 Tap **Sounds & Haptics** (<).

The Sounds & Haptics screen appears.

20 Repeat steps **7** to **19** to set other tones, such as text tones.

21 Set the **Keyboard Clicks** switch to On (⬤) or Off ( ), as needed.

22 Set the **Lock Sound** switch to On (⬤) or Off ( ), as needed.

23 Set the **System Haptics** switch to On (⬤) or Off ( ) to control whether your iPhone plays haptics for system controls and touches.

TIP

How do I use different ringtones for different callers?

The ringtone and text tone you set in the Ringtone area of the Sounds & Haptics screen are your standard tone for phone calls, FaceTime calls, and messaging calls. To set different tones for a contact, display the Home screen, tap **Phone** (📞), and then tap **Contacts**. In the Contacts list, tap the contact, tap **Edit**, and then tap **Ringtone**. On the Ringtone screen, tap the ringtone and then tap **Done**. You can also change other settings, such as the Text Tone vibration for the contact. Tap **Done** when you are finished.

Set Appearance, Brightness, and Wallpapers

Y ou can choose between a Light appearance and a Dark appearance for iOS, or you can set iOS to switch automatically between Light and Dark. You can adjust the screen's brightness to improve visibility, and you can turn the True Tone feature on to make colors appear consistent.

To make the screen look good, you can choose which picture to use as the wallpaper that appears in the background. You can use either a static wallpaper or a dynamic, changing wallpaper. You can set different wallpaper for the lock screen and for the Home screen.

Set Appearance, Brightness, and Wallpapers

1 Swipe up from the bottom of the screen to display the Home screen.

2 Tap **Settings** (⚙) to display the Settings screen.

3 Tap **Display & Brightness** (🔠).

4 In the Appearance area, select **Light** (✓) or **Dark** (✓), as appropriate.

A If you want iOS to switch between Light and Dark for you, set the **Automatic** switch to On (⚪). Tap **Options**; tap **Sunset to Sunrise**, or tap **Custom Schedule** and set custom times; and then tap **Back** (‹).

5 Drag the **Brightness** slider left or right to set brightness.

6 Set the **True Tone** switch to On (⚪) if you want colors to appear consistent in different lighting conditions.

7 Set the **Raise to Wake** switch to On (⚪) to make the iPhone wake when you raise it.

B You can tap **Text Size** to set your preferred text size.

C You can set the **Bold Text** switch to On (⚪) to make the system text bold.

8 Tap **Settings** (‹).

The Settings screen appears again.

9 Tap **Wallpaper** (🌼).

D You can set the **Dark Appearance Dims Wallpaper** switch to On (⚪) to make the Dark appearance dim the wallpaper.

10 Tap **Choose a New Wallpaper**.

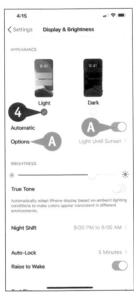

11 Tap **Dynamic**, **Stills**, or **Live** in the Apple Wallpaper area. This example uses **Stills**.

E To choose a picture from a different picture category, tap that category.

12 Tap the wallpaper you want to use.

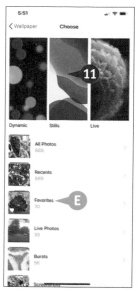

The Wallpaper Preview screen appears.

13 Tap **Perspective** (◎ or ▣) to toggle perspective on (◎) or off (▣). Perspective makes it appear that there is depth between the icons and the wallpaper.

14 Tap **Set**.

15 Tap **Set Lock Screen**, **Set Home Screen**, or **Set Both**. Tap **Cancel** if you do not want to proceed.

16 Swipe up from the bottom of the screen.

The Home screen appears.

If you changed the Home screen wallpaper, the new wallpaper appears.

Note: To see the lock screen wallpaper, press **Side**.

TIPS

How do I use only part of a picture as the wallpaper?
When you choose a photo as wallpaper, the iPhone displays the Move and Scale screen. Pinch in or out to zoom the photo out or in, and tap and drag to move the picture around. When you have chosen the part you want, tap **Set**.

How else can I make the screen more readable?
Try the Smart Invert Colors feature. From the Settings screen, tap **Accessibility** (⊕), tap **Display & Text Size** (AA), and then set the **Smart Invert** switch to On (◉).

Configure Night Shift and Display Zoom

Blue light from the screens of devices can prevent or disrupt your body's sleep, so the iPhone includes a feature called Night Shift that reduces blue light from the screen. You can configure Night Shift to run automatically each night, manually enable it until the next day, and adjust the color temperature to look more or less warm.

On large-screen iPhones, you can choose whether to zoom the display in to a larger size or to keep it at the standard size.

Configure Night Shift and Display Zoom

1 Swipe up from the bottom of the screen.

The Home screen appears.

2 Tap **Settings** (⚙).

The Settings screen appears.

3 Tap **Display & Brightness** (🔠).

The Display & Brightness screen appears.

4 Tap **Night Shift**.

The Night Shift screen appears.

5 Drag the **Color Temperature** slider along the Less Warm–More Warm axis to set the color temperature you want for Night Shift.

A You can set the **Manually Enable Until Tomorrow** switch to On (⚪) to enable Night Shift immediately.

6 Set the **Scheduled** switch to On (⚪) to run Night Shift each night.

7 Tap **From, To**.

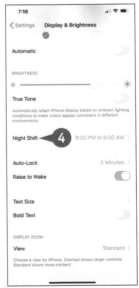

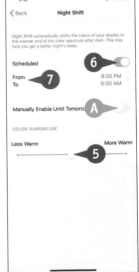

The Schedule screen appears.

8 Tap **Sunset to Sunrise** if you want Night Shift to follow sunset and sunrise times for your location; go to step **11**. Otherwise, tap **Custom Schedule**.

9 Tap **Turn On At** and set the time.

10 Tap **Turn Off At** and set the time.

11 Tap **Night Shift** (<).

The Night Shift screen appears.

12 Tap **Display & Brightness** (<).

The Display & Brightness screen appears.

13 Tap **View** in the Display Zoom area.

The Display Zoom screen appears.

14 Tap the unselected zoom type (changes to ✓).

The preview shows the zoom effect.

The preview cycles through several images to illustrate how the zoom types look.

15 Tap **Set**.

The Changing Display Zoom Will Restart iPhone dialog opens.

16 Tap **Use Zoomed** or **Use Standard**, depending on which button appears.

Your iPhone restarts, but you do not need to unlock it again.

The display appears with the zoom effect you chose.

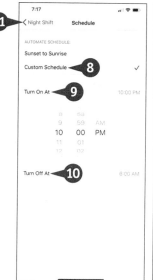
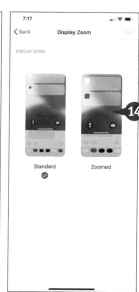

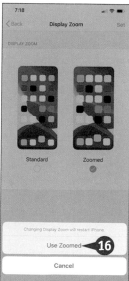

TIP

How does Night Shift know when sunset and sunrise are?
Your iPhone uses Location Services to determine your location, and then looks up the sunset time and sunrise time online. If you disable Location Services, you will need to turn on Night Shift on a custom schedule or manually.

Choose Privacy and Location Settings

Your iPhone contains a huge amount of information about you, the people you communicate with, what you do, and where you go. To keep this information secure, you need to choose suitable privacy and location settings.

Privacy settings enable you to control which apps can access your contacts, calendars, reminders, and photos. You can also choose which apps can use your iPhone's location services and which can track the iPhone's location via the Global Positioning System, or GPS.

Choose Privacy and Location Settings

1 Swipe up from the bottom of the screen.

The Home screen appears.

2 Tap **Settings** (⚙).

The Settings screen appears.

3 Tap **Privacy** (✋).

Note: To limit how ads can track your iPhone usage, tap **Advertising** at the bottom of the Privacy screen. On the Advertising screen, set the **Limit Ad Tracking** switch to On (⬤). Tap **Reset Advertising Identifier** and then tap **Reset Identifier** in the confirmation dialog.

The Privacy screen appears.

4 Tap the app or service you want to configure. This example uses **Photos** (✿).

The screen for the app or service appears.

5 For each app, tap the switch to display the app's screen, tap **Never** to prevent access or **Read and Write** to allow access, and then tap **Back** (‹).

6 Tap **Privacy** (‹).

The Privacy screen appears.

7 Configure other apps and services as needed.

8 Tap **Location Services** (➤).

The Location Services screen appears.

9 If you need to turn location services off completely, set the **Location Services** switch to Off ( ). Usually, you would leave it set to On ( ).

10 Tap the app or feature you want to configure.

11 In the Allow Location Access box, tap the appropriate button, such as **While Using the App** or **Never**.

Note: The buttons in the Allow Location Access box vary depending on the app or feature.

12 Tap **Back** (‹).

The Location Services screen appears again.

13 Set location access for other apps and features.

14 Tap **System Services** (⚙).

The System Services screen appears.

15 Set the switch for each system service to On ( ) or Off ( ), as needed. For example, set the **Location-Based Apple Ads** switch to Off ( ) to turn off ads based on your location.

16 Set the **Status Bar Icon** switch to On ( ) to see the Location Services icon in the status bar when an app requests your location.

Configure and Use Search

Your iPhone can put a huge amount of data in the palm of your hand, and you may often need to search to find what you need.

To make your search results more accurate and helpful, you can configure the Search feature. You can turn off searching for items you do not want to see in your search results.

Configure and Use Search

Configure Search

1 Swipe up from the bottom of the screen.

The Home screen appears.

2 Tap **Settings** (⚙️).

The Settings screen appears.

3 Tap **Siri & Search** (🔍).

The Siri & Search screen appears.

4 Set the **Suggestions in Search** switch to On (⬜) if you want to see Siri suggestions when you search.

5 Set the **Suggestions in Look Up** switch to On (⬜) if you want to see Siri suggestions when you use Look Up.

6 Set the **Suggestions on Lock Screen** switch to On (⬜) if you want to see Siri suggestions on the lock screen.

7 In the list of apps, tap the app you want to configure. This example uses **App Store** (🅰️).

The screen for that app appears.

8 Set the **Learn from this App** switch to On (⬜) if you want Siri to learn from your use of this app.

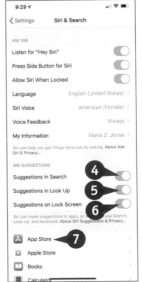

9 Set the **Show in Search** switch to On (◉) if you want this app's content to appear in searches.

10 Set the **Suggest Shortcuts** switch to On (◉) if you want this app to appear in results for Search and Look Up.

11 Set the **Show Siri Suggestions** switch to On (◉) if you want Siri suggestions to appear on the lock screen.

12 Tap **Siri & Search** (‹).

The Siri & Search screen appears again.

13 Tap the next app you want to configure.

Search for Items Using Search

1 Swipe up from the bottom of the screen.

The Home screen appears.

2 Tap near the top of the screen and pull down.

Ⓐ The Search panel appears, with the insertion point in it.

Note: You can also start a search by swiping right from the Home screen and then tapping the Search box at the top of the screen.

The keyboard appears.

3 Type your search term.

A list of results appears.

4 Tap the result you want to view or open.

Which items should I search?

This depends on what you need to be able to search for. For example, if you do not need to search for music, videos, or podcasts, you can exclude the Music apps, the Videos app, and the Podcasts app from Siri & Search Suggestions.

Choose Locking and Control Center Settings

After a period of inactivity whose length you can configure, your iPhone automatically locks itself. It then turns off its screen and goes to sleep to save battery power. Setting your iPhone to lock itself quickly helps preserve battery power, but you may prefer to leave your iPhone on longer so that you can continue to work, and then lock your iPhone manually. You can also choose which controls to display in Control Center and the order in which they appear.

Choose Locking and Control Center Settings

1 Swipe up from the bottom of the screen.

The Home screen appears.

2 Tap **Settings** (⚙).

The Settings screen appears.

3 Tap **Display & Brightness** (🔠).

Note: If your iPhone is managed by an administrator, you may not be able to set all the options explained here. For example, an administrator may prevent you from disabling automatic locking for security reasons.

The Display & Brightness screen appears.

4 Tap **Auto-Lock**.

The Auto-Lock screen appears.

5 Tap the interval — for example, **30 Seconds**.

Note: Choose **Never** for Auto-Lock if you need to make sure your iPhone never goes to sleep. For example, if you are playing music with the lyrics displayed, turning off auto-locking may be helpful.

6 Tap **Back** (<).

The Display & Brightness screen appears again.

7 Tap **Settings** (<).

The Settings screen appears again.

8 Tap **Control Center** (⊞).

The Control Center screen appears.

9 Set the **Access Within Apps** switch to On (⚪) if you want to be able to access Control Center from apps rather than only from the Home screen.

10 Tap **Customize Controls**.

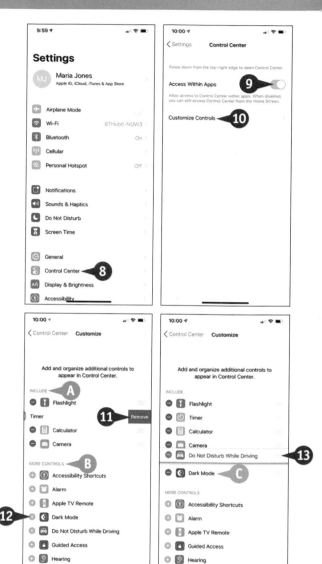

The Customize screen appears.

Ⓐ The Include section shows the controls currently in Control Center that you can remove.

Ⓑ The More Controls section shows controls you can add.

11 To remove a control from Control Center, tap **Remove** (⊖), and then tap the textual **Remove** button that appears.

Note: You can also remove a control by dragging it from the Include list to the More Controls list.

12 To add a control to Control Center, tap **Add** (⊕).

Ⓒ The control moves to the Include list.

13 To change the order of controls in Control Center, drag a control up or down by its handle (☰).

TIP

How do I put the iPhone to sleep manually?

You can put the iPhone to sleep at any point by pressing **Side**.

Putting the iPhone to sleep as soon as you stop using it helps to prolong battery life. If you apply a passcode or other means of locking, as discussed in the section "Secure Your iPhone with Face ID and a Passcode," later in this chapter, putting the iPhone to sleep also starts protecting your data sooner.

Set Up and Use Do Not Disturb Mode

When you do not want your iPhone to disturb you, turn on its Do Not Disturb Mode. You can configure Do Not Disturb Mode to turn on and off automatically at set times each day; you can also configure Do Not Disturb While Driving to run automatically. You can turn Do Not Disturb Mode on and off manually from Control Center.

You can allow particular groups of contacts to bypass Do Not Disturb Mode so they can contact you even when Do Not Disturb is on. You can also allow repeated calls to ring when Do Not Disturb is on.

Set Up and Use Do Not Disturb Mode

Configure Do Not Disturb Mode

1 Swipe up from the bottom of the screen.

The Home screen appears.

2 Tap **Settings** (⚙).

The Settings screen appears.

3 Tap **Do Not Disturb** (🌙).

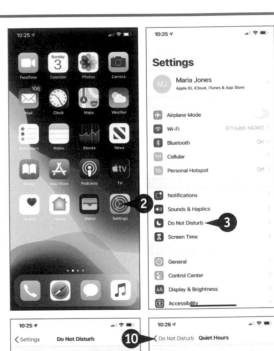

Ⓐ You can turn on Do Not Disturb manually by setting the **Do Not Disturb** switch to On (⬤).

Note: You can turn Do Not Disturb on and off more easily from Control Center. See the first tip in this section.

Ⓑ Set the **Dim Lock Screen** switch to On (⬤) if you want iOS to dim the lock screen and send notifications to Notification Center when Do Not Disturb is on.

4 Set the **Scheduled** switch to On (⬤).

5 Tap **From, To**.

6 Tap **From**.

7 Set the From time.

8 Tap **To**.

9 Set the To time.

🔟 Tap **Do Not Disturb** (‹).

The Do Not Disturb screen appears again.

48

11 In the Silence section, tap **Always** or **While iPhone is locked**, as needed.

12 Tap **Allow Calls From**.

13 Tap the group you will allow to call you when Do Not Disturb is on.

14 Tap **Do Not Disturb** (<).

15 Set the **Repeated Calls** switch to On (●) or Off ( ), as needed.

16 Tap **Activate** to display the Activate screen; choose settings for Do Not Disturb While Driving, such as **Automatically** or **When Connected to Car Bluetooth**; and then tap **Do Not Disturb** (<).

17 Choose Auto-Reply options for Do Not Disturb While Driving.

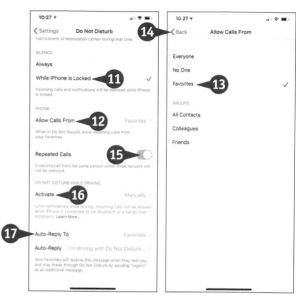

Turn Do Not Disturb Mode On or Off Manually

1 Swipe up from the bottom of the screen.

The Home screen appears.

2 Swipe down from the upper-right corner of the screen.

Control Center opens.

3 Tap **Do Not Disturb** to turn Do Not Disturb on (🌙 changes to 🌙) or off (🌙 changes to 🌙).

How can I tell whether Do Not Disturb is on?
Open Control Center and look at the Do Not Disturb icon (🌙 or 🌙). Also in Control Center, a crescent moon symbol appears in the status bar to the left of the battery readout when Do Not Disturb is on.

How can I allow multiple groups of people to call me when Do Not Disturb is on?
The Allow Calls From screen lets you select only one group. Unless you can put all the relevant contacts into a single group, the best solution is to create a new group and add the existing groups to it. This is easiest to do in your iCloud account by working in a web browser on a computer.

Customize Today View

Today View, which you display by swiping right on the first Home screen page, shows a list of widgets to provide you with quick information about the weather, the news, and your time commitments. You can configure Today View by removing widgets you do not need, adding widgets you find useful, and arranging the widgets into the order you find most helpful.

Customize Today View

1️⃣ Swipe up from the bottom of the screen.

The Home screen appears.

Note: If the first Home screen page does not appear at first, swipe up from the bottom of the screen again to display it.

2️⃣ Swipe right.

Today View appears.

3️⃣ Swipe up to scroll down to the bottom of the screen.

More items in Today View appear.

4️⃣ Tap **Edit**.

The Add Widgets screen appears.

5️⃣ Tap **Remove** (➖) to the left of a widget you want to remove.

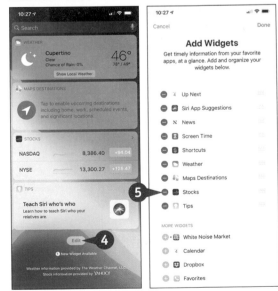

The textual Remove button appears.

6 Tap **Remove**.

The widget disappears from the list.

7 Swipe up.

The More Widgets list appears.

8 Tap **Add** (⊕) to the left of a widget you want to add to Today View.

The widget appears in the upper list.

9 Tap a widget's handle (≡) and drag up or down to rearrange the widgets.

10 Tap **Done**.

Today View appears, showing the widgets in the order you specified.

TIP

How do I get more widgets to add to Today View?

The widgets in Today View come built into apps, so the only way to get more widgets is to install more apps that have widgets.

When choosing an app to add to your iPhone, consider whether the app is one for which a widget in Today View would be useful. If so, look for an app that offers a widget.

Secure Your iPhone with Face ID and a Passcode

The primary method of unlocking your iPhone is Face ID, which uses depth cameras to scan your face in 3D and match it to stored data. During initial setup of your iPhone, iOS walks you through setting up Face ID, together with a passcode as a backup method of unlocking your iPhone for when Face ID does not work. After setup, you can configure Face ID, reset Face ID, or add an alternate appearance. For added security, you can set your iPhone to automatically erase its data after ten failed attempts to enter the passcode.

Secure Your iPhone with Face ID and a Passcode

1 Swipe up from the bottom of the screen.

The Home screen appears.

2 Tap **Settings** (⚙).

The Settings screen appears.

3 Tap **Face ID & Passcode** (😀).

Note: If the Enter Passcode screen appears, type your passcode.

The Face ID & Passcode screen appears.

4 Set the **iPhone Unlock** switch to On (⬤) to use Face ID to unlock your iPhone.

5 Set the **iTunes & App Store** switch to On (⬤) to use Face ID to authorize purchases on the iTunes Store and the App Store.

6 Set the **Apple Pay** switch to On (⬤) to use Face ID to authorize payments via Apple Pay.

7 Set the **Password AutoFill** switch to On (⬤) to use Face ID to authorize filling in passwords automatically.

8 If you want to add an alternate appearance, such as wearing glasses or makeup, tap **Set Up an Alternative Appearance** and follow the prompts.

A You can tap **Reset Face ID** if you want to redo Face ID, including any alternate appearance.

9 Set the **Require Attention for Face ID** switch to On (⬤) for added security.

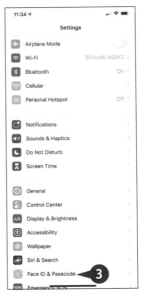

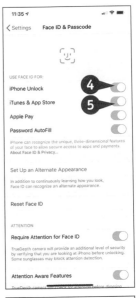

10 Set the **Attention Aware Features** switch to On (●) to have Face ID detect whether you are using the phone before it dims the screen or turns down alerts.

B To change the passcode type, you can tap **Change Passcode**, tap **Passcode Options**, and then tap **Custom Alphanumeric Code**, **Custom Numeric Code**, or **4-Digit Numeric Code**.

C iOS normally requires a passcode immediately after locking it. If your iPhone is configured via management policy, you may be able to tap **Require Passcode** and implement a delay, such as 30 Seconds.

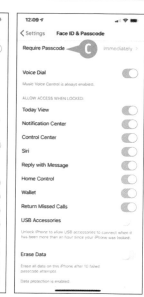

11 Set the **Voice Dial** switch to On (●) or Off ( ), as needed.

12 In the Allow Access When Locked area, set the switches to On (●) or Off ( ), as needed.

Note: Allowing access to Wallet when your iPhone is locked enables you to make payments and reach boarding passes and similar documents more quickly when you need them.

13 If you want the iPhone to erase all its data after ten failed passcode attempts, set the **Erase Data** switch to On (●).

The iPhone displays a confirmation dialog.

14 Tap **Enable**.

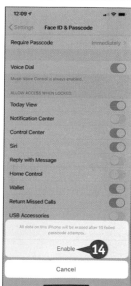

TIP

Which type of passcode should I use?

The default, a six-digit numeric passcode, provides reasonably good security and is easy to enter. But if you need strong security, choose **Custom Numeric Code** and use 12 or more digits. For extra-strong security, choose **Custom Alphanumeric Code** and create a passcode of 12 or more characters, including upper- and lowercase letters, numbers, and symbols.

Configure Screen Time and Restrictions

Mobile phones can be not only extremely useful, but great productivity tools as well — yet they can also be addictive time-sinks promoting disengagement and isolation. iOS provides the Screen Time feature to enable you to track and manage the time spent using an iPhone, enforce downtime away from the screen, and set limits on apps, either on your own iPhone or an iPhone you manage. You can also enforce restrictions on content and privacy — for example, preventing the iPhone's user from buying content in apps or watching adult-rated movies.

Access the Screen Time Features

To access the Screen Time features, first swipe up from the bottom of the screen to display the Home screen. Tap **Settings** (⚙) to display the Settings screen, and then tap **Screen Time** (⧗) to display the Screen Time screen.

The All Devices histogram shows your daily average usage for this week. You can tap **See All Activity** to display the All Devices screen, which breaks down the usage details.

Set Downtime Hours

To enforce downtime on the iPhone and other iOS devices, tap **Downtime** (🌙) on the Screen Time screen, and then work on the Downtime screen. Set the **Downtime** switch to On (⬤) to enable the controls, then either tap **Every Day** to use the same hours each day or tap **Customize Days** and tap a day to customize its hours. On the screen for a day, such as the Sunday screen, you can disable downtime by setting the switch to Off ( ), or simply specify custom hours.

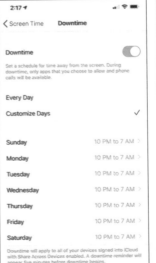

Set App Limits and Always Allowed

To set limits for app usage, tap **App Limits** (▣) on the Screen Time screen. On the App Limits screen, tap **Add Limit** to display the Choose Apps panel. Tap to select the app (changes to ✓), tap **Next**, specify the time limit, and then tap **Add**.

To allow anytime usage of some apps, tap **Always Allowed** (▣) on the Screen Time screen. On the Always Allowed screen, tap **Add** (➕) to move an app from the Choose Apps list to the Allowed Apps list, or tap **Remove** (➖) to remove an app from the Allowed Apps list.

Set Content and Privacy Restrictions

To set limits on the content the user can access and the degree to which the user can expose personal information, tap **Content & Privacy Restrictions** (⊘) on the Screen Time screen. On the Content & Privacy Restrictions screen, set the **Content & Privacy Restrictions** switch to On (⬤) to enable the controls. You can then configure the settings. For example, tap **Content Restrictions** and then use the controls on the Content Restrictions screen to set restrictions on movies, TV shows, books, apps, and other items.

Set Up Family Sharing and Add Members

Apple's Family Sharing feature enables you to share purchases from Apple's online services with other family members. You can also share photos and calendars, and you can use the Find My iPhone feature to find your iOS devices and Macs when they go missing.

This section assumes that you are the Family organizer, the person who gets to set up Family Sharing; invite others to participate; and pay for the content they buy on the iTunes Store, the iBooks Store, and the App Store.

Access the Family Sharing Controls

To set up Family Sharing, swipe up from the bottom of the screen to display the Home screen, and then tap **Settings** (⚙) to open the Settings app. Tap **Apple ID** — the button bearing your Apple ID name — at the top of the Settings screen to display the Apple ID screen, and then tap **Set Up Family Sharing** (⛅) to display the Family Sharing screen.

Tap **Get Started** to display the Get Started screen, which shows a list of the features you can share via Family Sharing: iTunes & App Store Purchases, Apple Music, iCloud Storage, Location Sharing, and Screen Time.

Set Up Shared Features

On the Get Started screen, tap the first feature you want to share with your family members, and then follow the prompts to set up the feature.

For example, if you want to share unlimited music with a Family subscription to the Apple Music service, tap **Apple Music** (♫) on the Get Started screen. The Share the Music with Your Family screen appears. Here, you can tap **Invite via Messages** to send a family member an invitation using the Messages app, or tap **Create an Account for a Child** to start the process of creating a child account.

Similarly, you can tap **Location Sharing** (📍) to display the Share Your Location with Your Family screen, and then tap **Share Your Location** to start the process of sharing your location information.

Add a Family Member to Family Sharing

To add a family member, first display the Family Sharing screen in the Settings app. Swipe up from the bottom of the screen to display the Home screen. Tap **Settings** (⚙️), tap **Apple ID** — the button bearing your Apple ID name — and then tap **Family Sharing** (☁️).

On the Family Sharing screen, tap **Add Family Member**. In the dialog that opens, tap **Invite via iMessage**, **Invite in Person**, or **Create a Child Account**, and then follow the prompts. For example, if you tap **Invite in Person**, the Family Member's Apple ID screen appears, and you can hand your iPhone to the family member so he or she can fill in his or her Apple ID and password.

Accept an Invitation to Family Sharing

When someone sends you an invitation to Family Sharing, tap the invitation's button in the message, and then tap **Join Family** on the You're Invited screen that appears.

If you do not want to accept the invitation, tap **Not Now** instead.

Choose Date, Time, and International Settings

To keep yourself on time and your data accurate, you need to make sure the iPhone is using the correct date and time.

To make dates, times, and other data appear in the formats you prefer, you may need to change the iPhone's International settings.

Choose Date, Time, and International Settings

Choose Date and Time Settings

① Swipe up from the bottom of the screen.

The Home screen appears.

② Tap **Settings** (⚙).

The Settings screen appears.

③ Tap **General** (⚙).

The General screen appears.

④ Tap **Date & Time**.

The Date & Time screen appears.

⑤ Set the **24-Hour Time** switch to On (🔘) if you want to use 24-hour times.

⑥ To set the date and time manually, set the **Set Automatically** switch to Off (⚪).

⑦ Tap the bar that shows the current date and time.

Controls for setting the date and time appear.

⑧ Use the controls to set the date and time.

⑨ Tap **General** (<).

The General screen appears.

Choose International Settings

1 From the General screen, tap **Language & Region**.

The Language & Region screen appears.

A The Region Format Example area shows examples of the time, date, currency, and number formats for the current region.

2 Tap **iPhone Language**.

The iPhone Language screen appears.

3 Tap the language you want to use.

A confirmation dialog opens.

4 Tap **Change To**.

The Language & Region screen appears.

5 Tap **Region**.

The Select Region screen appears.

6 Tap the region you want.

A confirmation dialog opens.

7 Tap **Continue**.

The Language & Region screen appears.

TIP

How does my iPhone set the date and time automatically?
Your iPhone sets the date and time automatically by using time servers, computers on the Internet that provide date and time information to computers that request it. The iPhone automatically determines its geographical location so it can request the right time zone from the time server.

CHAPTER 3

Using Voice, Accessibility, and Continuity

Your iPhone includes the Siri personal assistant, helpful accessibility features, and integration with your Mac and Apple Watch via the Continuity feature.

Give Commands with Siri

Often, speaking is even easier than using your iPhone's touch screen — especially when you are out and about or on the move. The powerful Siri feature enables you to take essential actions by using your voice to tell your iPhone what you want. Siri requires a fast Internet connection because the speech recognition runs on servers in Apple's data center.

You can use Siri either with the iPhone's built-in microphone or with the microphone on a headset. The built-in microphone works well in a quiet environment or if you hold your iPhone close to your face, but in noisy situations you will do better with a headset microphone.

Open Siri

You can open Siri from the Home screen or any app. Press and hold **Side** for several seconds. If you have connected a headset with a clicker button, you can also press and hold the headset clicker button for several seconds to invoke Siri. If you have chosen to allow Siri access when your iPhone is locked, you can also activate Siri while the lock screen is displayed.

The Siri screen appears. A tone indicates that Siri is ready to take your commands. If you enable the "Hey Siri" feature in the Settings app, you can also activate Siri by saying "Hey Siri."

Send an E-Mail Message

Say "E-mail" and the contact's name, followed by the message. Siri creates an e-mail message to the contact and enters the text. Review the message, and then tap **Send** to send it.

If you prefer, you can start the message by saying "E-mail" and the contact's name, and then pausing. Siri then prompts you for the subject and text of the message in turn.

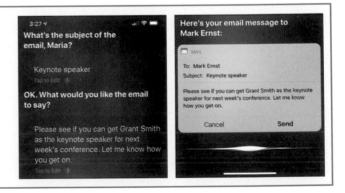

Set an Alarm

Say "Set an alarm for 4:30 a.m." and check the alarm that Siri displays.

You can turn the alarm off by tapping its switch (⬤ changes to ◯).

You can ask a question such as "Which alarms do I have set?" to make Siri display a list of your alarms.

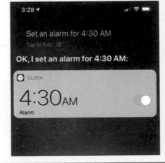

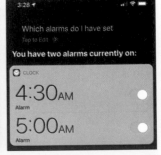

Set a Reminder for Yourself

Say "Remind me" and the details of what you want Siri to remind you of. For example, say "Remind me to take my iPad to work tomorrow morning." Siri listens to what you say and creates a reminder. Check what Siri has written. If the reminder is correct, simply leave it; if not, tap **Change** and edit it.

Send a Text Message

Say "Tell" and the contact's name. When Siri responds, say the message you want to send. For example, say "Tell Victor Kemp" and then "I'm stuck in traffic, so I'll be about 10 minutes late to the meeting. Please start without me." Siri creates a text message to the contact, enters the text, and sends the message when you say "Send" or tap **Send**.

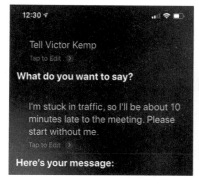

You can also say "Tell" and the contact's name followed immediately by the message. For example, "Tell Bill Sykes the package will arrive at 10 a.m."

Set Up a Meeting

Say "Meet with" and the contact's name, followed by brief details of the appointment. For example, say "Meet with Don Williamson at noon on Friday for lunch." Siri listens and warns you of any scheduling conflict. Siri then sends a meeting invitation to the contact if it finds an e-mail address, and adds the meeting to your calendar after you tap **Confirm** or say "Confirm."

Dictate Text Using Siri

One of Siri's strongest features is the capability to transcribe your speech quickly and accurately into correctly spelled and punctuated text. Using your iPhone, you can dictate into any app that supports the keyboard, so you can dictate e-mail messages, notes, documents, and more. To dictate, simply tap the microphone icon (🎤), speak after Siri beeps, and then tap **Done** or **Keyboard** (⌨).

To get the most out of dictation, it is helpful to know the standard terms for dictating punctuation, capitalization, symbols, layout, and formatting.

Insert Punctuation

To insert punctuation, use standard terms: "comma," "period" (or "full stop"), "semicolon," "colon," "exclamation point" (or "exclamation mark"), "question mark," "hyphen," "dash" (for a short dash, –), or "em dash" (for a long dash, —). You can also say "asterisk" (*), "ampersand" (&), "open parenthesis" and "close parenthesis," "open bracket" and "close bracket," and "underscore" (_).

For example, say "Buy eggs comma bread comma and cheese semicolon and maybe some milk period nothing else exclamation point" to enter the text shown here.

Insert Standard Symbols

To insert symbols, use these terms: "at sign" (@), "percent" (%), "greater than" (>) and "less than" (<), "forward slash" (/) and "backslash" (\), "registered sign" (®), and "copyright sign" (©).

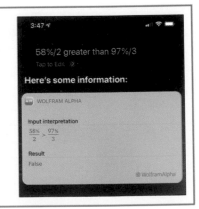

For example, say "Fifty-eight percent forward slash two greater than ninety-seven percent forward slash three" to enter the computation shown here.

Insert Currency Symbols

To insert currency symbols, say the currency name and "sign." For example, say "dollar sign" to insert $, "cent sign" to insert ¢, "euro sign" to insert €, "pound sterling sign" to insert £, and "yen sign" to insert ¥.

For example, say "Convert dollar sign two hundred to UK pounds sterling" to enter the calculation shown here.

Control Layout

You can control text layout by creating new lines and new paragraphs as needed. A new paragraph enters two line breaks, creating a blank line between paragraphs. To create a new line, say "new line." To create a new paragraph, say "new paragraph."

For example, say "Dear Anna comma new paragraph thank you for the parrot period new paragraph it's the most amazing gift I've ever had period" to enter the text shown here.

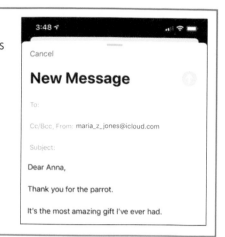

Control Capitalization

You can apply capitalization to the first letter of a word or to a whole word. You can also switch capitalization off temporarily to force lowercase:

Say "cap" to capitalize the first letter of the next word.

Say "caps on" to capitalize all the words until you say "caps off."

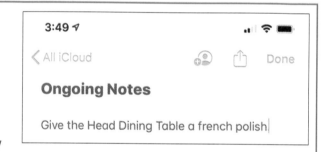

Say "no caps" to prevent automatic capitalization of the next word — for example, "no caps Monday" produces "monday" instead of "Monday."

Say "no caps on" to force lowercase of all words until you say "no caps off."

For example, say "Give the cap head cap dining cap table a no caps french polish period" to enter the text shown here.

Insert Quotes and Emoticons

To insert double quotes, say "open quotes" and "close quotes." To insert single quotes, say "open single quotes" and "close single quotes." To enter standard emoticons, say "smiley face," "frown face," and "wink face."

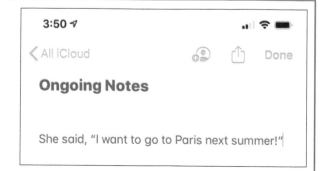

For example, say "she said comma open quotes I want to go to Paris next summer exclamation point close quotes" to enter the text shown here.

Gather and Share Information with Siri

You can use Siri to research a wide variety of information online — everything from sports and movies to restaurants worth visiting or worth avoiding. You can also use Siri to perform hands-free calculations. When you need to share information quickly and easily, you can turn to Siri. By giving the right commands, you can quickly change your Facebook status or post on your wall. Similarly, you can send tweets on your Twitter account.

Find Information About Sports

Launch Siri and ask a question about sports. For example:

"Siri, when's the next White Sox game?"

"Did the Lakers win their last game?"

"When's the end of the NBA season?"

"Can you show me the roster for the Maple Leafs?"

Find Information About Movies

Launch Siri and ask a question about movies. For example:

"Siri, where is the movie *Terminator: Dark Fate* playing in Indianapolis?"

"What's the name of Morgan Freeman's latest movie?"

"Who's the star of *Tigers Are Not Afraid*?"

"Is *Vita and Virginia* any good?"

Find a Restaurant

Launch Siri, and then tell Siri what type of restaurant you want. For example:

"Where's the best Mexican food in Palo Alto?"

"Where can I get sushi in Albuquerque?"

"Is there a brewpub in Minneapolis?"

"Is there any dim sum within 50 miles of here?"

Address a Query to the Wolfram Alpha Computational Knowledge Engine

Launch Siri, and then say "Wolfram" and your query. For example:

"Wolfram, minus 20 centigrade in Kelvin."

"Wolfram, what is the cube of 27?"

"Wolfram, tangent of 60 degrees."

"Wolfram, give me the chemical formula for hydrogen peroxide."

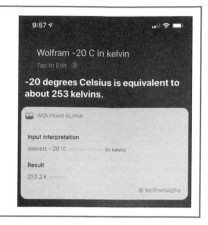

Find Out What Music You Are Listening To

Launch Siri and ask a question such as "What song is this?" or "Do you know what this music is called?" Siri monitors the microphone's input, consults the Shazam music-recognition service, and returns a result if there is a match.

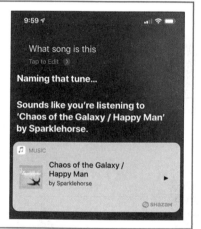

Translate to Another Language

Launch Siri, and then say "Translate to" and the name of the language, such as "Translate to Spanish." When Siri prompts you for the text, speak it. Siri announces the translated text and displays it on-screen, together with a Play button (▶) that you can tap to play the audio again.

Configure Siri to Work Your Way

To get the most out of Siri, spend a few minutes configuring Siri. You can set the language Siri uses and choose when Siri should give you voice feedback. You can also decide whether to use the Raise to Speak option, which activates Siri when you raise your iPhone to your face.

Most important, you can tell Siri which contact record contains your information, so that Siri knows your name, address, phone numbers, e-mail address, and other essential information.

Configure Siri to Work Your Way

1 Swipe up from the bottom of the screen.

The Home screen appears.

2 Tap **Settings** (⚙).

The Settings screen appears.

3 Tap **Siri & Search** (🔍).

The Siri & Search screen appears.

4 Set the **Listen for "Hey Siri"** switch to On (⬤) if you want to be able to activate Siri by saying "Hey Siri!"

5 Set the **Press Side Button for Siri** switch to On (⬤) if you want to be able to summon Siri by pressing and holding the Side button.

6 Set the **Allow Siri When Locked** switch to On (⬤) if you want to use Siri from the lock screen.

7 Tap **Language**.

The Language screen appears.

8 Tap the language you want to use.

9 Tap **Siri & Search** (〈).

The Siri & Search screen appears again.

10 Tap **Siri Voice**.

The Siri Voice screen appears.

⑪ In the Accent box, tap the accent you want Siri to use. For example, for English (United States), you can tap **American**, **Australian**, or **British**.

⑫ In the Gender box, tap **Male** or **Female**, as needed.

⑬ Tap **Siri & Search** (**<**).

The Siri & Search screen appears again.

⑭ Tap **Voice Feedback**.

The Voice Feedback screen appears.

⑮ Tap **Always On**, **Control with Ring Switch**, or **Hands-Free Only**, as needed.

⑯ Tap **Siri & Search** (**<**).

The Siri & Search screen appears again.

⑰ Tap **My Info**.

The Contacts screen appears, showing either the All Contacts list or the groups you have selected.

Note: If necessary, click Groups to display the Groups screen, select the groups you need, and then tap **Done**.

⑱ Tap the contact record that contains your information.

TIP

Does Apple store the details of what I ask Siri?

Yes, but not in a way that will come back to haunt you. When you use Siri, your iPhone passes your input to servers in Apple's data center in North Carolina, USA, for processing. The servers analyze your request and tell Siri how to respond to it. Apple's data center stores the details of your request and may analyze them to determine what people use Siri for and work out ways of making Siri more effective. Apple does not associate your Siri data with other data Apple holds about you — for example, the identity and credit card data you used to pay for iTunes Match.

Set Up VoiceOver to Identify Items On-Screen

If you have trouble identifying the iPhone's controls on-screen, you can use the VoiceOver feature to read them to you. VoiceOver changes your iPhone's standard finger gestures so that you tap to select the item whose name you want it to speak, double-tap to activate an item, and flick three fingers to scroll.

VoiceOver can make your iPhone easier to use. Your iPhone also includes other accessibility features, which you can learn about in the next section, "Configure Other Accessibility Features."

Set Up VoiceOver to Identify Items On-Screen

1 Swipe up from the bottom of the screen.

The Home screen appears.

2 Tap **Settings** (⚙).

The Settings screen appears.

3 Tap **Accessibility**.

The Accessibility screen appears.

4 Tap **VoiceOver**.

Note: You cannot use VoiceOver and Zoom at the same time. If Zoom is on when you try to switch VoiceOver on, your iPhone prompts you to choose which of the two to use.

The VoiceOver screen appears.

5 Set the **VoiceOver** switch to On (changes to).

6 Tap **VoiceOver Practice**.

A selection border appears around the button, and VoiceOver speaks its name.

7 Double-tap **VoiceOver Practice**.

The VoiceOver Practice screen appears.

8 Practice tapping, double-tapping, triple-tapping, swiping, and flicking. VoiceOver identifies each gesture and displays an explanation.

9 Tap **Done** to select the button, and then double-tap **Done**.

The VoiceOver screen appears again.

10 Swipe up with three fingers.

The screen scrolls down.

11 Tap **Speaking Rate** to select it, and then swipe up or down to adjust the rate. Swiping up or down is the VoiceOver gesture for adjusting the slider.

12 Tap **Speech**.

The Speech screen appears.

13 Choose options for voice, pronunciations, pitch, and languages.

14 Tap **VoiceOver** (〈).

The VoiceOver screen appears again.

15 Tap **Verbosity** and choose which items to have VoiceOver announce.

16 Set the **Always Speak Notifications** switch to On (⬤) or Off ( ), as needed.

17 Tap **Double-tap Timeout** and set the timeout for double-tapping.

18 Tap **Typing**.

The Typing screen appears.

19 Choose typing options, as needed. For example, you can tap **Typing Style** and then tap **Standard Typing**, **Touch Typing**, or **Direct Touch Typing**. You can tap **Typing Feedback** and choose which feedback to receive for software keyboards and which to receive for hardware keyboards.

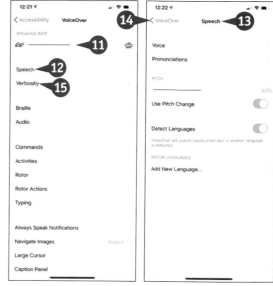

TIP

Is there an easy way to turn VoiceOver on and off?
Yes. You can set your iPhone to toggle VoiceOver on or off when you press **Side** three times in rapid sequence. At the bottom of the Accessibility screen, tap **Accessibility Shortcut** to display the Accessibility Shortcut screen. In the Triple-Click the Side Button For list, tap **VoiceOver**, placing a check mark next to it. Tap **Accessibility** (〈) to return to the Accessibility screen.

Configure Other Accessibility Features

To help you see the screen's contents, you can turn on the zoom capability and then triple-tap the screen to zoom in and out quickly. You can also display the Zoom Controller for easy control of zoom, choose the zoom region, and set the maximum zoom level.

Apart from the accessibility features explained in this section, your iPhone supports physical accessibility features such as Switch Control and AssistiveTouch. Switch Control enables you to control your iPhone through a physical switch you connect to it. AssistiveTouch lets you use an adaptive accessory to touch the screen.

Configure Other Accessibility Features

Display the Accessibility Screen and Configure Zoom Settings

1 Swipe up from the bottom of the screen to display the Home screen.

2 Tap **Settings** (⚙) to display the Settings screen.

3 Tap **Accessibility** (📷) to display the Accessibility screen.

4 Tap **Zoom** (⊕) to display the Zoom screen.

5 Set the **Zoom** switch to On (⬭ changes to ⬯).

A The Zoom window appears if the Zoom Region is set to Window Zoom.

6 Set the **Follow Focus** switch to On (⬯) to make the zoomed area follow the focus on-screen.

7 Set the **Smart Typing** switch to On (⬯) to make iOS switch to Window Zoom when a keyboard appears, so that text is zoomed but the keyboard is regular size.

8 Tap **Keyboard Shortcuts** to display the Keyboard Shortcuts screen.

9 Set the **Keyboard Shortcuts** switch to On (⬯) to enable keyboard shortcuts.

10 Specify which keyboard shortcuts you want to use by setting each switch to On (⬯) or Off (⬭).

11 Tap **Zoom** (‹) to display the Zoom screen again.

12 Tap **Zoom Controller** to display the Zoom Controller screen.

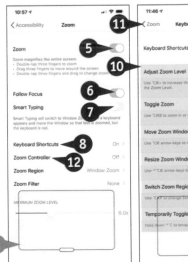

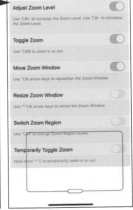

13 Set the **Show Controller** switch to On (⬤).

B The Zoom Controller (⬤) appears.

14 In the Controller Actions list, tap each button and choose the command for each action, or choose **None**. For example, tap **Single-Tap**, tap **Zoom In/Out**, and then tap **Zoom Controller** (〈).

15 Set the **Adjust Zoom Level** switch to On (⬤) if you want to adjust the zoom level by double-tapping the controller and sliding your finger.

C You can adjust the controller's color and its opacity when it is idle.

16 Tap **Zoom** (〈) to display the Zoom screen again.

17 Tap **Zoom Filter** to display the Zoom Filter screen.

18 Tap **None**, **Inverted**, **Grayscale**, **Grayscale Inverted**, or **Low Light**, as needed.

19 Tap **Zoom** (〈) to return to the Zoom screen.

20 Tap **Zoom Region** to display the Zoom Region screen; tap **Full Screen Zoom** or **Window Zoom**, as needed; and then tap **Zoom** (〈).

21 Drag the **Maximum Zoom Level** slider to set the maximum zoom level, such as 8×.

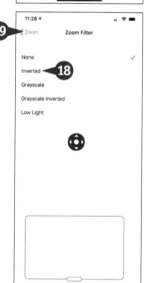

TIP

Is there an easy way to turn the Zoom feature on and off?

Yes. You can set your iPhone to toggle Zoom on or off when you press **Side** three times in rapid sequence. At the bottom of the Accessibility screen, tap **Accessibility Shortcut** to display the Accessibility Shortcut screen. In the Triple-Click the Side Button For list, tap **Zoom**, placing a check mark next to it, and then tap **Accessibility** (〈). You can also use the Side triple-press to access other features, such as VoiceOver, Smart Invert Colors, or Color Filters.

continued ▶

Your iPhone includes several display and text-size features to make the screen easier to view. These features include inverting the screen colors, reducing the white point to lessen the intensity of bright colors, and applying color filters for grayscale or for the protanopia, deuteranopia, or tritanopia color blindnesses.

You can also configure visual interface accessibility settings to make items easier to see. For example, you can set a larger text size, apply shading around text-only buttons, reduce the transparency of items, and darken colors.

Configure Other Accessibility Features (continued)

Configure Display and Text Size

1 On the Accessibility screen, tap **Display & Text Size** (🆎) to show the Display & Text Size screen.

2 Set the **Bold Text** switch to On (🔘) if you want to make text bold.

3 Tap **Larger Text** to display the Larger Text screen.

4 Set the **Larger Accessibility Sizes** switch to On (🔘).

5 Drag the slider to set the text size.

6 Tap **Back** (‹) to return to the Display & Text Size screen.

7 Set the **Button Shapes** switch to On (🔘) if you want iOS to underline navigation buttons, such as the Back button at the top of the left screen.

8 Set the **On/Off Labels** switch to On (🔘) if you want to display I and O labels on the switches.

9 Set the **Reduce Transparency** switch to On (🔘) or Off ( ), as needed.

10 Set the **Increase Contrast** switch to On (🔘) if you want to increase contrast.

11 Set the **Differentiate Without Color** switch to On (🔘) if you want visual differentiations to use other means than color.

12 Set the **Smart Invert** switch to On (🔘) if you want to invert the colors except for images, media files, and dark-themed apps.

Note: Enabling Invert Colors disables Night Shift.

D You can set the **Classic Invert** switch to On (🔘) if you want to invert all the colors.

13 Tap **Color Filters**.

The Color Filters screen appears.

E The color chart displays colors using the filtering you apply. Swipe left for other charts.

14 Set the **Color Filters** switch to On (◯).

The list of color filters appears.

15 Tap the filter you want to apply: **Grayscale**, **Red/Green Filter**, **Green/Red Filter**, **Blue/Yellow Filter**, or **Color Tint**.

16 If the Intensity slider appears, drag it to adjust the intensity.

17 For Color Tint, drag the **Hue** slider to adjust the hue.

18 Tap **Back** (‹).

The Display & Text Size screen appears again.

19 Set the **Reduce White Point** switch to On (◯) if you want to reduce the intensity of bright colors.

20 Drag the slider to adjust the white point.

21 Set the **Auto-Brightness** switch to On (◯) if you want iOS to adjust the screen brightness to suit the lighting conditions the iPhone detects.

Note: Auto-Brightness can improve battery life by saving power. Auto-Brightness may be enabled by default.

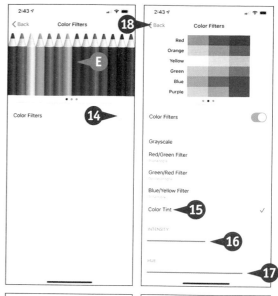

TIPS

How do I set up a hearing aid with my iPhone?
Tap **Hearing Devices** on the Accessibility screen to display the Hearing Devices screen. Here you can pair a hearing aid that conforms to the Made for iPhone standard; for other hearing aids, work on the Bluetooth screen, as for other Bluetooth devices.

What does the Reduce Motion feature do?
Reduce Motion reduces the amount of movement that occurs when you tilt the iPhone when displaying a screen such as the Home screen, where the icons appear to float above the background when perspective zoom is enabled.

continued ▶

Your iPhone includes a suite of interaction features designed to make it easier for you to interact with the touch screen and other hardware components, such as the accelerometers that detect and analyze the device's movements. Changes you can make include setting the tap-and-hold duration and the repeat interval, adjusting the pressure needed for 3D Touch, and configuring the double- and triple-click speed for the Side button. You can also choose your default audio device for call audio.

Configure Other Accessibility Features (continued)

Configure Interaction Accessibility Features

1 On the Accessibility screen, tap **Touch** (⬛) to display the Touch screen.

2 Set the **Reachability** switch to On (⬤) if you want to be able to bring the top of the screen down to about halfway by swiping down on the bottom edge of the screen.

F You can tap **Haptic Touch** and use the controls on the Haptic Touch screen to set the duration for haptic touch.

3 Tap **Touch Accommodations** to display the Touch Accommodations screen.

4 Set the **Touch Accommodations** switch to On (⬤) to enable touch accommodations.

Note: If the Important dialog opens, warning you that Touch Accommodations changes iPhone control gestures, tap **OK**.

G The zoom controller appears automatically when you enable touch accommodations.

5 Set the **Hold Duration** switch to On (⬤) if you need to adjust the hold duration.

6 Tap **+** or **−** to set the hold duration.

7 Tap **Swipe Gestures** to display the Swipe Gestures screen.

8 Set the **Swipe Gestures** switch to On (⬤) to use swipe gestures without waiting for the hold duration.

9 Tap the required movement distance for a swipe gesture.

10 Tap **Back** (**<**) to return to the Touch Accommodations screen.

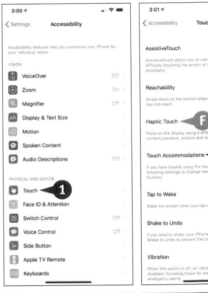

11 Set the **Ignore Repeat** switch to On (◯) if your iPhone detects false repeat touches.

12 Tap **+** or **–** to set the Ignore Repeat interval.

13 In the Tap Assistance box, tap **Off**, **Use Initial Touch Location**, or **Use Final Touch Location**, as needed, to specify how iOS should interpret touches that move across the screen.

14 Tap **Touch** (‹) to return to the Touch screen.

15 Set the **Tap to Wake** switch to On (◯) if you want to wake your iPhone by tapping the screen.

16 Set the **Shake to Undo** switch to On (◯) if you want to shake the iPhone to undo the last action.

17 Set the **Vibration** switch to Off (◯) if you want to disable all vibration.

18 Tap **Call Audio Routing**.

The Call Audio Routing screen appears.

19 Tap **Automatic**, **Bluetooth Headset**, or **Speaker** to specify the audio routing for phone calls and FaceTime audio.

20 Tap **Auto-Answer Calls**.

The Auto-Answer Calls screen appears.

21 Set the **Auto-Answer Calls** switch to On (◯) if you want the iPhone to answer calls automatically after a delay.

22 Tap **+** or **–** to set the delay before answering.

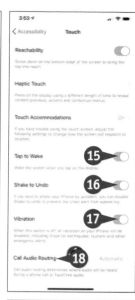

TIP

What are the Spoken Content accessibility settings?

You can have your iPhone speak selected text or the whole screen. To enable these features, tap **Spoken Content** (🔊) on the Accessibility screen and then set the **Speak Selection** switch or the **Speak Screen** switch to On (◯). Set the **Speak Screen** switch to On (◯) to enable swiping down the screen with two fingers to make your iPhone speak all the text on-screen. Tap **Voices** to choose the speaking voice and drag the **Speaking Rate** slider to set the speaking speed. To have your iPhone speak what you type, tap **Typing Feedback** and then choose settings on the Typing Feedback screen.

Using Your iPhone with Your Mac

If you have a Mac, you can enjoy the impressive integration that Apple has built into iOS and the Mac's operating system, macOS. Apple calls this integration Continuity. Continuity involves several features, including Handoff, which enables you to pick up your work or play seamlessly on one device exactly where you have left it on another device. For example, you can start writing an e-mail message on your Mac and then complete it on your iPhone.

Understanding Which iPhone Models and Mac Models Can Use Continuity

To use Continuity, your iPhone must be running iOS 8 or a later version. Your Mac must be running Yosemite, El Capitan, Sierra, High Sierra, Mojave, Catalina, or a later version. Your Mac must have Bluetooth 4.0 hardware. In practice, this includes a Mac mini or MacBook Air from 2011 or later, a MacBook Pro or iMac from 2012 or later, a Mac Pro from 2013 or later, or a MacBook from 2015 or later.

Enable Handoff on Your iPhone

To enable your iPhone to communicate with your Mac, you need to enable the Handoff feature. Display the Home screen, tap **Settings** (⚙) to open the Settings app, tap **General** (⚙) to display the General screen, and then tap **AirPlay & Handoff**. On the AirPlay & Handoff screen, set the **Handoff** switch to On (⬤).

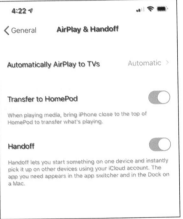

Enable Handoff on Your Mac

You also need to enable Handoff on your Mac. To do so, click on the menu bar and then click **System Preferences** to open the System Preferences window. Click **General** to display the General pane. Click **Allow Handoff between this Mac and your iCloud devices** (☐ changes to ☑). You can then click **System Preferences** on the menu bar and click **Quit System Preferences** to quit System Preferences.

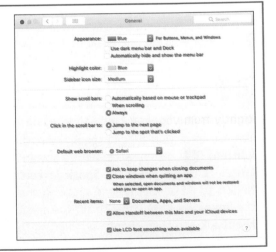

Make and Take Phone Calls on Your Mac

When you are using your Mac within Bluetooth range of your iPhone, Continuity enables you to make and take phone calls on your Mac instead of your iPhone. For example, when someone calls you on your iPhone, your Mac displays a call window automatically, and you can pick up the call on your Mac.

Send and Receive Text Messages from Your Mac

Your Mac can already send and receive messages via Apple's iMessage service, but when your iPhone's connection is available, your Mac can send and receive messages directly via Short Message Service (SMS) and Multimedia Messaging Service (MMS). This capability enables you to manage your messaging smoothly and tightly from your Mac.

Using Your iPhone with Your Apple Watch

Apple Watch puts timekeeping, notifications, and other essential information directly on your wrist. Apple Watch is an accessory for the iPhone — it requires an iPhone to set it up, to provide apps and data, and to give access to the cellular network and the Internet.

Apple Watch works with iPhone 5 and later models.

Pair Your Apple Watch with Your iPhone

You must pair Apple Watch with your iPhone before you can use the devices together. Press and hold the **side button** on Apple Watch until the Apple logo appears, and then wait while Apple Watch finishes starting up.

On your iPhone, display the Home screen, and then tap **Watch** (⊙) to open the Watch app. Tap **Start Pairing**, and then follow the prompts to hold Apple Watch up to your iPhone's rear camera so that the Watch app can recognize the pattern on the Apple Watch screen.

When the Your Apple Watch Is Paired screen appears, tap **Set Up Apple Watch** and complete the setup routine.

Configure Your Apple Watch Using Your iPhone

The Watch app on your iPhone enables you to configure your Apple Watch. On your iPhone, display the Home screen, tap **Watch** (⊙) to open the Watch app, and then tap **My Watch** (▣) to display the My Watch screen.

From here, you can choose a wide range of settings. For example, you can tap **App Layout** (▦) to configure the layout of the apps on your Apple Watch's screen, or you can tap **Notifications** (▤) to choose which notifications you receive on your Apple Watch.

Install Apps on Your Apple Watch

The Watch app on your iPhone enables you to install apps on your Apple Watch — and remove them if necessary.

When you install an iPhone app that has a companion app for Apple Watch, the app's name appears on the My Watch screen. Tap the app's name to display the app's screen. You can then set the **Show App on Apple Watch** switch to On (changes to) to install the app.

Receive Notifications on Your Apple Watch

When you receive a notification from an app you have permitted to raise notifications, your Apple Watch displays an icon showing the app and other information, such as the sender of an e-mail message. You can tap the notification to view its details.

Receive Calls on Your Apple Watch

When you receive a phone call, it rings on both your Apple Watch and your iPhone. You can tap **Accept** ( ) to pick up the call on Apple Watch or tap **Decline** ( ) to decline the call, sending it to voicemail.

CHAPTER 4

Setting Up Communications

In this chapter, you learn how to add your e-mail accounts to the Mail app and control how Mail displays your messages. This chapter also shows you how to control the way your iPhone displays your contacts; browse, search, create, and import contacts; choose options for your calendars; and set up Wallet and Apple Pay.

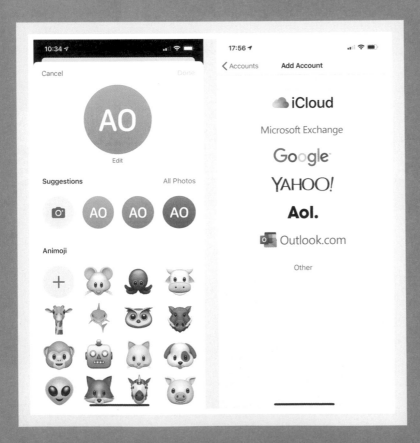

Set Up Your Mail Accounts

Usually, you set up your iCloud account while going through the initial setup routine for your iPhone. You can set up other e-mail accounts as explained here.

To set up an e-mail account, you need to know the e-mail address and password, as well as the e-mail provider. You may also need to know the addresses of the mail servers the account uses. For Microsoft Exchange, including Office 365, you may need the domain name as well; see "Connect Your iPhone to Exchange Server" in Chapter 12.

Set Up Your Mail Accounts

1 Swipe up from the bottom of the screen.

The Home screen appears.

2 Tap **Settings** (⚙).

The Settings screen appears.

Note: If you have not yet set up an e-mail account on the iPhone, you can also open the Add Account screen by tapping **Mail** on the iPhone's Home screen.

Note: If you primarily use Microsoft's e-mail services, such as Outlook and Exchange, consider trying Microsoft's Outlook mail app, which integrates tightly with these services but also works with other e-mail services.

3 Tap **Passwords & Accounts** (🔑).

The Passwords & Accounts screen appears.

4 Tap **Add Account**.

The Add Account screen appears.

5 Tap the kind of account you want to set up. For example, tap **Google**.

Note: Some account types have fields other than those shown here. For example, some accounts include a field for entering your name the way you want it to appear on outgoing messages. Some include a field for changing the description displayed for the account.

The screen for setting up that type of account appears.

Ⓐ You can tap **Create account** to create a new account.

❻ Tap **Enter your email** and type the e-mail address.

Note: For a Google address ending gmail.com, you need not type *gmail.com*.

❼ Tap **Next**.

The Password screen appears.

❽ Type your password.

Ⓑ You can tap **Show** (👁) to display the password you have typed.

❾ Tap **Next**.

❿ If another security screen appears, such as the 2-Step Verification screen shown here, enter the required information and tap **Next**.

The configuration screen for the account appears.

⓫ Make sure the **Mail** switch is set to On (⬤).

⓬ Set the **Contacts** switch, **Calendars** switch, **Notes** switch, and any other switches to On (⬤) or Off (⬤), as needed.

⓭ Tap **Save**.

The account appears on the Passwords & Accounts screen.

TIP

How do I set up a Hotmail account?

Hotmail is one of the services that Microsoft has integrated into its Outlook.com service. Tap **Outlook.com** on the Add Account screen, enter your e-mail address on the Outlook screen that appears, and tap **Next**. On the Enter Password screen, type your password and tap **Sign In**. After Mail verifies the account, set the **Mail** switch, **Contacts** switch, **Calendars** switch, and **Reminders** switch to On (⬤) or Off (⬤), as needed, and then tap **Save**.

Control How Your E-Mail Appears

In the Mail app, you can choose how many lines to include in message previews, decide whether to display the To and Cc label, and control whether Mail prompts you before deleting a message. You can change the minimum font size. You can also choose whether to load remote images in messages; whether to mark e-mail addresses outside a particular domain, such as that of your company or organization; and whether to increase the indentation on messages you reply to or forward.

Control How Your E-Mail Appears

① Swipe up from the bottom of the screen.

The Home screen appears.

② Tap **Settings** (⚙).

The Settings screen appears.

③ Tap **Mail** (✉).

The Mail screen appears.

④ Set the **Cellular Data** switch to On (⬤) if you want to allow Mail to transfer data across the cellular connection. This is good for synchronization but increases use of data and battery power.

⑤ Tap **Preview**.

The Preview screen appears.

⑥ Tap the number of preview lines you want.

⑦ Tap **Mail** (‹).

The Mail screen appears again.

⑧ Set the **Show To/Cc Labels** switch to On (⬤) or Off (◯), as needed.

⑨ Set the **Ask Before Deleting** switch to On (⬤) or Off (◯), as needed.

⑩ Set the **Load Remote Images** switch to On (⬤) or Off (◯), as needed.

⑪ Tap **Swipe Options**.

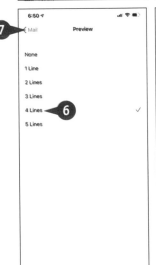
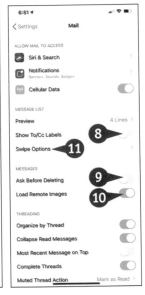

The Swipe Options screen appears.

12 Tap **Swipe Left**; tap **None**, **Mark as Read**, **Flag**, or **Move Message**; and then tap **Swipe Options** (<).

13 Tap **Swipe Right**; tap **None**, **Mark as Read**, **Flag**, **Move Message**, or **Archive**; and then tap **Swipe Options** (<).

14 Tap **Mail** (<).

The Mail screen appears again.

15 Tap **Mark Addresses**.

The Mark Addresses screen appears.

16 In the Mark Addresses Not Ending With box, type the domain name of your company or organization, such as surrealmacs.com.

17 Tap **Mail** (<).

The Mail screen appears again.

18 Tap **Increase Quote Level**.

The Increase Quote Level screen appears.

19 Set the **Increase Quote Level** switch to On (◉) or Off (◯), as needed.

20 Tap **Mail** (<).

TIPS

Why might I want to turn off Load Remote Images?

Loading a remote image may let the sender know that you have opened the message. When Mail requests the remote image, the server that provides the image can log the date and time and your Internet connection's IP address, which reveals your approximate location.

What is Always Bcc Myself useful for?

Most e-mail services automatically put a copy of each outgoing message into a folder with a name such as Sent. If your e-mail service does not use a Sent folder, set the **Always Bcc Myself** switch to On (◉) to send a bcc copy — a "blind carbon copy," in typewriter terminology — of each message to yourself for your records.

Organize Your E-Mail Messages by Threads

The Mail app gives you two ways to view e-mail messages. You can view the messages as a simple list, or you can view them with related messages organized into *threads*, which are sometimes called *conversations*.

Having Mail display your messages as threads can help you navigate your Inbox quickly and find related messages easily. You may find threading useful if you tend to have long e-mail conversations, because threading reduces the number of messages you see at once.

Organize Your E-Mail Messages by Threads

Set Mail to Organize Your Messages by Thread

1 Swipe up from the bottom of the screen.

The Home screen appears.

2 Tap **Settings** (⚙).

The Settings screen appears.

3 Tap **Mail** (✉).

The Mail screen appears.

4 Set the **Organize by Thread** switch to On (⬤).

5 Set the **Collapse Read Messages** switch to On (⬤) if you want Mail to save space by collapsing messages you have read.

6 Set the **Most Recent Message on Top** switch to On (⬤) if you want the newest message in each thread to appear at the top of the screen. This option is often helpful for keeping up with your messages.

7 Set the **Complete Threads** switch to On (⬤) if you want each thread to show all its messages, even if you have moved some to other mailboxes. This option is usually helpful.

8 Tap **Muted Thread Action** to display the Muted Thread Action screen, and then tap **Mark as Read** or **Archive or Delete** to specify which action Mail should take when you mute a thread.

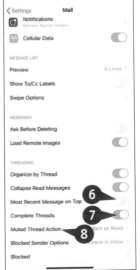

Read Messages Organized into Threads

1 Swipe up from the bottom of the screen.

The Home screen appears.

2 Tap **Mail** (✉).

The Mailboxes screen appears.

Note: If Mail displays the contents of a mailbox, tap **Back** (‹) to return to the Mailboxes screen.

3 Tap the mailbox you want to open.

The Inbox for the account appears.

The Expand Thread icon on the right, a chevron in a circle (⊙), indicates a thread.

4 Tap **Expand Thread** (⊙ changes to ⊙).

The thread expands, showing the messages it contains from other people.

You can get an overview of the thread's contents.

5 Tap the message you want to view.

The thread opens.

Ⓐ The bar at the top of the screen shows the number of messages in the thread.

6 Tap the message you want to display.

TIP

Is there a quick way to enter my name and information at the end of a message?
Yes. You can create one or more e-mail signatures, which are sections of predefined text that Mail can insert at the end of messages. From the Home screen, tap **Settings** (⚙), and then tap **Mail** (✉). Scroll down to the Composing section and tap **Signature** to display the Signature screen. Tap **All Accounts** to use the same signature for each account, or tap **Per Account** to use a different signature for each account. Then type the text to use for the signature or signatures.

Set Your Default E-Mail Account

If you set up two or more e-mail accounts on your iPhone, make sure that you set the right e-mail account to be the default account. The default account is the one from which the Mail app sends messages when you start creating a message from another app. For example, if you open the Photos app and choose to share a photo via Mail, Mail uses your default account.

You can quickly set your default e-mail account on the Mail screen in the Settings app.

Set Your Default E-Mail Account

1. Swipe up from the bottom of the screen.

   The Home screen appears.

2. Tap **Settings** (⚙).

   The Settings screen appears.

3. Tap **Mail** (✉).

   The Mail screen appears.

4. In the Composing section, tap **Default Account**.

   The Default Account screen appears.

5. Tap the account you want to make the default.

6. Tap **Mail** (〈).

Note: To change the e-mail account for a message you are sending, tap **Cc/Bcc, From** to expand the Cc, Bcc, and From fields. Next, tap **From**, and then tap the address on the list that appears at the bottom of the screen.

Control How Your Contacts Appear

To swiftly and easily find the contacts you need, you can make your iPhone sort and display the contacts in your preferred order. Your iPhone can sort contacts either by first name, putting Abby Brown before Bill Andrews, or by last name, putting Bill Andrews before Abby Brown. Your iPhone can display contacts either as first name followed by last name or as last name followed by first name. You can also specify how you want your iPhone to display short names for contacts.

Control How Your Contacts Appear

1 Swipe up from the bottom of the screen.

The Home screen appears.

2 Tap **Settings** (⚙).

The Settings screen appears.

3 Tap **Contacts** (🖼).

The Contacts screen appears.

4 In the Contacts section, tap **Sort Order** or **Display Order**, depending on which order you want to set. This example uses Sort Order.

The Sort Order screen or the Display Order screen appears.

5 Tap **First, Last** or **Last, First**, as needed.

6 Tap **Contacts** (<).

The Contacts screen appears again.

7 Tap **Short Name**.

The Short Name screen appears.

8 Set the **Short Name** switch to On (⬤).

9 Tap **First Name & Last Initial**, **First Initial & Last Name**, **First Name Only**, or **Last Name Only** to specify the format for short names.

10 Set the **Prefer Nicknames** switch to On (⬤) or Off (   ), as needed.

11 Tap **Contacts** (<).

The Contacts screen appears again.

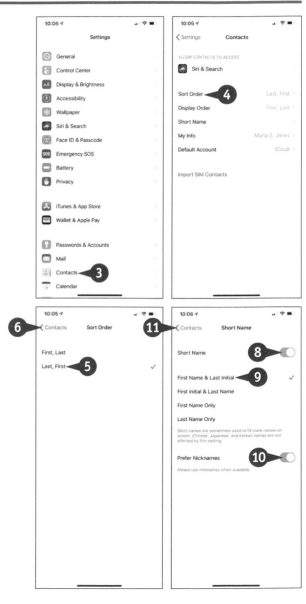

Browse or Search for Contacts

Your iPhone's Contacts app enables you to store contact data that you sync from your computer or online accounts or that you enter directly on your iPhone. You can access the contacts either via the Contacts app itself or through the Contacts tab in the Phone app.

To locate a particular contact, you can browse through the list of contacts or through selected groups, such as your friends, or use the Search feature.

Browse or Search for Contacts

Browse Your Contacts

1 Swipe up from the bottom of the screen.

The Home screen appears.

2 Tap **Contacts** (🔘).

The Contacts screen appears, showing either all contacts or your currently selected groups.

Note: You can also access your contacts by displaying the Home screen, tapping **Phone** (📞), and then tapping **Contacts** (🔘 changes to 🔘).

A To navigate the screen of contacts quickly, tap the letter on the right that you want to jump to. To navigate more slowly, scroll up or down.

3 Tap the contact whose information you want to view.

The contact's screen appears.

Note: From the contact's screen, you can quickly phone the contact by tapping the phone number you want to use.

4 If necessary, tap and drag up to scroll down the screen to display more information.

B You can tap **Edit** to open the contact record for editing.

5 Tap **Contacts** (❮) when you want to return to the Contacts screen.

Choose Which Groups of Contacts to Display

1 From the Contacts screen, tap **Groups**.

The Groups screen appears.

2 Tap **Show All Contacts**.

Contacts displays a check mark next to each group.

Note: When you tap **Show All Contacts**, the Hide All Contacts button appears in place of the Show All Contacts button. You can tap **Hide All Contacts** to remove all the check marks.

3 Tap a group to apply a check mark to it or to remove the existing check mark.

4 Tap **Done**.

The Contacts screen appears, showing the contacts in the groups you selected.

Search for Contacts

1 From the Contacts screen, tap **Search** (Q).

The Search screen appears.

2 Start typing the name you want to search for.

3 From the list of matches, tap the contact you want to view.

The contact's information appears.

TIP

What is a linked contact?

A *linked contact* is a contact record that the Contacts app has created by combining contact records from two or more separate sources. For example, if your iCloud account and your Gmail account each contain a contact called Ron Brown, Contacts creates a linked contact called Ron Brown. To unlink a linked contact, tap **Edit** at the top of the screen for a contact. In the Linked Contacts area, tap **Remove** (●) for the appropriate contact record, and then tap **Unlink**. Alternatively, tap **Edit** and then tap **link contacts** (●) in the Linked Contacts area to link another contact record to the current record.

Create a New Contact

A s well as syncing your existing contacts via cloud services such as iCloud or Yahoo!, you can create new contact records directly on your iPhone. For example, if you meet someone you want to remember, you can create a contact record for that person — and take a photo using the iPhone's camera. You can then sync that contact record online, adding it to your other contacts.

Create a New Contact

1 Swipe up from the bottom of the screen.

The Home screen appears.

2 Tap **Phone** (📞).

The Phone app opens.

3 Tap **Contacts** (👤 changes to 👤).

The Contacts screen appears.

Note: You can also access the Contacts app by tapping **Contacts** (👤) on the Home screen.

4 Tap **Add** (+).

The New Contact screen appears.

5 Tap **First name** and type the first name.

6 Tap **Last name** and type the last name.

7 Fill in other information, such as a company or phone numbers.

8 Tap **Add Photo**.

The Add Photo screen appears.

A You can tap a suggested logo or photo to use instead of taking a photo.

B You can tap a suggested animoji or tap **New** (+) to create a new animoji.

9 Tap **Take Photo** (📷).

The Take Photo screen appears.

10 Compose the photo, and then tap **Take Photo** (⭕).

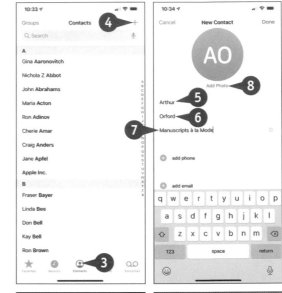

The Move and Scale screen appears.

11 Position the part of the photo you want to use in the middle.

Note: Pinch in with two fingers to zoom the photo out. Pinch out with two fingers to zoom the photo in.

C You can tap **Retake** to take another photo.

12 Tap **Use Photo**.

The Select a Filter screen appears.

13 Tap the filter you want to apply, such as **Vivid Warm**.

D Tap **Original** to skip applying a filter.

The photo appears in the contact record.

14 Tap **Done**.

The contact record closes.

15 Tap **Contacts**.

The Contacts screen appears again.

How do I assign my new contact an existing photo?
On the Add Photo screen, tap **All Photos** to display the Photos screen. You can then tap a photo container, such as an album, to display its contents. Tap the photo you want to use, and it appears on the Move and Scale screen. Position and scale the photo as needed within the frame, and then tap **Choose**.

Import Contacts from a SIM Card

If you have stored contacts on a SIM card, you can import them into your iPhone. If the SIM card is a nano-SIM, the smallest common size, you can insert the SIM card in the iPhone temporarily and import the contacts. Alternatively, you can insert the iPhone's SIM card in an unlocked cell phone, copy the contacts to the SIM card, and then put the SIM card back in the iPhone. This approach enables you to use a SIM adapter to make the iPhone's nano-SIM fit in a micro-SIM or full-size SIM slot.

Import Contacts from a SIM Card

1 Swipe up from the bottom of the screen.

The Home screen appears.

2 Tap **Settings** (⚙).

The Settings screen appears.

3 Tap **Contacts** (👤).

The Contacts screen appears.

4 In the Contacts section, tap **Import SIM Contacts**.

5 If the Import SIM Contacts to Account dialog appears, tap the account in which you want to put the contacts.

Your iPhone imports the contacts from the SIM.

Ⓐ If you want your iPhone to suggest creating contacts from names and data found in e-mail messages, incoming calls, or contact data, tap **Siri & Search** (🔍) to display the Siri & Search screen, and then set the **Show Siri Suggestions for Contacts** switch to On (⚪).

Choose Default Alert Options for Calendar Events

Your iPhone enables you to sync your calendars via iCloud and other online services. To help keep on schedule, you can set default alert times for calendar events. You can set a different alert time for each type of event — for example, 15 minutes' notice for a regular event and a week's notice for a birthday. You can also turn on the Time to Leave feature to make the Calendar app allow travel time based on your location and current traffic.

Choose Default Alert Options for Calendar Events

1 Swipe up from the bottom of the screen to display the Home screen.

2 Tap **Settings** (⚙️) to display the Settings screen.

3 Tap **Calendar** (📅) to display the Calendar screen.

Ⓐ If you want your iPhone to suggest creating events from apparent event data found in apps such as Mail and Messages, tap **Siri & Search** (🔍) to display the Siri & Search screen, and then set the **Show Siri Suggestions in App** switch to On (⚪).

Ⓑ Set the **Location Suggestions** switch to On (⚪) if you want Calendar to suggest locations for events.

4 Tap **Default Alert Times**.

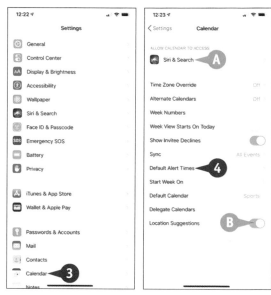

The Default Alert Times screen appears.

5 Tap the event type for which you want to set the default alert time. For example, tap **Events**.

The Events screen, Birthdays screen, or All-Day Events screen appears.

6 Tap the amount of time for the alert.

7 Tap **Back** (‹).

The Default Alert Times screen appears again.

8 Set default alert times for other event types by repeating steps **5** to **7**.

9 Set the **Time to Leave** switch to On (⚪) if you want Calendar to suggest leave times based on your location and current traffic information.

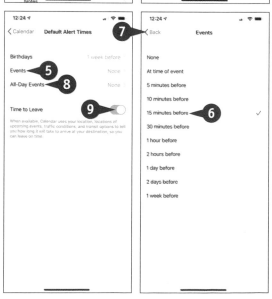

Set Up and Use Wallet and Apple Pay

Your iPhone enables you to make payments using the Apple Pay system and the Wallet app on your iPhone. Apple Pay can be faster and more convenient than paying with cash. It can also be more secure than paying with a credit card or debit card.

Understanding Apple Pay and Wallet

Apple Pay is Apple's electronic-payment and digital-wallet service. After setting up Apple Pay with one or more credit cards or debit cards, you can make payments using your iPhone either at contactless payment terminals or online. If you have an Apple Watch, you can use Apple Pay on that device as well. You can also set up the Apple Cash service and use it to make peer-to-peer payments via apps such as Messages.

Wallet is the app you use on your iPhone to manage Apple Pay and the digital documents you want to carry with you, such as airline tickets or store rewards cards.

Set Up Wallet

Swipe up from the bottom of the screen to display the Home screen, and then tap **Wallet** (⬛) to open the Wallet app.

If you have not yet set up a credit card or debit card, tap **Add** (➕) at the top of the Wallet screen. Follow the prompts to add a card to Wallet. You can add the card either by lining it up within an on-screen frame and using the camera to recognize it or by typing in the details manually; if the card is one you already use with Apple, you may need to provide only the CVV, the card verification code.

Complete the card registration by selecting the correct billing address. For some cards, you may need to contact the card provider to confirm you are setting up Apple Pay.

After you add cards, they appear at the top of the Wallet screen.

Set Apple Pay to Use Face ID

After setting up Apple Pay, you can set your iPhone to use Face ID instead of your Apple ID password for buying items. Face ID enables you to authenticate yourself and approve a purchase by looking at your iPhone. This is much more convenient than typing a password, especially when you are shopping in the physical world rather than online.

To set your iPhone to use Face ID for Apple Pay, swipe up from the bottom of the screen to display

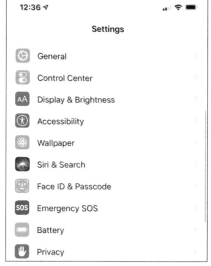

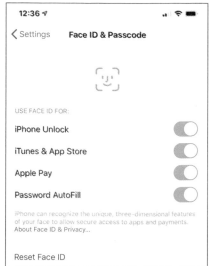

the Home screen, and then tap **Settings** (⚙) to display the Settings screen. Tap **Face ID & Passcode** (😀), and then type your passcode when prompted, to display the Face ID & Passcode screen. Then go to the Use Face ID For section and set the **Apple Pay** switch to On (⚪).

While in the Settings app, you may want to tap **Wallet & Apple Pay** (▭) to display the Wallet & Apple Pay screen. Here, you can set the **Double-Click Side Button** switch to On (⚪) to give yourself instant access to your cards and passes.

Make a Payment with Apple Pay

Now that you have set up Apple Pay and configured your iPhone to use it, you can make payments by bringing your iPhone close to the contact area on a payment terminal.

When the Near Field Communication (NFC) chips on the two devices make contact, a tone sounds. Your iPhone then displays details of the transaction and prompts you to confirm it using Face ID.

Set Up and Use eSIMs

SIM is the acronym for Subscriber Identity Module, a container that holds unique information used to identify a phone to cellular providers and to specify what it is allowed to do through their networks. A SIM can be either physical — a SIM card — or virtual, an electronic SIM, or eSIM for short.

Your iPhone contains a slot for a single physical SIM card — specifically, a nano-SIM. But as well as this SIM card, or instead of it, you can use one or more eSIMs, which enables you to use different cellular plans on the same phone. Before using an eSIM, you must add it to your iPhone and configure it. Only one eSIM can be active at a time, but you can easily switch back and forth between eSIMs.

Determine Whether You Can Use eSIMs

First of all, determine whether you can use eSIMs with your iPhone.

If your iPhone is an unlocked model — one that is not bound to a particular carrier — you should be able to use eSIMs freely. But if your iPhone is locked to a carrier, you will only be able to use eSIMs from that carrier. If that carrier does not support eSIMs, you will not be able to use eSIMs with your iPhone.

The simplest way to find out whether your carrier supports eSIMs in your region is to check the Apple website. Alternatively, consult your carrier.

Get and Add an eSIM

Once you have determined that you can use eSIMs with your iPhone, evaluate your options for getting an eSIM.

If your iPhone is locked to a particular carrier, you must use that carrier's method of adding an eSIM. But if your iPhone is unlocked, you may have multiple options for adding an eSIM. In this case, your next step is to identify the eSIM plan you want to buy. Go to Apple's website and look at the list of carriers per region that support eSIM to determine your choice of carriers, and then explore the eSIM plans they offer.

After choosing your plan, you need to add it to your iPhone. You can add an eSIM to your iPhone in four different ways, depending on your carrier and how it handles eSIMs:

- If the carrier provides a card with a QR code, scan the QR code on the Add Cellular Plan screen. A Cellular Plan Detected notification appears. Tap the notification, tap **Continue**, and then tap **Add Cellular Plan**.

- If the carrier provides an app, tap **App Store** (A) on the Home screen. In the App Store app, search for the carrier's app, and then download and install it. Tap the app's icon on the Home screen, and then follow the prompts to buy a cellular plan.

Get and Add an eSIM (continued)

- If the carrier assigns cellular plans "over the air," your iPhone will display a Carrier Cellular Plan Ready to Be Installed notification. Tap this notification to open the Settings app, and then tap **Carrier Cellular Plan Ready to Be Installed**. Tap **Continue**, and follow the prompts.

- If the carrier tells you to enter the eSIM details manually, tap **Settings** (⚙), on the Home screen, tap **Cellular** (📶) on the Settings screen, and then tap **Add Cellular Plan** on the Cellular screen. Next, tap **Enter Details Manually** at the bottom of the Add Cellular Plan screen.

Configure an eSIM

You configure an eSIM while installing it, but you can also change its configuration later. During the initial configuration of the eSIM, you decide which SIM — the eSIM you are adding or the physical SIM card — plays which roles in your iPhone. You can assign a descriptive label to each SIM to make them easy to identify.

For each contact, you can configure the Preferred Line setting between Last Used and the two SIMs, the SIM card and the active eSIM. This feature lets you continue using the number with which a contact is familiar, so that the contact can see who the call is coming from.

To control which number is used for calling or messaging anyone not in your contacts, you set the default line. You can subsequently change this by changing the Default Voice Line setting from the Cellular screen in the Settings app.

On the "Add to iMessage, FaceTime, Apple ID" screen, you can choose which SIMs you want to associate with your Apple ID. This lets you control the number on which people can contact you through Apple ID–connected services such as iMessage and FaceTime. You can change these settings later by tapping **Settings** (⚙), tapping **Messages** (💬), tapping **Send & Receive**, and then working on the iMessage screen.

On the Cellular Data screen, you can choose which SIM's plan to use as the default for transferring data across the cellular network. You can also set the **Allow Cellular Data Switching** switch to On (🔵) to enable the iPhone to fall back on the other SIM's plan when the default SIM's plan cannot maintain a data connection. Be aware that enabling cellular data switching may inadvertently exhaust the secondary plan's allowance or run up charges.

CHAPTER 5

Making Calls and Messaging

You can make calls by holding your iPhone to your face, by using the speakerphone, or by using a headset or your car's audio system. You can also make calls using Favorites and recent numbers, send and receive text and multimedia messages, and chat using the FaceTime feature.

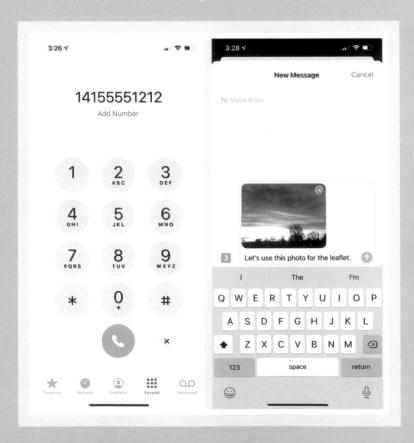

Make Phone Calls and FaceTime Audio Calls

With your iPhone, you can make cellular phone calls anywhere you have a connection to the cellular network; you can make audio or video calls via FaceTime across Wi-Fi connections as well. You can dial a phone number using the iPhone's keypad, but you can place calls more easily by tapping the appropriate phone number for a contact, using the Phone app's Recents screen, using the Favorites list, or using Siri. When other people near you need to be able to hear the call, you can switch on your iPhone's speaker; otherwise, you can use the headset for privacy.

Make Phone Calls and FaceTime Audio Calls

Open the Phone App

1 Swipe up from the bottom of the screen.

The Home screen appears.

2 Tap **Phone** (📞).

The Phone app opens and displays the screen you used last — for example, the Contacts screen.

A Your contact card appears at the top of the Contacts list for quick reference. You can tap it to see your phone number and other details.

Note: You can dial a call by activating Siri and speaking the contact's name or the number. See Chapter 3 for instructions on using Siri.

Dial a Call Using the Keypad

1 Tap **Keypad** (⚏ changes to ⚏).

The Keypad screen appears.

Note: On the Keypad screen, you can tap **Call** (📞) without dialing a number to display the last number dialed.

2 Tap the number keys to dial the number.

Note: You can tap **Add to Contacts** (⊕) to add this number to your Contacts list.

B If you dial a contact's number, the contact's name and phone type appear.

3 Tap **Call** (📞).

Your iPhone makes the call.

4 Tap **End** (📞) when you are ready to end the call.

Place a Call to a Contact

1 Tap **Contacts** (👤 changes to 👤).

The Contacts list appears.

2 Tap the contact you want to call.

The contact's info appears.

3 If FaceTime (📞) appears, tap **FaceTime Audio** (📞) to place a FaceTime Audio call. Otherwise, tap **Call** (📞).

Ⓒ You can tap a number to place a phone call to that number.

Note: You can also place a call to a phone number that the iPhone has identified — for example, by tapping an underlined phone number on a web page or in an e-mail message.

Your iPhone places the call.

Ⓓ In a FaceTime Audio call, you can tap **FaceTime** (📷) to switch to a FaceTime Video call.

4 When you are ready to end the call, tap **End** (📞).

Your iPhone ends the call.

The Call Ended screen appears for a moment.

The screen from which you placed the call appears — for example, the Contacts screen.

Note: To end a call for which you are using the headset, press the clicker button.

Can I use the iPhone as a speaker phone?

Yes. Tap **speaker** (🔊 changes to 🔊) on the screen that appears while you are making a phone call; if you are using an audio device, tap **Audio** (🔊), and then tap **speaker** (🔊 changes to 🔊). The iPhone starts playing the phone call through the speaker on the bottom instead of the small speaker at the top. Tap **speaker** (🔊 changes to 🔊) to switch off the speaker.

What is Dial Assist?

Dial Assist is a feature that automatically determines the correct local prefix or international prefix when you place a call. To turn Dial Assist on or off, press **Home**, tap **Settings** (⚙️), tap **Phone** (📞), and then set the **Dial Assist** switch to On (🔵) or Off ( ).

Using a Wireless Headset or Car System

Instead of using the headset that came with your iPhone, you can use a Bluetooth headset. Similarly, you can use a car system with a Bluetooth connection when using your iPhone in your vehicle, perhaps also connecting the iPhone to a power source to charge it. For example, many new cars have systems that include Apple's CarPlay standard, which enables the car system to act as the display and controller for a connected iPhone.

You must first pair the Bluetooth headset or car system with your iPhone, as discussed in Chapter 6.

Using a Wireless Headset or Car System

1 Turn on the wireless headset or connection and make sure it works.

2 Swipe up from the bottom of the screen.

The Home screen appears.

3 Tap **Phone** (📞).

The Phone app opens.

4 Dial the call. For example, tap **Contacts**, tap the contact, tap **Call** (📞), and then tap the appropriate phone number.

Note: You can also tell Siri to place the call for you.

Your iPhone places the call.

The Audio dialog opens.

5 Tap the headset or other device you want to use.

Ⓐ If you have enabled Handoff, your Mac or Macs may appear.

The Audio dialog closes.

Ⓑ You can tap **audio** (🔊) to display the Audio dialog and switch to another audio device.

Note: If you are playing audio or video on a Bluetooth headset when you receive a call, your iPhone automatically pauses the audio or video and plays the ringtone on the headset.

Mute a Call or Put a Call on Hold

When you are on a call, you may need to mute your iPhone's microphone so that you can confer with people near you without the person at the other end of the phone call hearing.

You may also need to put a call on hold so that you can make another call or take a break from the call.

Mute a Call or Put a Call on Hold

1 Establish the phone call as usual. For example, call a contact.

2 Tap **mute** (changes to).

The iPhone mutes the call.

3 When you are ready to unmute the call, tap **mute** again (changes to).

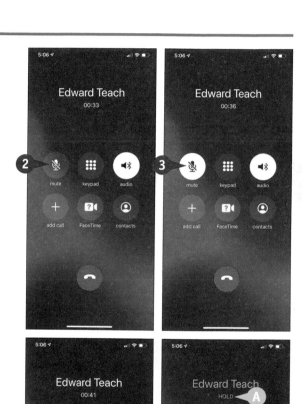

The iPhone turns off muting.

4 To put the call on hold, tap and hold **mute** (changes to) for several seconds.

The iPhone puts the call on hold.

Ⓐ The HOLD readout appears in place of the call time.

Note: After placing a call on hold, you can make another call if necessary.

5 When you are ready to take the call off hold, tap **hold** (changes to).

Make a Conference Call

As well as making phone calls to one other phone at a time, your iPhone can make calls to multiple phones at once, making either cellular calls or FaceTime audio calls, but not mixing the two. To make a conference call, you call the first participant, and then add each other participant in turn. During a conference call, you can talk in private to individual participants. You can also drop a participant from the call.

Make a Conference Call

1 Swipe up from the bottom of the screen.

The Home screen appears.

2 Tap **Phone** (📞).

The Phone app opens.

3 Tap **Contacts** (👤 changes to 👤).

The Contacts screen appears.

4 Tap the contact you want to call first.

The contact's record appears.

5 Tap **Call** (📞) on the phone number to use.

Note: You can also add a contact to the call by using Favorites, Recents, or Keypad.

Your iPhone establishes the call.

6 Tap **add call** (➕).

The Contacts screen appears.

7 Tap the contact you want to add.

The contact's record appears.

8 Tap **Call** (📞).

Ⓐ The iPhone places the first call on hold and makes the new call.

9 Tap **merge calls** (🧍).

The iPhone merges the calls and displays the participants' names at the top of the screen. You can now speak to both participants.

Ⓑ You can add more participants by tapping **add call** (➕), specifying the contact or number, and then merging the calls.

10 To speak privately to a participant, tap **Information** (ⓘ).

The Conference screen appears, showing a list of the participants.

11 Tap **Private** next to the participant.

The iPhone places the other caller or callers on hold.

Ⓒ You can tap **swap** (⇄) to swap the caller on hold and the active caller.

12 When you are ready to resume the conference call, tap **merge calls** (🧍).

The iPhone merges the calls, and all participants can hear each other again.

13 When you finish the call, tap **End** (☎).

The iPhone ends the call.

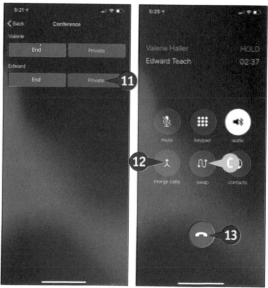

How do I drop a participant from a conference call?
Tap **Information** (ⓘ) to display the Conference screen, and then tap **End** next to the participant you want to drop.

How many people can I add to a conference call?
This depends on your carrier, not on your iPhone. Ask your carrier what the maximum number of participants can be.

Make Video Calls Using FaceTime

By using your iPhone's FaceTime feature, you can enjoy video chats with any of your contacts who have an iOS device — an iPhone, iPad, or iPod touch — running iOS 7 or later, an iPad running iPadOS, or a Mac with the FaceTime for Mac app.

To make a FaceTime call, you and your contact must both have Apple IDs. Your iPhone must be connected to either a wireless network or the cellular network. Using a wireless network is preferable because you typically get better performance and do not use up your cellular data allowance.

Make Video Calls Using FaceTime

Receive a FaceTime Call

1 When your iPhone receives a FaceTime request, and the screen shows who is calling, aim the camera at your face, and then tap **Accept** ( ).

The Connecting screen appears.

When the connection is established, your iPhone displays the caller full-screen, with your video inset.

2 Start your conversation.

3 Tap the screen.

The controls appear.

4 If you need to mute your microphone, tap **Mute** (changes to).

5 Tap **Mute** again (changes to) when you want to turn muting off.

6 Tap **End** ( ) when you are ready to end the FaceTime call.

Make a FaceTime Call

1 Swipe up from the bottom of the screen.

The Home screen appears.

2 Tap **FaceTime** (▢).

The FaceTime app opens.

3 Tap the contact you want to call.

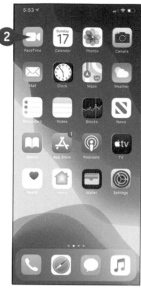
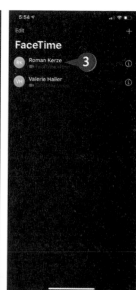

The FaceTime app starts a video call.

4 When your contact answers, smile and speak.

A If you need to show your contact something using the rear-facing camera, tap **Switch Cameras** (▣).

B Tap **Effects** (⬠) to access a variety of visual effects, such as replacing your head with a cartoon animal's head or motion-tracking animated stickers to a location on the screen.

5 When you are ready to end the call, tap **End** (⬤).

TIP

Are there other ways of starting a FaceTime call?

Yes. Here are two easy ways to start a FaceTime call:

• Ask Siri to call a contact via FaceTime. For example, press and hold **Side** to summon Siri, and then say "FaceTime John Smith."

• During a phone call, tap **FaceTime** (◯).

Save Time with Call Favorites and Recents

Y ou can dial phone numbers easily from your Contacts list, but you can save time and effort by using the Favorites and Recents features built into the Phone app.

Favorites are phone numbers that you mark as being especially important to you. Recents are phone numbers you have called and received calls from recently.

Save Time with Call Favorites and Recents

Add a Contact to Your Favorites List

1 Swipe up from the bottom of the screen.

The Home screen appears.

2 Tap **Phone** ( ).

The Phone app opens.

3 Tap **Contacts** (changes to).

The Contacts list appears.

4 Tap the contact you want to add.

The contact's record appears.

5 Tap **Add to Favorites**.

The Add to Favorites dialog opens.

6 Tap the heading for the type of favorite you want to add. This example uses **Call**.

The list of phone numbers for the contact appears.

7 Tap the phone number you want to add to your Favorites list.

The Add to Favorites dialog closes, and the iPhone creates a favorite for the contact.

Call a Favorite

1 In the Phone app, tap **Favorites** (⭐ changes to ⭐).

The Favorites list appears.

2 Tap the Favorite you want to call.

Your iPhone places the call.

A To display the contact's record, tap **Information** (ⓘ) instead of tapping the contact's button. You can then tap a different phone number for the contact if necessary.

Call a Recent

1 In the Phone app, tap **Recents** (🕓 changes to 🕓).

The Recents screen appears. Red entries indicate calls you missed.

B Tap **Missed** if you want to see only recent calls you missed.

C To delete some recents, tap **Edit**; tap **Delete** (➖) to the left of the recent, and then tap the textual **Delete** button; and then tap **Done**.

2 Tap the recent you want to call.

Your iPhone places the call.

Note: If you want to clear the Recents list, tap **Edit** and then tap **Clear**. In the dialog that opens, tap **Clear All Recents**.

TIP

How do I remove a contact from my Favorites?

Tap **Favorites** (⭐ changes to ⭐) to display the Favorites list, and then tap **Edit**. Tap **Delete** (➖) next to the contact, and then tap the textual **Delete** button. You can also rearrange your favorites by tapping the handle (☰) and dragging up or down. Tap **Done** when you have finished changing your favorites.

Send Text and Multimedia Messages

Your iPhone can send instant messages using the Short Message Service, abbreviated SMS; the Multimedia Messaging Service, MMS; or Apple's iMessage service. An SMS message consists of only text, whereas an MMS message can contain text, videos, photos, sounds, or other data. An iMessage can contain text, multimedia content, emoji, animations, handwriting, and other features. The Messages app automatically chooses the appropriate type — SMS, MMS, or iMessage — for the messages you create and the ways you send them.

Send Text and Multimedia Messages

1 Swipe up from the bottom of the screen.

The Home screen appears.

2 Tap **Messages** (💬).

The Messages screen appears.

3 Tap **New Message** (✏️).

Note: Before sending an SMS or MMS message, make sure the recipient's phone number can receive such messages. Typically, you do not receive an alert if the message cannot be delivered.

The New Message screen appears.

4 Tap **Add Contact** (⊕).

The Contacts list appears.

5 Tap the contact to whose phone you want to send the message.

Note: If the contact's record contains multiple phone numbers, Messages displays the contact record. Tap the phone number to use.

Note: iMessage is available only for communicating with other users of Apple devices using their Apple IDs. SMS and MMS work with any device, but may use up your messaging allowance from your carrier.

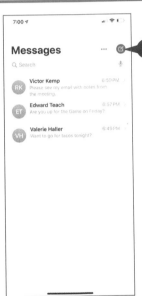

The contact's name appears in the To field of the New Message screen.

6 Tap the text field.

The text field expands, and the More button appears.

7 Tap in the text field, and then type your message.

8 Tap **More** (▶).

The other buttons reappear.

Ⓐ To take a photo and add it, tap **Photo** (⌾).

Note: Messages from contacts sent via iMessage appear in blue balloons. Messages from contacts sent via SMS or MMS appear in green balloons.

9 Tap **Apps** (Ⓐ).

The Apps bar appears.

10 Tap **Photos** (✷).

The Recent Photos list appears.

Ⓑ You can tap **All Photos** to select a photo from your photo library.

11 Tap a recent photo to add it. Scroll left to view other recent photos.

Ⓒ The photo appears in the message.

Ⓓ You can tap **Remove** (⊗) to remove the photo from the message.

12 Tap **Send** (⬆).

Messages sends the message and the photo.

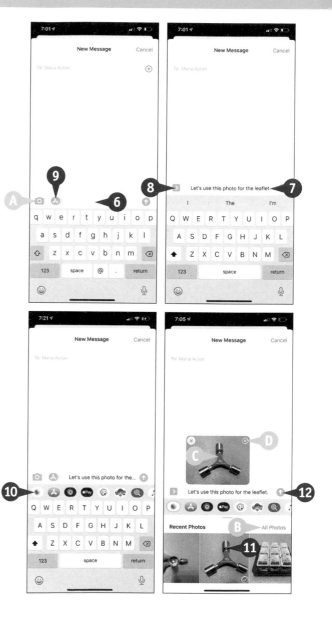

TIPS

How can I respond quickly to an instant message?

When Messages displays a notification for an instant message, tap and hold the notification to display the Quick Reply box. You can then type a reply and tap **Send** to send it.

Is there another way to send a photo or video?

Yes. You can start from the Camera app or the Photos app. Select the photo or video you want to share, and then tap **Share** (⬆). On the Share sheet, tap **Message**. Your iPhone starts a new message containing the photo or video. You can then address and send the message.

Using Emoji and iMessage Features

The Messages app makes it easy to include *emoji* — graphical characters — in your messages. You can send emoji to users of most instant-messaging services, not just to iMessage users.

When you are sending a message to another user of the iMessage service, you can also use a wide range of features that are not available for SMS messages and text messages. These features include stickers, handwriting and sketches, animations, and Digital Touch, which enables you to send a pattern of taps or your heartbeat. You can also respond quickly to a message by using the Tapback feature.

Add Emoji to Messages

The Messages app makes it easy to add emoji to your messages. After typing text, tap **Emoji** (😊) on the keyboard. Messages highlights with color any words in the message that you can replace with emoji; tap a word to insert the corresponding emoji icon, such as 👍 for "great!"

You can also insert other emoji manually by tapping them on the emoji keyboard. Tap the buttons at the bottom of the screen, or simply scroll the emoji panel left or right, to browse the available emoji.

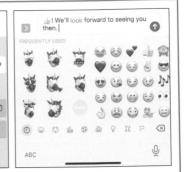

Send a Handwritten Message or Sketch

To send a handwritten message or sketch, tap **New** (📝) to begin a new message. Address the message to an iMessage user, tap **Apps** (🅰), and then tap **Digital Touch** (●) to display the Digital Touch controls.

Tap **Expand** (—) to expand the panel to full screen, tap the color you want, and then write or draw what you want to send. Tap **Send** (⬆) to send the message.

Send Heartbeats or Taps

To send heartbeats or taps, tap **New** (📝) to begin a new message. Address the message to an iMessage user, tap **Apps** (🅰), and then tap **Digital Touch** (●) to display the Digital Touch controls.

To send a heartbeat, tap and hold with two fingers on the screen. Messages displays a heartbeat graphic and sends a heartbeat; you do not need to tap **Send** (⬆).

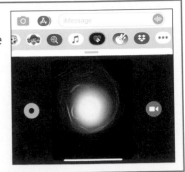

Send a Message with Effect

To send a message with effect, write the text for the message, and then tap and hold **Send** (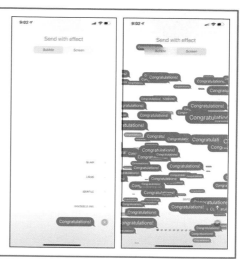). The Send with Effect screen appears. At the top of the screen, tap **Bubble** if you want to send a bubble with an effect such as Slam or Invisible Ink, and then tap the button for the effect; a preview then plays. To send text with a full-screen effect, tap **Screen** at the top of the screen, and then swipe left or right to reach the effect you want; again, a preview plays. When you are ready to send the message, tap **Send** (⬆).

Responding Quickly Using the Tapback Feature

iMessage enables you to respond quickly to an incoming message by tapping and holding it. The Tapback panel opens, and you can tap the icon you want to send as an instant response.

Share the Music You Are Listening To

With iMessage, you can quickly share links to the music you are enjoying on Apple Music. Tap **New** (✏) to begin a new message, and then address the message to an iMessage user. Tap **Apps** (Ⓐ) to display the Apps panel. Swipe left or right if necessary to display the Music panel, and then tap the item you want to share. A button for the item appears in the message box. Type any explanatory or exhortatory text needed, and then tap **Send** (⬆).

Send a Payment

With iMessage, you can send a payment to a contact. Tap **New** (✏) to begin a new message, and then address the message to an iMessage user. Tap **Apps** (Ⓐ) to display the Apps panel. Swipe left or right if necessary to display the Apple Pay button, and then tap **Apple Pay** (Pay). Use the controls to specify the amount, and then tap **Pay**. The payment ticket appears in the message box. Tap **Send** (⬆) to send it.

Manage Your Instant Messages

Messages is great for communicating quickly and frequently with your nearest and dearest and with your colleagues, so it may not take long before the interface is so full of messages that it becomes hard to navigate.

To keep your messages under control, you can forward messages to others and delete messages you do not need to keep. You can either delete messages from a conversation, leaving the conversation's other messages, or delete the entire conversation.

Manage Your Instant Messages

Delete an Entire Conversation

1 Swipe up from the bottom of the screen.

The Home screen appears.

2 Tap **Messages** (⬭).

The Messages screen appears.

3 Tap **More** (⋯).

A dialog opens.

4 Tap **Select Messages**.

The Messages screen switches to Edit Mode.

5 Tap the selection button (⬭ changes to ✓) for each conversation you want to delete.

The Delete button appears.

6 Tap **Delete**.

Messages deletes the conversation.

Ⓐ You can also delete a conversation by swiping it to the left and then tapping **Delete**.

Ⓑ You can suppress alerts for a contact by swiping a message left and then tapping **Hide Alerts**.

7 When you finish deleting conversations, tap **Done**.

Messages turns off Edit Mode.

Forward or Delete One or More Messages from a Conversation

1 On the Messages screen, tap the conversation that contains the message or messages you will forward.

The conversation appears.

Note: You can tap in a conversation and slide your finger left to display the time of each message.

2 Tap and hold a message.

A dialog opens.

3 Tap **More**.

A selection button ( ) appears to the left of each message.

4 Tap the selection button (changes to ✓) for each message you want to affect.

5 Tap **Forward** (↪).

Messages starts a new message containing the message or messages you selected.

Ⓒ Instead of forwarding the selected messages, you can tap **Delete** (🗑) to delete them from the conversation.

Ⓓ You can also tap **Delete All** to delete all the messages.

6 Address the message.

7 Type any extra text needed.

8 Tap **Send** (⬆) to send the message.

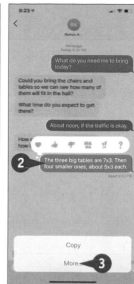

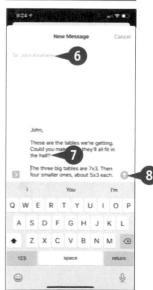

TIP

Can I resend a message?

Yes, you can resend a message in either of these ways:

- If a red icon with an exclamation point appears next to the message, the message has not been sent. Tap the icon to try sending the message again.

- If the message has been sent, you can forward it as described in this section. Alternatively, tap and hold the message text, and then tap **Copy** to copy it. Tap and hold in the message text field, and then tap **Paste** to paste the text. Tap **Send** to send the message.

Choose Settings for Messages

essages includes many settings that you can configure to control the way the app looks and behaves. These settings include whether to send messages as SMS if the iMessage service is unavailable, whether to use MMS messaging, and how long to keep messages.

A key setting is whether to send read receipts for the messages you receive. You can turn read receipts on or off for Messages as a whole, but you can also make exceptions for individual contacts.

Choose Settings for Messages

1 Swipe up from the bottom of the screen.

The Home screen appears.

2 Tap **Settings** (⚙).

The Settings screen appears.

3 Tap **Messages** (💬).

4 Set the **iMessage** switch to On (⬤) to use the iMessage service.

5 Set the **Show Contact Photos** switch to On (⬤) to display contact photos.

6 Set the **Send Read Receipts** switch to On (⬤) or Off ( ) to control whether Messages sends read receipts for all messages.

7 Tap **Send & Receive**.

The iMessage screen appears.

8 Verify that this list shows the correct phone number and address.

9 Tap the phone number or e-mail address from which to start new conversations.

10 Tap **Messages** (<).

The Messages screen appears again.

11 Set the **Send as SMS** switch to On (⬤) to send iMessage messages as SMS or MMS messages when iMessage is unavailable.

12 Tap **Text Message Forwarding**.

The Text Message Forwarding screen appears.

13 Set the switch to On (⬤) for each Mac or device you want to allow to send text messages via the iPhone.

14 Tap **Back** (**<**).

The Messages screen appears again.

15 Set the **MMS Messaging** switch to On (⬤) to enable MMS messaging.

16 Set the **Show Subject Field** switch to On (⬤) or Off ( ), as needed.

17 Set the **Character Count** switch to On (⬤) or Off ( ), as needed.

18 Tap **Keep Messages**.

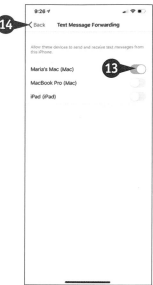

The Keep Messages screen appears.

19 Tap **30 Days**, **1 Year**, or **Forever**, as needed.

20 Tap **Messages** (**<**).

The Messages screen appears again.

21 Set the **Filter Unknown Senders** switch to On (⬤) if you want to keep messages from unknown senders separate.

22 Tap **Expire** and choose **After 2 Minutes** or **Never** for audio messages.

23 Set the **Raise to Listen** switch to On (⬤) or Off ( ).

24 Set the **Low Quality Image Mode** switch to On (⬤) or Off ( ), as needed.

TIP

How do I control read receipts for individual contacts?

First, on the Messages screen in the Settings app, set the **Send Read Receipts** switch to On (⬤) or Off ( ) to control whether Messages sends read receipts by default.

Next, in the Messages app, open a message to or from the appropriate contact. Tap the contact's icon, then tap **Info** (ⓘ) to display the Details screen. Set the **Send Read Receipts** switch to On (⬤) or Off ( ), as needed, and then tap **Done**.

Block and Unblock Senders

Messages enables you to block any sender from whom you do not want to receive communications. You can implement blocking from the Messages app or from the Phone app. Whichever app you start from, blocking the contact prevents you from receiving notifications when the contact phones or messages you.

You can review your list of blocked senders and unblock any sender from whom you want to receive messages again.

Block and Unblock Senders

Block a Sender from the Messages App

1 Swipe up from the bottom of the screen.

The Home screen appears.

2 Tap **Messages** (○).

The Messages screen appears.

Note: If the screen for a contact appears, tap **Back** (<) to display the Messages screen.

3 Tap a conversation with the contact you want to block.

The conversation opens.

4 Tap the contact's icon.

The Audio button, FaceTime icon, and Info icon appear.

5 Tap **Info** (ⓘ).

The Details screen appears.

6 Tap the contact's name.

The contact record opens.

7 Tap **Block this Caller**.

A confirmation dialog opens.

8 Tap **Block Contact**.

View Your Blocked List and Unblock Senders

1 Swipe up from the bottom of the screen.

The Home screen appears.

2 Tap **Settings** (⚙).

The Settings screen appears.

3 Tap **Messages** (💬).

The Messages screen appears.

4 In the SMS/MMS section, tap **Blocked Contacts**.

The Blocked screen appears, showing the list of contacts you have blocked.

Ⓐ You can tap **Add New** to display the Contacts screen, and then tap the contact you want to block. Blocking the contact blocks all the means of contact, but you can then unblock any means of contact you wish to allow.

5 To unblock a means of contact, swipe its button to the left.

The Unblock button appears.

6 Tap **Unblock**.

How do I block a contact in the Phone app?

In the Phone app, tap **Contacts** (👤 changes to 👤), tap the contact to display the contact record, and then tap **Block this Caller**. In the confirmation dialog that opens, tap **Block Contact**.

Set Up and Use the Emergency SOS Feature

The iPhone's Emergency SOS feature can either display the Emergency SOS screen or dial emergency services automatically when you give the Emergency SOS shortcut, five quick presses on the Side button. Emergency SOS can also automatically text a group of emergency contacts to tell them you have dialed emergency services.

To be ready for an emergency, enable the Emergency SOS feature, configure its settings, and then set up your emergency contacts in the Health app.

Set Up and Use the Emergency SOS Feature

Set Up the Emergency SOS Feature

1 Swipe up from the bottom of the screen to display the Home screen.

2 Tap **Settings** (⚙) to display the Settings screen.

3 Tap **Emergency SOS** (🆘).

The Emergency SOS screen appears.

4 Set the **Call with Side Button** switch to On (◉) if you want to make an emergency call by pressing **Side** five times in quick succession.

5 Set the **Auto Call** switch to On (◉) if you want to invoke the Emergency SOS shortcut to place the emergency call. Set the **Auto Call** switch to Off ( ) to display the Emergency SOS screen instead.

6 If you set the **Auto Call** switch to On (◉), set the **Countdown Sound** switch to On (◉) to receive a 3-second countdown before your iPhone dials emergency services.

7 Tap **Set up Emergency Contacts in Health**.

The Medical ID screen in the Health app appears.

8 Tap **Edit**.

The Medical ID screen opens for editing.

9 Tap **add emergency contact** (➕).

The Contacts screen appears.

Ⓐ If the contact you want does not appear, tap **Groups**, select the appropriate groups, and then tap **Done**.

10 Tap the contact you want to designate an emergency contact.

The Relationship screen appears.

11 Tap the button for the term that describes the contact's relationship to you, such as **mother**, **sister**, or **partner**.

The Medical ID screen appears again.

You can add other contacts by repeating steps **8** to **10**.

12 Tap **Done**.

Use the Emergency SOS Feature

1 When you need to place an emergency call, press **Side** five times in quick succession.

Ⓑ If you set the **Auto Call** switch to On (◉), your iPhone starts placing an emergency call.

Ⓒ If you set the **Countdown Sound** switch to On (◉), a 3-second countdown starts.

Ⓓ You can tap **Stop** (⊗) to stop the call.

Ⓔ If you set the **Auto Call** switch to Off ( ), the Power Off screen appears.

Ⓕ You can swipe **Emergency SOS** (sos) right to place the emergency call.

TIP

How can I quickly disable Face ID to prevent someone from forcing me to unlock my iPhone?
You can temporarily disable Face ID by pressing and holding **Side** and **Volume Up** or **Side** and **Volume Down** for two seconds. The Power Off screen appears. At this point, Face ID is disabled, and you will need to enter your passcode to enable it again.

CHAPTER 6

Networking and Social Networking

You can control which cellular and wireless networks your iPhone uses and enjoy social networking wherever you go.

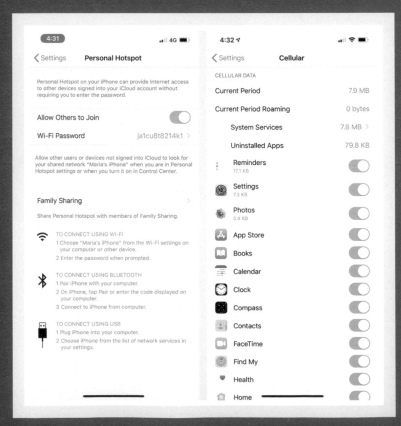

Using Airplane Mode

Normally, you will want to keep your iPhone connected to the cellular network so that you can make or receive phone calls and access the Internet. But when you do not need or may not use the cellular network, you can turn on the iPhone's Airplane Mode feature to cut off all connections.

Turning on Airplane Mode turns off Wi-Fi as well, but you can turn Wi-Fi on and off separately when you need to.

Using Airplane Mode

① Swipe down from the upper-right corner of the screen to open Control Center.

Note: You can open Control Center from within most apps. If an app blocks Control Center, first display the Home screen, and then open Control Center. If all apps block you opening Control Center, tap **Settings** (⚙), tap **Control Center** (🎛), and then set the **Access Within Apps** switch to On (⬤).

Ⓐ You can tap **Airplane Mode** (✈ changes to ✈) to turn Airplane Mode on quickly.

② Tap and hold the upper-left box.

The pop-up panel opens.

③ Tap **Airplane Mode** (✈ changes to ✈).

Your iPhone turns off all cellular and wireless connections.

④ To turn on Wi-Fi, tap **Wi-Fi** (📶 changes to 📶).

⑤ Tap the screen above the pop-up panel.

The pop-up panel closes.

⑥ Tap the screen at the top of Control Center.

Control Center closes.

Note: When your iPhone has a wireless network connection, it uses that connection instead of the cellular connection. This helps keep down your cellular network usage and often gives a faster connection.

Monitor Your Cellular Network Usage

I f you use your iPhone extensively, you may need to monitor your usage of the cellular network to avoid incurring extra charges beyond your data allowance. You can check your current data usage and roaming data usage in the Cellular Data Usage area of the Cellular screen in the Settings app. However, you should also see if your carrier provides an app for monitoring data usage, because such apps frequently offer extra features, such as warning you when your phone is using data quickly.

Monitor Your Cellular Network Usage

1 Swipe up from the bottom of the screen to display the Home screen.

2 Tap and hold **Settings** (⚙) to open the pop-up panel.

The pop-up panel opens.

3 Tap **Cellular Data** (📶) to display the Cellular screen.

Note: You can also display the Cellular screen by displaying the Home screen, tapping **Settings** (⚙), and then tapping **Cellular** (📶) on the Settings screen.

4 Set the **Cellular Data** switch to On (◉) to enable cellular data.

A The readouts in the Cellular Data Usage area show your cellular data usage since last resetting the statistics and how much roaming data you have used.

B The readouts in the Call Time area show the amount of time you have spent making calls since last resetting the statistics and during your phone's lifetime.

C You can reset your usage statistics by tapping **Reset Statistics** at the bottom of the Cellular screen.

D You can set the **Wi-Fi Assist** switch to On (◉) to make your iPhone automatically use cellular data when the phone's Wi-Fi connection is poor. This switch may be set to On (◉) by default. The readout shows the amount of cellular data used.

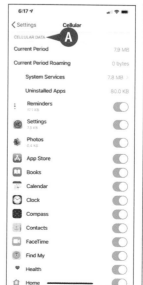

Control Cellular Data and Background Refresh

To control your iPhone's use of cellular data, you can turn cellular data on and off, and you can specify which apps can use cellular data. You can determine which apps and services use the most data, and then turn off greedy apps.

You can also use the Background App Refresh feature to control which apps refresh their content via Wi-Fi or cellular connections when running in the background rather than the foreground.

Control Cellular Data and Background Refresh

① Swipe up from the bottom of the screen to display the Home screen.

② Tap **Settings** (⚙) to display the Cellular screen.

③ Tap **Cellular** (📶) to display the Cellular screen.

Note: Turning off cellular data does not affect cellular voice services: You can still make phone calls, and GPS tracking still works.

④ If you need to turn cellular data off altogether, set the **Cellular Data** switch to Off (⚪ changes to ⚪).

⑤ Tap **Cellular Data Options**.

The Cellular Data Options screen appears.

⑥ Tap **Voice & Data** to display the Voice & Data screen.

Note: The options on the Voice & Data screen vary depending on your carrier and region.

⑦ Tap the button for the service or services you want to use. In the example, you might tap **4G, VoLTE On** to enable 4G cellular with Voice over LTE.

⑧ Tap **Back** (‹).

The Cellular Data Options screen appears again.

⑨ Tap **Cellular** (‹).

The Cellular screen appears again.

10 If cellular data is enabled, set each app's switch to On (⬤) or Off (   ), as needed.

11 To see which system services have been using cellular data, tap **System Services**.

The System Services screen appears.

12 Browse the list to identify any services that hog cellular data.

13 Tap **Cellular** (⟨).

The Cellular screen appears.

14 Tap **Settings** (⟨).

The Settings screen appears.

15 Tap **General** (⚙).

The General screen appears.

16 Tap **Background App Refresh**.

The Background App Refresh screen appears.

17 Tap **Background App Refresh**; tap **Off**, **Wi-Fi**, or **Wi-Fi & Cellular Data**, as needed; and then tap **Background App Refresh** (⟨).

18 Assuming you chose Wi-Fi or Wi-Fi and Cellular Data, set each individual app switch to On (⬤) or Off (   ), as needed.

19 Tap **General** (⟨).

The General screen appears.

20 Tap **Settings** (⟨).

The Settings screen appears.

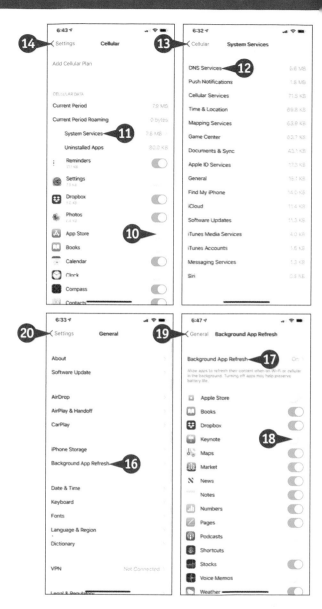

TIP

Which apps should I allow to use Background App Refresh?

Normally, you should restrict Background App Refresh to those apps for which it is important to have updated information immediately available each time you access the app. For example, if you use your iPhone for navigation, getting updated map and GPS information in the background is a good idea, whereas updating magazine subscriptions is usually a waste of cellular data.

Connect Your iPhone to a Different Carrier

Your iPhone's SIM card makes it connect automatically to a particular carrier's network, such as the AT&T network or the Verizon network. If your iPhone is not locked to a particular carrier's network, you can connect the iPhone to a different carrier's network when you go outside the area your carrier covers. For example, if you travel to the United Kingdom, you can connect your iPhone to carriers such as O2, Vodafone, Three, or EE. You may need to change the iPhone's SIM card to connect to another network.

Connect Your iPhone to a Different Carrier

1 Swipe up from the bottom of the screen.

The Home screen appears.

2 Tap **Settings** (⚙️).

The Settings screen appears.

3 Tap **Cellular** (📶).

The Cellular screen appears.

4 Tap **Network Selection**.

Note: To connect to a different carrier's network, you may need to set up an account with that carrier or pay extra charges to your standard carrier. You may also need to insert a different SIM card in your iPhone.

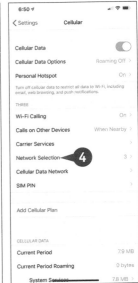

The Network Selection screen appears.

5 Set the **Automatic** switch to Off (⬤ changes to ◯).

The list of available carriers appears.

6 Tap the carrier you want to use.

Note: When you want to switch back to your regular carrier, set the **Automatic** switch on the Network Selection screen to On (◯ changes to ⬤).

Turn Data Roaming On or Off

When you need to use your iPhone somewhere your carrier does not provide Internet service, you can turn on data roaming, which enables you to access the Internet using other carriers' networks. Data roaming may incur extra charges, especially when you use it in another country, so keep data roaming turned off and turn it on only when you need it. Normally, you will want to use data roaming only when no wireless network connection is available.

Turn Data Roaming On or Off

1 Swipe up from the bottom of the screen.

The Home screen appears.

2 Tap and hold **Settings** (⚙️).

The pop-up panel opens.

3 Tap **Cellular Data** (📶).

The Cellular screen appears.

A You can also turn off cellular data altogether by setting the **Cellular Data** switch to Off ( ). Do this when you need to ensure that all apps use Wi-Fi rather than cellular connections.

4 Tap **Cellular Data Options**.

The Cellular Data Options screen appears.

5 Set the **Data Roaming** switch to On (changes to 🔵).

Note: When you need to turn data roaming off again, set the **Data Roaming** switch on the Cellular Data Options screen to Off (🔵 changes to).

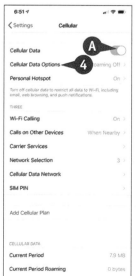

Connect Bluetooth Devices to Your iPhone

To extend your iPhone's functionality, you can connect devices to it that communicate using the wireless Bluetooth technology.

For example, you can connect a Bluetooth headset and microphone so that you can listen to music and make and take phone calls. Or you can connect a Bluetooth keyboard so that you can quickly type e-mail messages, notes, or documents. You can also connect your iPhone to another phone, to a tablet, to many cars' infotainment unit, or to a computer via Bluetooth.

Connect Bluetooth Devices to Your iPhone

Set Up a Bluetooth Device

1 Swipe up from the bottom of the screen.

The Home screen appears.

2 Tap and hold **Settings** (⚙).

The pop-up panel opens.

3 Tap **Bluetooth** (✳).

The Bluetooth screen appears.

4 Set the **Bluetooth** switch to On (changes to ⬤).

5 Turn on the Bluetooth device and make it discoverable.

Note: Read the Bluetooth device's instructions to find out how to make the device discoverable via Bluetooth.

Ⓐ Devices in the My Devices list are already paired with your iPhone. You can tap a device to connect it.

6 Tap the device's button.

Ⓑ For a device such as a keyboard or a computer, the Bluetooth Pairing Request dialog opens.

7 Type the pairing code on the device.

The iPhone pairs with the device and then connects to it.

Ⓒ The My Devices list shows the device as Connected. You can start using the device.

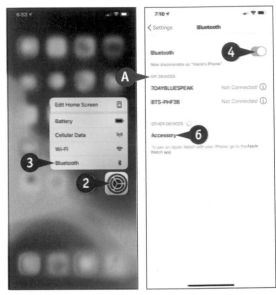

Choose the Device for Playing Audio or Taking a Call

1 Swipe down from the upper-right corner of the screen.

Note: This example uses the Music app.

Control Center opens.

2 Tap and hold the audio controls box.

The pop-up panel opens.

3 Tap **AirPlay** ().

The list of devices appears.

4 Tap the device you want to use.

C You can tap **Audio Controls** (▶️) to display the audio controls box again.

5 Tap outside the pop-up panel.

The pop-up panel closes.

6 Tap the screen at the top of Control Center.

Control Center closes.

TIP

How do I stop using a Bluetooth device?

When you no longer need to use a particular Bluetooth device, tell your iPhone to forget it. Swipe up from the bottom of the screen to display the Home screen, and then tap **Settings** (⚙️). Tap **Bluetooth** (🔵), and then tap **Info** (ⓘ) for the device. On the device's screen, tap **Forget This Device**, and then tap **Forget Device** in the confirmation dialog.

Share Items via AirDrop

AirDrop enables you to share files quickly and easily with iOS devices and Macs near your iPhone. For example, you can use AirDrop to share a photo, a contact record, or an item from Wallet. You can use AirDrop in any app that displays a Share button (⬆).

You can turn AirDrop on when you need it and off when you do not. When AirDrop is on, you can choose between accepting items only from your contacts or from everyone.

Share Items via AirDrop

Turn AirDrop On or Off

1 Swipe down from the upper-right corner of the screen.

Control Center opens.

2 Tap and hold the upper-left box.

The pop-up panel opens.

A The readout shows AirDrop's status: *AirDrop: Receiving Off*; *AirDrop: Contacts Only*; or *AirDrop: Everyone*.

3 Tap **AirDrop** (◉).

Note: AirDrop uses Wi-Fi or Bluetooth to transfer files wirelessly without the devices having to be on the same wireless network.

The AirDrop panel opens.

4 Tap **Receiving Off**, **Contacts Only**, or **Everyone**, as needed.

The AirDrop panel closes.

B The AirDrop readout shows the AirDrop setting you chose.

5 Tap the screen above the pop-up panel.

The pop-up panel closes.

6 Tap the screen at the top of Control Center.

Control Center closes.

Share an Item via AirDrop

1 Open the app that contains the item. For example, tap **Photos** (🌸) on the Home screen.

2 Navigate to the item you want to share. For example, tap a photo to open it.

3 Tap **Share** (⬆️).

The Share sheet appears.

C In some apps, you can select other items to share at the same time. For example, in Photos, you can select other photos.

4 In the AirDrop area, tap **AirDrop** (◉).

The AirDrop panel opens.

5 Tap the icon for the device to which you want to send the item.

AirDrop sends the item.

D The Sent readout appears below the icon for the device.

6 Tap **Done**. The app and the share sheet appear again.

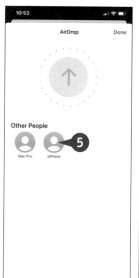
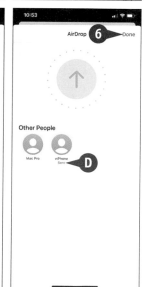

TIPS

How do I receive an item via AirDrop?
When someone tries to send you an item via AirDrop, the AirDrop dialog opens. Tap **Accept** if you want to receive the item; otherwise, tap **Decline**.

Does AirDrop pose a security threat to my iPhone and data?
AirDrop encrypts files so it can transfer them securely. When using AirDrop, you choose which files — if any — you want to share from your iPhone and accept on it; other iOS devices and Macs cannot use AirDrop to grab files from your iPhone.

Share Internet Access via Personal Hotspot

Your iPhone can not only access the Internet itself from anywhere it has a suitable connection to the cellular network, but it can also share that Internet access with your computer and other devices. This feature is called *Personal Hotspot*.

For you to use Personal Hotspot, your iPhone's carrier must permit you to use it. Some carriers charge an extra fee per month on top of the standard data plan charge.

Share Internet Access via Personal Hotspot

Set Up Personal Hotspot

1 Swipe up from the bottom of the screen.

The Home screen appears.

2 Tap **Settings** (⚙️).

The Settings screen appears.

3 Tap **Personal Hotspot** (📶).

The Personal Hotspot screen appears.

4 Tap **Wi-Fi Password**.

The Wi-Fi Password screen appears.

5 Tap **Delete** (×) to delete the default password.

6 Type the password you want to use.

7 Tap **Done**.

The Personal Hotspot screen appears again.

8 Set the **Allow Others to Join** switch to On (🔘) if you want to allow people other than Family Sharing members to use the hotspot.

9 Tap **Family Sharing**.

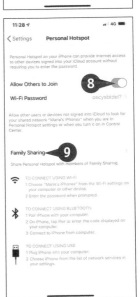

The Family Sharing screen appears.

10 Set the **Family Sharing** switch to On (⬤) if you want to let Family Sharing members use the hotspot.

11 Tap the family member whose access you want to configure.

The screen for that family member appears.

12 Tap **Ask for Approval** or **Automatic**, as appropriate.

13 Tap **Back** (‹).

The Family Sharing screen appears again.

14 Tap **Back** (‹).

The Personal Hotspot screen appears again.

You can now connect your computer or other devices.

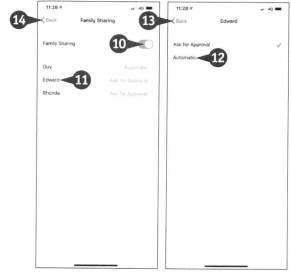

Stop Using Personal Hotspot

1 Swipe up from the bottom of the screen.

The Home screen appears.

Ⓐ The blue background for the clock readout indicates that Personal Hotspot is active and has one or more connections.

2 Tap the clock readout with the blue background.

The Personal Hotspot screen appears.

3 Set the **Allow Others to Join** switch to Off (⬤ changes to ⬜).

TIP

How else can I connect a PC or Mac to Personal Hotspot?

Usually, you can connect a PC to Personal Hotspot by simply connecting your iPhone to the PC via USB. Windows automatically detects the iPhone's Internet connection as a new network connection and installs any software needed.

Similarly, you can connect a Mac via USB, but you may need to configure the network connection. [Control] + click or right-click **System Preferences** (⚙) on the Dock and click **Network** on the contextual menu to open the Network preferences pane. In the left pane, click **iPhone USB**. If the Apply button is dark, click **Apply**.

If you cannot get USB to work, connect the computer via Wi-Fi or Bluetooth, if your computer has either of those features.

Connect to Wi-Fi Networks and Hotspots

To conserve your data allowance, use a Wi-Fi network instead of the cell phone network whenever you can. Your iPhone can connect to both private Wi-Fi networks and to public Wi-Fi hotspots. Use public Wi-Fi hotspots with caution, because they may not be secure.

The first time you connect to a Wi-Fi network, you must provide the network's password. After that, the iPhone stores the password, so you can connect to the network without entering the password again.

Connect to Wi-Fi Networks and Hotspots

Connect to a Network Listed on the Wi-Fi Screen

1 Swipe up from the bottom of the screen.

The Home screen appears.

2 Tap and hold **Settings** (⚙).

The pop-up panel opens.

3 Tap **Wi-Fi** (📶).

The Wi-Fi screen appears.

4 If Wi-Fi is off, set the **Wi-Fi** switch to On (changes to ⬤).

The list of networks appears.

Ⓐ A lock icon (🔒) indicates the network has security such as a password.

5 Tap the network you want to connect to.

Note: If the network does not have a password, your iPhone connects to it without prompting you for a password.

Note: When connecting to a Wi-Fi hotspot, you may need to enter login information in Safari. In this case, Safari usually opens automatically and prompts you to log in.

The Enter Password screen appears.

6 Type the password.

7 Tap **Join**.

Your iPhone connects to the wireless network.

Ⓑ The Wi-Fi screen appears again, showing a check mark (✓) next to the network the iPhone has connected to.

Connect to a Network Not Listed on the Wi-Fi Screen

1 On the Wi-Fi screen, tap **Other**.

The Other Network screen appears.

2 Type the network name.

Note: If the network does not use security, tap **Join**.

C The Wi-Fi signal icons (📶) on the Wi-Fi screen and in the status bar show the strength of the Wi-Fi signals. The more bars that appear in black rather than gray, the stronger a signal is.

3 Tap **Security**.

The Security screen appears.

4 Tap the security type — for example, **WPA2/WPA3**.

5 Tap **Other Network** (‹).

The Other Network screen appears.

6 Type the password.

7 Tap **Join**.

Your iPhone joins the network.

TIPS

What does Ask to Join Networks do?

Your iPhone automatically connects to networks it "knows" — those it has connected to before. Tap **Ask to Join Networks** to display the Ask to Join Networks screen, and then tap **Notify** to have iOS notify you of available networks, tap **Ask** to have iOS prompt you to connect to available networks, or tap **Off** to have iOS take no action.

How do I stop using a particular wireless network?

Tap **Info** (ⓘ) to the right of the network's name on the Wi-Fi screen. On the network's screen, tap **Forget This Network**. In the dialog that opens, tap **Forget**.

Always forget a Wi-Fi hotspot you will not use again. Forgetting the hotspot helps prevent your iPhone from connecting to a malevolent hotspot that mimics the genuine hotspot.

Set Up and Enjoy Social Networking

Always in your pocket or purse if not in your hand, your iPhone is the perfect device for keeping in touch with family, friends, and acquaintances via social networking. You can install apps such as Facebook, Twitter, or WhatsApp; post updates or browse what others have posted; and share content easily from many apps, such as Photos.

To protect your account and data, it is a good idea to enable two-factor authentication for any social-networking app or other app that offers this security feature.

Install the Social Networking Apps You Need

To start with, install the social networking apps you want to use. Swipe up from the bottom of the screen to display the Home screen, and then tap **App Store** () to launch the App Store app. To find a specific app, tap **Search** (Q changes to Q), type the app's name, and then tap the appropriate search result. On the screen showing the app, tap **Get** and follow the procedure for installing the app.

Configure Settings for a Social Networking App

Many social networking apps have settings that you can configure in the Settings app. To do so, swipe up from the bottom of the screen to display the Home screen, tap **Settings** (), and then tap the app's button — for example, tap **Facebook** () to display the settings screen for the app. You can then configure the controls. Many apps have standard settings such as the Siri & Search screen, the Notifications screen, and the Background App Refresh switch. Some have other settings, such as the Upload HD switches in the Facebook app, which controls whether the app uploads high-definition videos and photos.

Some apps also have settings that you can configure within the app itself. For example, in Facebook, tap **Menu** (≡) to open the menu, and then tap **Settings & Privacy** ().

Launch and Sign In to a Social Networking App

When you are ready to start using a social networking app, launch it by tapping its icon on the Home screen. For example, tap **Twitter** ( ). Follow the prompts to sign in or log in. For example, in Twitter, enter your username or Twitter handle, enter your password, and then tap **Log in**.

The app then opens, and you can start using it as normal. For example, in Twitter, tap **Tweet** ( ) to start writing a new tweet.

Share Content with a Social Networking App

You can easily share content from other apps with your social networking apps. To do so, first open the appropriate app and select the item you want to share. For example, tap **Photos** ( ) and select a photo to share. Next, tap **Share** ( ) to open the Share sheet, tap the social networking app on the Activities bar, and then follow the prompts to post the photo.

If the app does not appear on the Activities bar, tap **More** (···) at the right end of the Activities bar to display the Apps screen. Tap **Edit**, set the app's switch to On ( ) in the Suggestions list, and optionally drag the app by its handle ( ) to the Favorites list. Then tap **Done**.

CHAPTER 7

Working with Apps

iOS enables you to customize the Home screen, putting the icons you need most right at hand and organizing them into folders. You can switch instantly among the apps you are running, find the apps you need on Apple's App Store, and update and remove apps. You can also work easily with text and take notes.

Customize the Home Screen

From the Home screen, you run the apps on your iPhone. You can customize the Home screen to put the apps you use most frequently within easy reach. You can create additional Home screen pages as needed and move the app icons among them so that the app icons are arranged in the way you find fastest and most convenient to use.

Customize the Home Screen

Unlock the Icons for Customization

1 Swipe up from the bottom of the screen.

The Home screen appears.

2 Swipe left or right to display the Home screen page you want to customize.

Ⓐ You can also tap the dots, or to their left or right, to move from one page to the previous or next page.

3 Tap and hold any app's icon on that Home screen page.

The pop-up menu opens.

4 Tap **Edit Home Screen** (▯).

The icons start to jiggle, indicating that you can move them.

Move an Icon Within a Home Screen

1 After unlocking the icons, drag the icon to where you want it.

The other icons move out of the way.

2 When the icon is in the right place, drop it.

Ⓑ The icon stays in its new position.

Move an Icon to a Different Home Screen

1 After unlocking the icons, drag the icon to the left edge of the screen to display the previous Home screen page or to the right edge to display the next page.

The previous page or next page appears.

2 Drag the icon to where you want it.

If the page contains other icons, they move out of the way as needed.

3 Drop the icon.

C The icon stays in its new position.

Stop Customizing the Home Screen

1 Tap **Done**.

The icons stop jiggling.

TIP

How can I put the default apps back into their original Home screen locations?
Swipe up from the bottom of the screen — to display the Home screen, tap **Settings** (⚙️), and then tap **General** (⚙️). At the bottom of the General screen, tap **Reset**. On the Reset screen, tap **Reset Home Screen Layout**, and then tap **Reset Home Screen** in the dialog that opens. Swipe up from the bottom of the screen to return to the Home screen.

Organize Apps with Folders

To organize the Home screen pages, you can arrange the items into folders. The iPhone's default Home screen layout includes a folder named Utilities, which contains items such as the Calculator app and the Compass app, but you can create as many other folders as you need. Like the Home screen, each folder can have multiple pages, with up to nine apps on each page, so you can put many apps in a folder.

Organize Apps with Folders

Create a Folder

① Display the Home screen page that contains the icon you want to put into a folder.

② Tap and hold an icon.

The pop-up menu opens.

③ Tap **Edit Home Screen** (▦).

The icons start to jiggle, indicating that you can move them.

Note: When creating a folder, you may find it easiest to first put both items you will add to the folder on the same page.

④ Drag the icon to the other icon you want to place in the folder you create.

The iPhone creates a folder, puts both icons in it, and assigns a default name based on the genre, if it can identify a genre.

⑤ Tap **Delete** (⊗) to delete the folder name.

The keyboard appears.

⑥ Type the new name for the folder.

⑦ Tap outside the folder.

The iPhone applies the name to the folder.

⑧ Tap **Done**.

The icons stop jiggling.

Note: You can quickly rename a folder by pressing it, tapping **Rename**, typing the new name, and then tapping outside the folder.

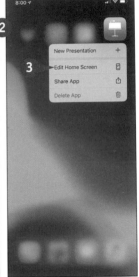

Open an Item in a Folder

1 Display the Home screen page that contains the folder.

2 Tap the folder's icon.

The folder's contents appear, and the items outside the folder fade and blur.

3 If necessary, swipe left or right or tap to the left or right of the dots to navigate to another page in the folder.

4 Tap the item you want to open.

The item opens.

Add an Item to a Folder

1 Display the Home screen page that contains the item.

2 Tap and hold an icon.

The pop-up menu opens.

3 Tap **Edit Home Screen** (📱).

The icons start to jiggle, indicating that you can move them.

4 Drag the icon on top of the folder and drop it there.

Note: If the folder is on a different Home screen page from the icon, drag the icon to the left edge to display the previous page or to the right edge to display the next page.

The item goes into the folder.

5 Tap **Done** to stop the icons jiggling.

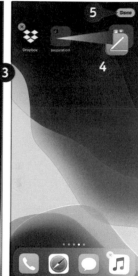

TIPS

How do I take an item out of a folder?

Tap the folder to display its contents, and then tap and hold an icon until the pop-up menu opens. Tap **Edit Home Screen** (📱). The icons start to jiggle. Drag the icon out of the folder, drag it to where you want it on the Home screen, and then drop it. When you remove the last icon, iOS deletes the folder automatically.

How do I create another page in a folder?

Open the folder, and then tap and hold an icon until the pop-up menu opens. Tap **Edit Home Screen** (📱). The icons start jiggling. Drag the icon to the right side of the current page. A new page appears automatically.

Switch Quickly from One App to Another

You can run many apps on your iPhone at the same time, switching from one app to another as needed.

You can switch apps by displaying the Home screen and then tapping the icon for the next app. But the iPhone also has an app-switching screen that enables you to switch quickly from one running app to another running app. From the app-switching screen, you can also easily close one or more running apps.

Switch Quickly from One App to Another

1 Swipe up from the bottom of the screen.

The Home screen appears.

2 Tap the app you want to launch. This example uses **Maps** (🧭).

The app's screen appears.

3 Start using the app as usual.

Note: You can also switch quickly from one app to another by swiping left or right on the invisible bar at the bottom of the screen.

4 Swipe up from the bottom of the screen to the middle, and then pause momentarily.

A The app-switching screen appears, showing a carousel of thumbnails of the open apps.

B The icons identify the app thumbnails.

5 Swipe left or right to scroll until you see the app you want.

Note: The last app you used appears on the right side of the app-switching screen. To its right is the Home screen. To its left are the apps you have used most recently.

6 Tap the app.

The app appears.

7 When you are ready to switch back, display the app-switching screen again. Swipe up from the bottom of the screen to the middle, and then pause momentarily.

8 Scroll left or right as needed, and then tap the app to which you want to return.

The app appears, ready to resume from where you stopped using it.

TIP

TIP

How do I stop an app that is not responding?
If an app stops responding, you can quickly close it from the app-switching screen. Display the app-switching screen by swiping up from the bottom of the screen and pausing. Scroll to the problem app and then drag it upward so it disappears off the screen. Tap the app you want to use, or tap at the top or bottom of the screen to return to the Home screen.

You can use this move to close any app that you no longer want to use, whether or not it has stopped responding. For example, if an app seems to be devouring battery power, you can use this technique to close it.

Find Apps on the App Store

The iPhone comes with essential apps, such as Safari for surfing the web, Mail for e-mail, and Calendar for keeping track of your schedule. But to get the most out of your iPhone, you will likely need to add other apps.

To get apps, you use the App Store, which provides apps that Apple has approved as correctly programmed, suitable for purpose, and free of malevolent code. Before you can download any apps, including free apps, you must create an App Store account.

Find Apps on the App Store

1 Swipe up from the bottom of the screen.

The Home screen appears.

2 Tap **App Store** ( ).

The App Store screen appears.

Usually, the Today screen appears at first.

3 Tap **Apps** (changes to).

Ⓐ You can tap **Games** (changes to) if you want to browse games instead of apps.

The Apps screen appears.

Ⓑ You can tap **See All** for a list to see the whole list.

4 Swipe up to scroll down until the Top Categories section appears.

Note: The Top Free Apps list shows the free apps that App Store users are downloading. The Top Paid Apps list shows the apps that App Store users are buying.

5 Tap **See All** in the Top Categories section.

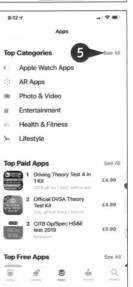

The Categories screen appears.

6 Tap the category you want to see. This example uses the **Business** category.

The category's screen appears.

C You can tap **See All** to view the full list.

7 Tap the app you want to view.

Note: To understand what an app does and how well it does it, look at the app's rating, read the description, and read the user reviews. Swipe the images to see screen captures from the app.

The app's screen appears.

8 Tap the price button or the **Get** button.

Note: If the iPhone prompts you to sign in, type your password and then tap **OK**.

Note: If you have not created an App Store account already, the iPhone prompts you to create one now.

The iPhone downloads and installs the app.

9 Tap **Open**.

Note: If you switch to another app while the new app downloads and installs, launch the new app from the Home screen instead.

The app opens, and you can start using it.

TIP

Why does App Store not appear on the Home screen or when I search for it?

If App Store (🅐) does not appear on the Home screen, and if searching for it does not show a result, the iPhone has restrictions applied that prevent you from installing apps. You can remove these restrictions if you know the restrictions passcode. Swipe up from the bottom of the screen to display the Home screen, tap **Settings** (⚙), and then tap **Screen Time** (⏳). On the Screen Time screen, tap **Content & Privacy Restrictions** (🚫), and then tap **iTunes & App Store Purchases**. Tap **Installing Apps**, and then tap **Allow**.

Update and Remove Apps

To keep your iPhone's apps running smoothly, you should install app updates when they become available. Most minor updates for paid apps are free, but you must often pay to upgrade to a new version of the app.

When you no longer need an app you have installed on your iPhone, you can remove it, thus recovering the space it occupied. You can remove some but not all of the built-in apps.

Update and Remove Apps

Update One or More Apps

1 Swipe up from the bottom of the screen.

The Home screen appears.

A The badge on the App Store icon shows the number of available updates.

2 Tap **App Store** (icon).

The App Store screen appears.

3 Tap **Account** (icon or your chosen picture).

Note: You can go straight to the Updates screen by tapping and holding **App Store** (icon) on the Home screen and then tapping **Updates** (icon) on the pop-up panel.

The Updates screen appears.

4 Tap **Update All** to apply all the available updates now.

B You can tap **Update** to update a single app.

C You can tap **Purchased** to display the Purchased screen, from which you can install apps you have bought previously but not yet installed on this iPhone.

5 Tap **Done**.

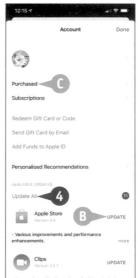

Remove an App from the iPhone

1 Swipe up from the bottom of the screen.

The Home screen appears.

2 Display the Home screen that contains the app you want to delete.

3 Tap and hold the app you want to delete.

The pop-up menu appears.

4 Tap **Delete App** (🗑).

The Delete dialog appears.

5 Tap **Delete**.

The iPhone deletes the app, and the app's icon disappears.

TIP

Can I set my iPhone to update its apps automatically?
Yes. Swipe up from the bottom of the screen to display the Home screen, and then tap **Settings** (⚙).
Tap **iTunes & App Store** (🅰) to display the iTunes & App Stores screen, go to the Automatic Downloads section, and then set the **App Updates** switch to On (🔘).

Type, Cut, Copy, and Paste Text

You can easily type text on your iPhone's keyboard, either by tapping each letter or by sliding your finger from letter to letter, using the QuickPath feature; you can also dictate text using Siri. If the text already exists, you can copy and paste it instead.

If the text is in a document you can edit, you can either copy the text or cut it. If the text is in a document you cannot edit, you can only copy the text.

Type, Cut, Copy, and Paste Text

Type Text

1 Open an app that supports text entry. To follow this example, tap **Notes** (⬜) on the Home screen, and then tap **New** (✏️) to start a new note.

2 Type a word by placing your finger on the first letter and then sliding it to each successive letter. Lift your finger off the screen when the word is complete.

A If the suggestion bar shows the word you want, tap it to enter it.

3 Type a word by tapping each letter in turn.

4 Press **return** to create a new line.

5 Type some more text to use for the copy-and-paste example.

Copy Text

1 Tap and hold a word in the section of text you want to copy or cut.

The word becomes highlighted.

B Selection handles appear around the selection.

C The formatting bar appears.

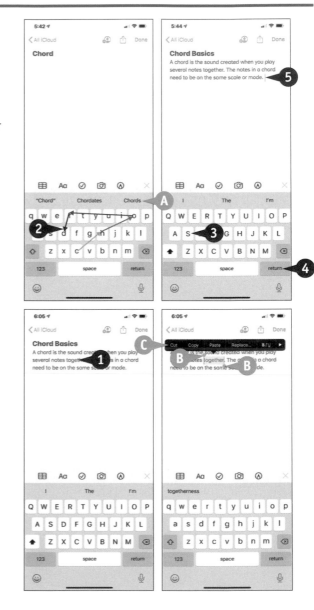

2 Drag the start handle (⬆) to the beginning of the text you want.

3 Drag the end handle (⬇) to the end of the text you want.

4 Tap **Copy**.

D You can tap **Cut** if you want to remove the selected text from the document.

The formatting bar disappears.

Your iPhone places the text on the Clipboard, a hidden storage area.

5 If you no longer need the text to be selected, tap outside the text to deselect it.

Paste the Content You Have Copied or Cut

1 Open the app and document into which you want to paste the text. This example uses a new note in the Notes app.

2 Tap where you want to paste the text.

The formatting bar appears.

3 Tap **Paste**.

E The pasted text appears in the document.

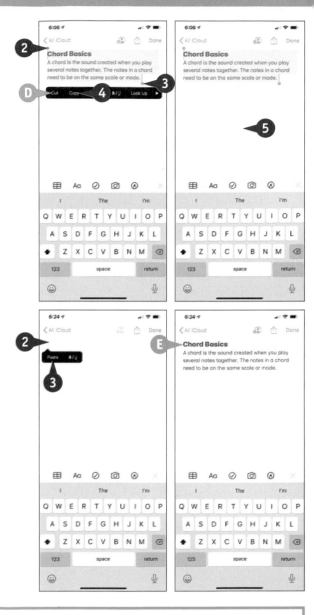

TIPS

How many items can I store on the Clipboard?

You can store only one item on the Clipboard at a time. Each item you cut or copy replaces the existing item on the Clipboard. But until you replace the existing item on the Clipboard, you can paste it as many times as needed.

Can I transfer the contents of the Clipboard to my computer?

If your computer is a Mac, you have enabled the Handoff feature in the General category of System Preferences, and the Mac is signed into the same iCloud account as the iPhone, the Universal Clipboard feature synchronizes Clipboard content across devices automatically. Otherwise, transfer the Clipboard contents indirectly — for example, paste it into an e-mail message and send it to yourself.

Format and Replace Text

Some apps enable you to add text formatting such as boldface, underline, or italics to text to make parts of it stand out. For example, you can apply formatting in e-mail messages you create using the Mail app on some e-mail services and in various apps for creating word-processing documents.

To apply formatting, you first select the text, and then choose options from the pop-up formatting bar. Some apps also offer other text commands, such as replacing a word or phrase from a menu of suggestions.

Format and Replace Text

Apply Bold, Italics, or Underline

1. Tap and hold the text to which you want to apply bold, italics, or underline.

   Part of the text becomes highlighted, and the selection handles appear.

   The formatting bar appears.

2. Drag the start handle (⬆) to the beginning of the text you want.

3. Drag the end handle (⬇) to the end of the text you want.

4. Tap **B***I*U on the formatting bar.

   The formatting bar displays formatting options.

5. Tap **Bold**, **Italic**, or **Underline**, as needed.

   The text takes on the formatting you chose.

6. Tap outside the selected text to deselect it.

Note: Some apps have their own formatting tools, many of which are more extensive than the standard formatting tools shown here.

Note: Some e-mail services and notes services do not support formatting.

Replace Text with Suggested Words

1 Double-tap the word you want to replace.

The word becomes highlighted and selection handles appear around it.

The formatting bar appears.

2 Tap **Replace**.

The formatting bar displays suggested replacement words.

3 Tap the word with which you want to replace the selected word.

The word you tapped appears in the text.

Note: Tap **More** (▶) to display more commands on the formatting bar. For example, in some apps, you can insert photos and videos.

TIP

What does the Quote Level button on the pop-up formatting bar in Mail do?
Tap **Quote Level** when you need to increase or decrease the quote level of your selected text. You may need to tap **More** (▶) to display the Quote Level button. When you tap Quote Level, the formatting bar displays an Increase button and a Decrease button. Tap **Increase** to increase the quote level, indenting the text more and adding a colored bar to its left, or **Decrease** to decrease the quote level, reducing the existing indent and removing a colored bar.

CHAPTER 8

Browsing the Web and E-Mailing

Your iPhone is fully equipped to browse the web and send e-mail via a Wi-Fi connection or via the cellular network.

Browse the Web with Safari

Your iPhone comes equipped with the Safari app, which enables you to browse the web. You can quickly go to a web page by entering its address in the Address box or by following a link.

Although you can browse quickly by opening a single web page at a time, you may prefer to open multiple pages and switch back and forth among them. Safari makes this easy to do. You can also install other browsers, such as Google Chrome or Microsoft Edge, from the App Store and use them instead of, or as well as, Safari.

Browse the Web with Safari

Open Safari and Navigate to Web Pages

1. Swipe up from the bottom of the screen.

   The Home screen appears.

2. Tap **Safari** (⊘).

   Safari opens and loads the last web page that was shown.

3. Tap the Address box.

Note: You can enter widely used domain extensions, such as .com and .net, by tapping and holding**.** (the period key) and tapping the extensions on the pop-up panel that appears.

   Safari selects the current contents of the Address box, and the keyboard appears.

4. Tap **Delete** (×) if you need to delete the contents of the Address box.

5. Type the address of the page you want to open.

   Ⓐ You can also tap a search result that Safari displays below the Address box.

6. Tap **go**.

   Safari displays the page.

7. Tap a link on the page.

   Safari displays that page.

   Ⓑ After going to a new page, tap **Back** (〈) to display the previous page. You can then tap **Forward** (〉) to go forward again.

Open Multiple Pages and Navigate Among Them

1 Tap **Pages** (▢).

Safari displays the list of open pages, each bearing a Close button (✕).

C Below the list of open pages, you can find a list of recent pages you opened on other devices that use the same iCloud account.

2 Tap **New Page** (➕).

Note: In landscape orientation, a large-screen iPhone displays a tab bar at the top of the screen. Tap the tab for the page you want to view.

Safari opens a new page and displays your bookmarks.

3 Tap the Address box, and then go to the page you want.

Note: You can also go to a page by using a bookmark, as described in the next section, "Access Websites Quickly with Bookmarks."

The page appears.

4 To switch to another page, tap **Pages** (▢).

Safari displays the list of pages.

5 Tap the page you want to see.

D You can tap **Close** (✕) to close a page.

TIPS

How do I search for information?

Tap the Address box to select its current contents, and then type your search terms. Safari searches as you type; you can type further to narrow down the results, and stop as soon as you see suitable results. Tap the result you want to see, and then tap a link on the results page that Safari opens.

How can I reopen a tab I closed by mistake?

Tap **Pages** (▢) to display the list of open pages, and then tap and hold **New Page** (➕). On the Recently Closed Tabs screen that appears, tap the page you want to reopen.

Access Websites Quickly with Bookmarks

Typing web addresses can be laborious, even with the help that the iPhone's keyboard adds, so you will probably want to use bookmarks to access websites you visit often.

By syncing your existing bookmarks from your computer or online account, as described in Chapter 1, you can instantly provide your iPhone with quick access to the web pages you want to visit most frequently. You can also create bookmarks on your iPhone, as discussed in the next section, "Create Bookmarks."

Access Websites Quickly with Bookmarks

Open the Bookmarks Screen

1 Swipe up from the bottom of the screen.

The Home screen appears.

2 Tap **Safari** (🧭).

Safari opens.

3 If the navigation bar at the bottom is hidden, tap at the top of the screen.

The navigation bar appears.

Note: You can also scroll up a short distance to display the navigation bar.

4 Tap **Bookmarks** (📖).

The Bookmarks screen appears.

Note: You can display the Bookmarks screen quickly from the Home screen by tapping and holding **Safari** (🧭) and then tapping **Show Bookmarks** (📖) on the pop-up panel.

Explore Your History

1 On the Bookmarks screen, tap **History** (🕐).

The History screen appears, showing a list of the web pages you have recently visited.

Ⓐ You can tap a time or a day to display the list of web pages you visited then.

Ⓑ You can tap **Search History** (🔍) and type search terms to search for particular pages.

Note: If the Search History box is hidden, swipe down at the top of the list of pages.

Ⓒ You can tap a page's button to display that page.

2 Tap **Bookmarks** (📖) when you want to return to the Bookmarks screen.

Open a Bookmarked Page and Use the Toolbar

1 On the Bookmarks screen, tap the bookmarks folder or category you want to see. This example uses the **Books** folder.

The contents of the folder or category appear. For example, the contents of the Books folder appear.

D You can delete a bookmark by swiping it to the left and then tapping **Delete**.

2 When you find the bookmark for the web page you want to open, tap the bookmark.

E The web page opens.

3 If you need to change your view of the page, tap **Show/Hide Toolbar** (AA).

The toolbar opens.

F Tap **Smaller** (A) to zoom out.

G Tap **Larger** (A) to zoom in.

H Tap **Show Reader View** (≡) to switch to Reader View for ease of reading.

I Tap **Request Desktop Website** (🖥) to request the desktop site instead of the mobile version.

J Tap **Hide Toolbar** (↖) or tap **Show/Hide Toolbar** (AA) again when you no longer need the toolbar.

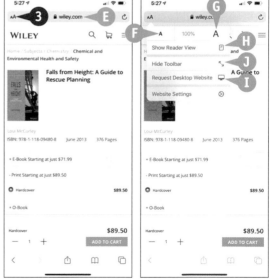

TIP

How can I quickly access a website?
Creating a bookmark within Safari — as discussed in the next section, "Create Bookmarks" — is good for sites you access now and then. But if you access a site frequently, create an icon for it on your Home screen. Open the site in Safari. Tap **Share** (⬆), tap **Add to Home Screen** (⊕), type the name on the Add to Home Screen panel, and then tap **Add**. You can then go straight to the page by tapping its icon on the Home screen.

Create Bookmarks

When you want to access a web page again easily, create a bookmark for it. If you have set your iPhone to sync bookmarks with your iCloud account, the bookmark becomes available on your computer or online account as well when you sync.

If you create many bookmarks, it is usually helpful to create multiple folders in which you can organize the bookmarks. You can create folders easily on the iPhone and choose the folder in which to store each bookmark.

Create Bookmarks

Create a Bookmark

1 Swipe up from the bottom of the screen.

The Home screen appears.

2 Tap **Safari** ( ).

Safari opens and displays the last web page you were viewing.

3 Navigate to the web page you want to bookmark.

4 Tap **Share** ( ).

The Share sheet appears.

5 Tap **Add Bookmark** ( ).

The Add Bookmark screen appears.

6 Edit the suggested name, or type a new name, as needed.

7 Tap the current folder under the Location heading.

The Choose a Folder screen appears.

8 Tap the folder in which to store the bookmark.

The Add Bookmark screen appears.

9 Tap **Save**.

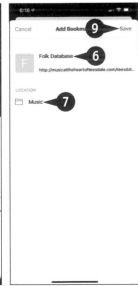

Create a New Folder for Bookmarks

1 In Safari, tap **Bookmarks** (□).

The Bookmarks screen appears.

2 Tap **Edit**.

The editing controls appear.

A You can drag a handle ( ) to change the order of the bookmark folders.

B You can tap **Delete** (⊖) and then tap the textual **Delete** button to delete a bookmark folder and its contents.

3 Tap **New Folder**.

The Edit Folder screen appears.

4 Type the name for the folder.

5 Tap the folder under the Location heading.

A screen showing the list of folders appears.

6 Tap the folder in which to store the bookmark folder.

The Edit Folder screen appears again.

7 Tap **All** (<).

The Bookmarks screen appears, still with editing controls displayed.

8 Tap **Done**.

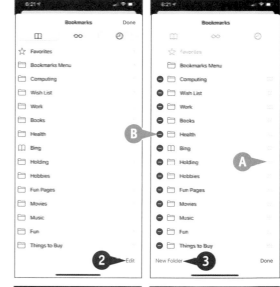

TIP

Can I change a bookmark I have created?

Yes. Tap **Bookmarks** (□) to display the Bookmarks screen, and then navigate to the bookmark you want to change. Tap **Edit** to switch to Editing Mode. You can then tap a bookmark to open it on the Edit Bookmark screen, where you can change its name, address, or location. In Editing Mode, you can also delete a bookmark by tapping **Delete** (⊖) and then tapping **Delete**, or rearrange your bookmarks by dragging the handle ( ) up or down the list. Tap **Done** when you finish editing bookmarks.

Keep a Reading List of Web Pages

afari's Reading List feature enables you to save a web page for later without creating a bookmark. You can quickly add the current web page to Reading List by using the Share sheet. Once you have added pages, you access Reading List through the Bookmarks feature. When viewing Reading List, you can display either all the pages it contains or only those you have not read.

Keep a Reading List of Web Pages

Add a Web Page to Reading List

1 Swipe up from the bottom of the screen.

The Home screen appears.

2 Tap **Safari** (⊘).

Safari opens and displays the last web page you were viewing.

3 Navigate to the web page you want to add to Reading List.

A If the navigation bar is hidden, tap at the top of the screen to display it.

4 Tap **Share** (⬆).

The Share sheet appears.

5 Tap **Add to Reading List** (∞).

The first time you give the Add to Reading List command, the Automatically Save Reading List Articles for Offline Reading? dialog opens.

6 Tap **Save Automatically** if you want to save the articles so you can read them when you do not have an Internet connection, which is usually helpful. If not, tap **Don't Save Automatically**.

Safari adds the web page to Reading List.

Note: To change the Automatically Save Offline setting later, display the Home screen, tap **Settings** (⚙), and then tap **Safari** (⊘). Scroll down to the Reading List section and set the **Automatically Save Offline** switch to On (🔵) or Off (⚪), as needed.

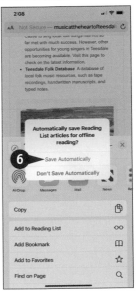

Open Reading List and Display a Page

1 In Safari, tap **Bookmarks** (🔖).

The Bookmarks screen appears.

2 Tap **Reading List** (∞).

Note: You can quickly display the Reading List screen from the Home screen by tapping and holding **Safari** (🧭) and then tapping **Show Reading List** on the pop-up panel.

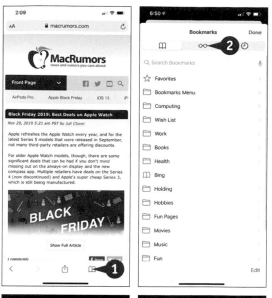

The Reading List screen appears.

3 Tap **Show All**.

Reading List displays all the pages it contains, including those you have read.

B Pages you have read appear with gray shading.

C You can tap **Show Unread** to display only unread pages.

4 Tap the page you want to open.

D If you decide not to open a page from Reading List, tap **Done** to hide the Reading List screen.

TIP

How do I remove an item from Reading List?

To remove an item from Reading List, swipe it left and then tap the textual **Delete** button that appears.

You can also swipe an item right. When you do so, the Mark Read button also appears if you have not read the item; the Mark Unread button appears if you have read it. You can tap **Mark Read** or **Mark Unread** to switch the item's read status.

Navigate Among Open Web Pages Using Tabs

If you browse the web a lot, you will probably need to open many web pages in Safari at the same time. Safari presents your open pages as a list of scrollable tabs, making it easy to navigate from one page to another.

You can change the order of the tabs to suit your needs, and you can quickly close a tab by either tapping its **Close** button or simply swiping it off the list.

Navigate Among Open Web Pages Using Tabs

Open Safari and Display the List of Tabs

1 Swipe up from the bottom of the screen.

The Home screen appears.

2 Tap **Safari** ().

Safari opens or becomes active.

Note: If Safari has hidden the on-screen controls, tap at the top of the screen to display them. Alternatively, scroll up the screen a short way.

3 Tap **Pages** (⧉).

The list of pages appears.

Close Pages You Do Not Need to Keep Open

1 Tap **Close** (⊠) on the tab for a page you want to close.

The page closes, and the tab disappears from the list.

2 Alternatively, you can tap a tab and swipe it left off the screen.

The page closes, and the tab disappears from the list.

Note: You can turn a large-screen iPhone to landscape orientation and then tap **Close** (⊠) to close the current tab.

Change the Order of the Pages

1 Tap and hold the tab for a page you want to move.

The tab moves to the foreground.

2 Drag the tab to where you want it to appear in the list, and then release it.

Find a Page and Display It

1 Tap the tab for the page you want to display.

The page opens.

Note: You can also turn a large-screen iPhone to landscape orientation to display the tab bar at the top of the screen. You can then tap the tab you want to view.

TIP

How do I return from the list of tabs to the page I was viewing before?

To return to the page you were viewing before, either tap the page's tab in the list of tabs, or tap **Done** in the lower-right corner of the screen.

Tighten Up Safari's Security

To protect yourself against websites that infect computers with malware or try to gain your sensitive personal or financial information, turn on Safari's Fraudulent Website Warning feature. You can also turn off the JavaScript programming language, which can be used to attack your iPhone. Additionally, you can block pop-up windows, which some websites use to display unwanted information; block new cookies and data; and set Safari to prevent cross-site tracking.

Tighten Up Safari's Security

1 Swipe up from the bottom of the screen.

The Home screen appears.

2 Tap **Settings** (⚙).

The Settings screen appears.

3 Tap **Safari** (🧭).

The Safari screen appears.

A The AutoFill feature enables you to save information — such as your name, address, and credit card details — for filling out web forms quickly.

4 Set the **Block Pop-ups** switch to On (🔘) to block unwanted pop-up windows.

5 Set the **Prevent Cross-Site Tracking** switch to On (🔘) or Off ( ), as needed.

6 Set the **Block All Cookies** switch to On (🔘) or Off ( ), as needed.

7 Set the **Fraudulent Website Warning** switch to On (🔘).

8 Set the **Check for Apple Pay** switch to On (🔘) to let websites check whether Apple Pay is enabled.

9 Tap **Clear History and Website Data**.

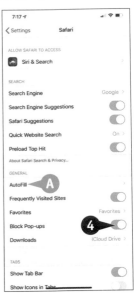

Note: If the Clear History and Website Data button is dimmed and unavailable, your iPhone has restrictions applied. If you manage the iPhone, you may be able to remove these restrictions through Screen Time.

A dialog opens.

10 Tap **Clear History and Data**.

The dialog closes.

Safari clears your browsing history and data.

11 Tap **Advanced**.

The Advanced screen appears.

12 Set the **JavaScript** switch to On (⬤) or Off ( ), as needed.

Note: Turning off JavaScript may remove some or most functionality of harmless sites.

13 Tap **Website Data**.

The Website Data screen appears.

Ⓑ You can tap **Remove All Website Data** to remove all website data.

14 Tap **Edit**.

A Delete icon (⊖) appears to the left of each website.

15 To delete a website's data, tap **Delete** (⊖), and then tap the textual **Delete** button that appears.

16 Tap **Done**.

TIP

What are cookies, and what threat do they pose?
A *cookie* is a small text file that a website places on a computer to identify that computer in the future. This is helpful for many sites, such as shopping sites in which you add items to a shopping cart, but when used by intrusive or malevolent sites, cookies can pose a threat to your privacy. You may want to set the **Block All Cookies** switch to On (⬤) to stop Safari from accepting cookies, but be warned that doing so will prevent some legitimate sites from working properly.

Manage Your App and Website Passwords

Your iPhone can store your app and website passwords so that Safari and other apps can enter them automatically when needed, reducing the need for you to type passwords manually.

The App & Website Passwords screen in the Settings app enables you to view the list of password entries your iPhone has stored. You can view and edit a password entry, which lets you copy the password, update it, or change the sites for which it is used; delete a password; or add a new password entry.

Manage Your App and Website Passwords

1 Swipe up from the bottom of the screen.

The Home screen appears.

2 Tap **Settings** (⚙).

The Settings screen appears.

3 Tap **Passwords & Accounts** (🔑).

The Passwords & Accounts screen appears.

4 Tap **Website & App Passwords**.

Note: Before displaying the Passwords screen, the iPhone authenticates you. Normally, this happens via Face ID and takes only moments. If Face ID repeatedly fails, you will need to enter your passcode.

The Passwords screen appears.

A You can tap **Search** (🔍) and type a search term to search for a particular password.

5 Tap the password entry you want to view.

The screen for the password entry appears.

B You can copy the username or password by tapping and holding it and then tapping **Copy** on the pop-up toolbar.

6 If you need to edit the username, password, or list of websites, tap **Edit**.

The fields open for editing.

7 Edit the username or password as needed.

8 To remove a website, tap **Delete** (⊖) and then tap the textual **Delete** button.

9 Tap **Done**.

Editing Mode closes.

10 Tap **Passwords** (‹).

The Passwords screen appears again.

Note: You can delete a password entry by swiping it left and then tapping **Delete**.

11 To add a new password, tap **Add Password** (+).

The Add Password screen appears.

12 Type or paste the website address.

13 Type or paste the username.

14 Type or paste the password.

15 Tap **Done**.

The Passwords screen appears again.

TIP

What does the Edit button on the Passwords screen enable me to do?
The Edit button on the Passwords screen enables you to delete multiple password entries at once instead of one at a time. Tap **Edit** to switch the Passwords screen to Editing Mode. You can then tap the selection circle (changes to ✓) for each password you want to delete, and then tap **Delete**.

Using the Sign In with Apple Feature

Many apps and websites require you to create an account and sign in to it before you can use them. Each account typically requires a valid e-mail address and a password; ideally, each password should be unique, but the more passwords you have, the harder it is to remember them.

One solution to this problem is to use a password manager, but your iPhone offers a neater solution: the Sign In with Apple feature, which simplifies the process of signing into apps and websites — and even lets you hide your e-mail address from apps and websites.

Understanding the Requirements for Sign In with Apple

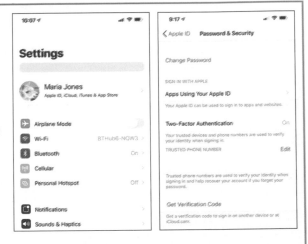

Sign In with Apple uses your existing Apple ID, the credentials you use to sign in to iCloud. Normally, you configure your iPhone to use your Apple ID when first setting up the iPhone. You can verify that your iPhone is using your Apple ID by tapping **Settings** (⚙) on the Home screen and making sure that "Apple ID" appears on the Apple ID button, the one that bears your name and picture at the top of the Settings screen.

Sign In with Apple requires you to have enabled two-factor authentication on your iPhone. Two-factor authentication is a security feature that requires you to use a trusted device to receive a verification code when signing in to your account on a new device for the first time. Until you enable two-factor authentication, your iPhone prompts you relentlessly to do so; and once you have enabled two-factor authentication, you cannot disable it again. You can verify that your iPhone has two-factor authentication enabled by tapping **Settings** (⚙), tapping **Apple ID**, and then tapping **Password & Security**. On the Password & Security screen, check that the Two-Factor Authentication button shows On.

Sign In to an App or Website Using Sign In with Apple

When you go to sign in to an app or website that supports Sign In with Apple, a button such as Continue with Apple or Sign In with Apple appears. Tap this button to start creating an account using your Apple ID. Enter your name the way you want it to appear. Then tap **Share My Email** (changes to ✓) if you want to use your e-mail address, or tap **Hide My Email** (changes to ✓) if you want to have Apple create a unique address on its relay service and forward messages from the app or website to your e-mail address. Tap **Continue** and follow any other prompts that appear.

See Which Apps Are Using Your Apple ID

To see which apps are using your Apple ID, tap **Settings** (⚙) on the Home screen. On the Settings screen, tap **Apple ID**, the button at the top that contains your name and picture. On the Apple ID screen, tap **Password & Security** to display the Password & Security screen. Here, tap **Apps Using Your Apple ID** to display the Apps Using Apple ID screen, which contains a list of the apps.

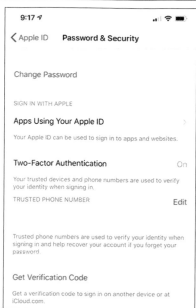

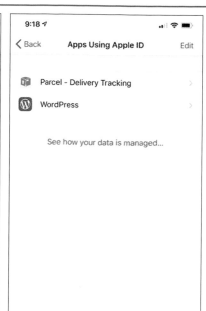

Block Forwarded Messages or Stop Using Sign In with Apple for an App

To stop using Sign In with Apple for a particular app, follow the instructions in the previous section to display the Apps Using Apple ID screen.

Tap the app you want to stop using. A screen for that app appears, such as the WordPress screen shown here.

If you configured the Hide My Email feature for this app, the Hide My Email section appears. Here, the This App Received button shows the e-mail address that Apple used for this app. The Forward To button shows the address to which messages from the app are forwarded. You can set the **Forward To** switch to Off (   ) to stop receiving messages from the app.

To stop using Sign In with Apple for this app, tap **Stop Using Apple ID** and then tap **Stop Using** in the confirmation dialog box that opens.

Read E-Mail

After you have set up Mail during the initial setup routine, as described in Chapter 1, or by adding other accounts, as explained in Chapter 4, you are ready to send and receive e-mail messages using your iPhone. This section shows you how to read your incoming e-mail messages. You learn to reply to messages and write messages from scratch later in this chapter.

Read E-Mail

Read a Message and View an Attached File

1 Swipe up from the bottom of the screen.

The Home screen appears.

A The badge shows the number of unread messages.

2 Tap **Mail** (✉).

The Mailboxes screen appears.

Note: If Mail does not show the Mailboxes screen, tap **Back** (‹) until the Mailboxes screen appears.

3 Tap the inbox you want to open.

B To see all your incoming messages together, tap **All Inboxes**.

C A blue dot indicates an unread message.

D A paperclip icon (📎) indicates one or more attachments.

E A gold star indicates the message's sender is one of your VIPs. See the second tip for information about VIPs.

F You can tap **Filter** (⊜) to filter the messages by Unread status, displaying only unread messages. You can then tap **Unread** to apply a different filter.

4 Tap a message.

The message opens.

G You can tap **Previous** (⌃) or **Next** (⌄) to display another message.

5 If the message has an attachment, tap it.

The attachment opens in the viewer.

Note: Mail's viewer can display many types of attached files, but not all files.

Note: If Mail has hidden the controls at the top of the screen, tap the screen to display the controls.

6 If you want to send the file to an app or share it with others, tap **Share** (⬆️).

The Share sheet opens.

7 Tap the means of sharing, such as **Copy to Pages** (◪) for a Word document.

8 Tap **Done**.

The message appears again.

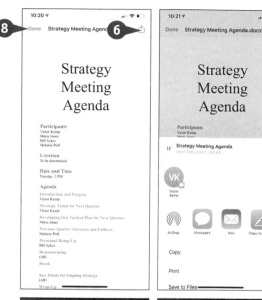

Access New Messages Quickly from the Home Screen

1 Swipe up from the bottom of the screen.

The Home screen appears.

2 Tap and hold **Mail** (✉️).

The pop-up panel opens.

H You can also tap another button, such as **VIP**.

I You can tap a contact whose icon bears a badge to display a new message from that contact.

3 Tap **All Inboxes**.

The All Inboxes screen appears.

TIPS

How do I view the contents of another mailbox?

From an open message, tap **Inbox** (<) or **All Inboxes** (<) to return to the inbox or the screen for all the inboxes. Tap **Back** (<) to go back to the Mailboxes screen. You can then tap the mailbox you want to view.

What is the VIP inbox on the Mailboxes screen?

The VIP inbox is a tool for identifying important messages. You mark particular contacts as being very important people to you, and Mail then adds messages from these VIPs to the VIP inbox. To add a VIP, tap the sender's name in an open message, tap the linked name after the From readout, and then tap **Add to VIP** on the Sender screen.

Reply To or Forward an E-Mail Message

Mail makes it easy to reply to an e-mail message or forward it to others. If the message had multiple recipients, you can choose between replying only to the sender of the message and replying to the sender and all the other recipients in the To field and the Cc field, if there are any. Recipients in the message's Bcc field, whose names you cannot see, do not receive your reply.

Reply To or Forward an E-Mail Message

Open the Message You Will Reply To or Forward

1 Swipe up from the bottom of the screen.

The Home screen appears.

2 Tap **Mail** (✉).

The Mailboxes screen appears.

Note: When you launch Mail, the app checks for new messages. This is why the number of new messages you see on the Mailboxes screen sometimes differs from the number on the Mail badge on the Home screen.

3 Tap the inbox you want to see.

The inbox opens.

4 Tap the message you want to open.

The message opens.

5 Tap **Action** (⤺).

The Action dialog opens.

Note: You can also reply to or forward a message by using Siri. For example, say "Reply to this message" or "Forward this message to Alice Smith," and then tell Siri what you want the message to say.

Reply To the Message

1 In the Action dialog, tap **Reply**.

A To reply to all recipients, tap **Reply All**. Reply to all recipients only when you are sure that they need to receive your reply. Often, it is better to reply only to the sender.

A screen containing the reply appears.

B Mail automatically adds your signature, if you have one.

2 Type your reply to the message.

3 Tap **Send** (↑).

Mail sends the message.

Forward the Message

1 In the Action dialog, tap **Forward**.

A screen containing the forwarded message appears.

2 Type the recipient's address.

C Alternatively, you can tap **Add Contact** (⊕) and choose the recipient in your Contacts list.

3 Type a message if needed.

4 Tap **Send** (↑).

Mail sends the message.

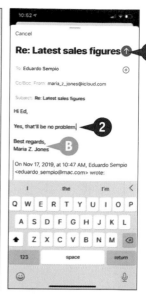

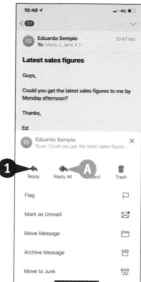

TIPS

Can I reply to or forward only part of a message?
Yes. The quick way to do this is to select the part of the message you want to include before tapping **Action** (↰). Mail then includes only your selection. Alternatively, you can start the reply or forwarded message, and then delete the parts you do not want to include.

How do I check for new messages?
In a mailbox, tap and drag your finger down the screen, pulling down the messages. When a progress circle appears at the top, lift your finger. Mail checks for new messages.

Organize Your Messages in Mailbox Folders

To keep your inbox or inboxes under control, you should organize your messages into mailbox folders.

You can quickly move a single message to a folder after reading it or after previewing it in the message list. Alternatively, you can select multiple messages in your inbox and move them all to a folder in a single action. You can also delete any message you no longer need.

Organize Your Messages in Mailbox Folders

Open Mail and Move a Single Message to a Folder

1 Swipe up from the bottom of the screen.

The Home screen appears.

2 Tap **Mail** (✉).

The Mailboxes screen appears.

3 Tap the mailbox you want to open.

The mailbox opens.

A The Replied arrow (↩) indicates you have replied to the message.

B The Forwarded arrow (➙) indicates you have forwarded the message.

4 Swipe left on the message you want to move.

The swipe controls appear.

C You can delete the message by tapping **Trash** (🗑).

5 Tap **More** (⋯).

The Action dialog opens.

6 Tap **Move Message**.

Note: If the message is from a VIP, the Move Message dialog opens. Tap **Move to "Starred"** to move the message to the Starred mailbox, or tap **Other Mailbox** to display the Move This Message to a New Mailbox screen.

The Move This Message to a New Mailbox screen appears.

7 Tap the mailbox to which you want to move the message.

Mail moves the message.

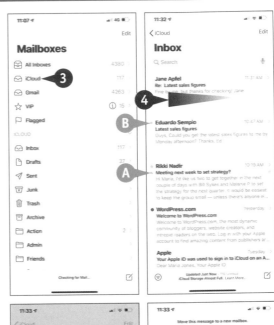

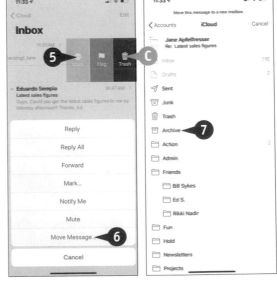

Move Multiple Messages to a Folder

1 In the mailbox, tap **Edit**.

2 Tap the selection button (changes to ✓) next to each message you want to move.

3 Tap **Move**.

The Move These Messages to a New Mailbox screen appears.

4 Tap the destination mailbox.

D To move the messages to a mailbox in another account, tap **Accounts**. On the Accounts screen, tap the appropriate account to display the mailboxes in the account, then tap the destination mailbox.

Note: Mail studies your history of moving messages so it can suggest the folder you may want for a particular message, saving you scrolling through all your folders.

The mailbox appears again, now without the messages you moved.

TIP

What does the Mark command in the Action dialog do?

Tap **Mark** to display the Mark dialog. You can then tap **Flag** to set a flag on the message — for example, to indicate that you need to pay extra attention to it. The flag (🚩) then appears on the message. In the Mark dialog, you can also tap **Mark as Unread** to mark the message as not having been read, even though you have opened it; if the message is marked as unread, you can tap **Mark as Read** instead. You can also mark a message as unread or read by tapping it in the message list, swiping right, and then tapping **Unread** (✉) or **Read** (✉), as appropriate.

Write and Send E-Mail Messages

Your iPhone is great for reading and replying to e-mail messages you receive, but you will likely also need to write new messages. When you do, you can use the data in the Contacts app to address your outgoing messages quickly and accurately. If the recipient's address is not one of your contacts, you can type the address manually.

You can attach one or more files to an e-mail message to send those files to the recipient. This works well for small files, but many mail servers reject files larger than several megabytes in size.

Write and Send E-Mail Messages

1 Swipe up from the bottom of the screen.

The Home screen appears.

2 Tap and hold **Mail** (✉).

The pop-up panel appears.

3 Tap **New Message** (✎).

Note: You can also tap **Mail** (✉) and then tap **New Message** (✎) to start a new message.

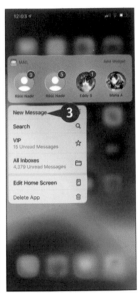

The New Message screen appears.

4 Tap **Add Contact** (⊕).

The Contacts list appears.

Note: If necessary, change the Contacts list displayed by tapping **Groups**, making your choice on the Groups screen, and then tapping **Done**.

Ⓐ If the person you are e-mailing is not a contact, type the address in the To area. You can also start typing here and then select a matching contact from the list that the Mail app displays.

Note: Contacts that appear in gray have no e-mail address.

5 Tap the contact you want to send the message to.

B The contact's name appears in the To area.

Note: You can add other contacts to the To area by repeating steps **4** and **5**.

6 If you need to add a Cc or Bcc recipient, tap **Cc/Bcc, From**.

The Cc, Bcc, and From fields expand.

7 Tap the Cc area or Bcc area, and then follow steps **4** and **5** to add a recipient.

C To change the e-mail account you are sending the message from, tap **From**, and then tap the account to use.

8 Tap **Subject**, and then type the message's subject.

D You can tap **Notifications** (🔔 changes to 🔔) to receive notifications when someone responds to the e-mail conversation.

9 Tap below the Subject line, and then type the body of the message.

Note: If you need to stop working on a message temporarily, tap its title bar and drag it down to the bottom of the screen. You can then work with other messages. To resume work on the parked message, tap its title bar.

10 Tap **Send**.

Mail sends the message.

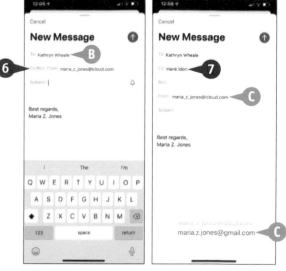

TIP

How do I attach a file to a message?
To attach a photo or video, tap and hold the message body area to display the contextual menu, and then tap **Insert Photo or Video**. On some iPhone models, you may need to tap **More** (▶) before tapping **Insert Photo or Video**.

To attach a file from iCloud Drive, tap and hold the message body area to display the contextual menu, and then tap **Add Document**. On some iPhone models, you may need to tap **More** (▶) before tapping **Add Document**.

To attach other types of files, start the message from the app that contains the file. Select the file, tap **Share** (⬆️), and then tap **Mail** (✉️). Mail starts a message with the file attached. You then address the message, add a subject and any text needed, and send the message.

CHAPTER 9

Keeping Your Life Organized

Your iPhone includes many apps for staying organized, such as the Calendars app, the Reminders app, and the Wallet app. Other apps help you find your way, stay on time, and track stock prices, weather forecasts, and your own health.

Browse Existing Events in Your Calendars

Your iPhone's Calendar app gives you a great way of managing your schedule and making sure you never miss an appointment.

After setting up your calendars to sync using iCloud or other calendar services, you can take your calendars with you everywhere and consult them whenever you need to. You can view either all your calendars or only those you choose.

Browse Existing Events in Your Calendars

Browse Existing Events in Your Calendars

① Swipe up from the bottom of the screen.

② Tap **Calendar** ( ).

Ⓐ In Light Mode, the black circle indicates the day shown; in Dark Mode, the circle is white. When the current date is selected, the circle is red.

Ⓑ Your events appear on a scrollable timeline.

Ⓒ An event's background color indicates the calendar it belongs to.

Ⓓ You can tap **Today** to display the current day.

③ Tap the day you want to see.

The events for the day appear.

④ Tap the month.

The calendar for the month appears.

Ⓔ You can tap the year to display the calendar for the full year, in which you can navigate quickly to other months.

⑤ Scroll up or down as needed, and then tap the date you want.

The date's appointments appear.

6 Tap **List** (:≡ changes to ▤).

The appointments appear as a list, enabling you to see more.

7 Tap an event to see its details.

The Event Details screen appears.

8 To edit the event, tap **Edit**.

The Edit screen appears, and you can make changes to the event. When you finish, tap **Done**.

Choose Which Calendars to Display

1 Tap **Calendars**.

2 Tap to place or remove a check mark next to a calendar you want to display or hide.

F Tap **Show All** to place a check mark next to each calendar for all accounts. Tap **Hide All** to remove all check marks.

G Similarly, tap **Show All** or **Hide All** for an account to display or hide the account's calendars.

H The Birthdays calendar automatically displays birthdays of contacts whose contact data includes the birthday.

I You can set the **Show Declined Events** switch to On (⬤) to include invitations you have declined.

3 Tap **Done**.

The calendars you chose appear.

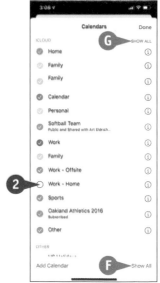

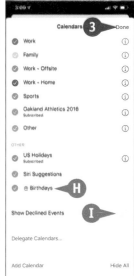

TIP

How can I quickly find an event?
In the Calendar app, tap **Search** (🔍). Calendar displays a list of your events. Type your search term. When Calendar displays a list of matches, tap the event you want to view.

Create New Events in Your Calendars

You can create calendar events on your computer, or online using a web interface such as that of iCloud, and then sync the events to your iPhone. But you can also create new events directly on your iPhone.

You can create either a straightforward, one-shot appointment or an appointment that repeats on a schedule. You can also choose the calendar in which to store the appointment.

Create New Events in Your Calendars

1 Swipe up from the bottom of the screen to display the Home screen.

2 Tap **Calendar** (📅) to display the Calendar screen.

3 Tap the day on which you want to create the new event.

Note: From the Home screen, tap and hold **Calendar** (📅) to display the pop-up panel and then tap **Add Event** to start creating a new event. You will need to select the date.

Note: You can also leave the current date selected, and then change the date when creating the event.

4 Tap **New** (+).

Note: If New (+) is disabled, tap **Settings** (⚙) on the Home screen, tap **Passwords & Accounts** (🔑), tap the appropriate account, and verify that the Calendars switch is On (⬤).

The New Event screen appears.

5 Tap **Title** and type the title of the event.

6 Tap **Location**.

Note: If the Allow "Calendar" to Access Your Location While You Use the App? dialog opens when you tap **Location**, tap **Allow** to use locations.

The Location screen appears.

A You can tap **Current Location** to use the current location.

7 Start typing the location.

8 Tap the appropriate match.

9 Tap **Starts**.

The time and date controls appear.

10 Tap the date and time controls to set the start time.

11 Tap **Ends**.

12 Tap the date and time controls to set the end time.

B If this is an all-day appointment, set the **All-day** switch to On (⬤).

C If you need to change the time zone, tap **Time Zone**, type the city name, and then tap the time zone.

13 Tap **Alert**.

The Alert screen appears.

14 Tap **Time to Leave** if you want Calendar to calculate when you should leave, based on your location, the event's location, and the traffic conditions. Otherwise, tap the timing for the alert, such as **30 minutes before**.

The New Event screen appears.

15 Tap **Calendar**.

The Calendar screen appears.

16 Tap the calendar for the event.

The New Event screen appears again.

17 Tap **Add**.

The event appears on your calendar.

TIPS

How do I set up an event that repeats every week?

On the New Event screen, tap **Repeat**. On the Repeat screen, tap **Every Week**, placing a check mark next to it, and then tap **Done**.

How do I set a time to the exact minute instead of to the nearest 5 minutes?

On the New Event screen, tap **Starts** to display the time and date controls. Double-tap the time readout — either the hours or the minutes — to switch the minutes between 5-minute intervals and single minutes.

Work with Calendar Invitations

As well as events you create yourself, you may receive invitations to events that others create. When you receive an event invitation attached to an e-mail message, you can choose whether to accept the invitation or decline it. If you accept the invitation, you can add the event automatically to your calendar.

Work with Calendar Invitations

Respond to an Invitation from an Alert

1 When an invitation alert appears, tap and hold it.

The pop-up panel displays the event's details, together with buttons for responding to the event.

2 Tap **Accept**, **Maybe**, or **Decline**, as needed.

Ⓐ You can tap **Close** (❌) to close the pop-up panel without tapping one of the response buttons.

Respond to an Invitation from the Inbox Screen

1 Swipe up from the bottom of the screen.

The Home screen appears.

2 Tap **Calendar** (📅).

The Calendar screen appears.

3 Tap **Inbox**.

The Inbox screen appears.

Ⓑ You can tap **Accept**, **Maybe**, or **Decline** to deal with the invitation without viewing the details.

4 Tap the invitation whose details you want to see.

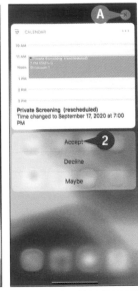

The Event Details screen appears.

5 Tap **Calendar** if you decide to accept the invitation.

The Calendar screen appears.

6 Tap the calendar to which you want to assign the event.

The Event Details screen appears again.

7 Tap **Alert**.

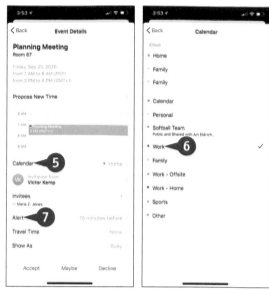

The Alert screen appears.

8 Tap the button for the alert interval. For example, tap **1 hour before**.

The Event Details screen appears again.

Note: To control how the event's time appears in your calendar, tap **Show As**, and then tap **Busy** or **Free**, as appropriate, on the Show As screen.

9 Tap **Accept**.

Your calendar appears, showing the event you just accepted.

TIP

In what other ways can I respond to an invitation?

You can also respond to an invitation by tapping and holding its alert on the lock screen and then tapping **Accept**, **Maybe**, or **Decline** in the Pop-up panel.

If you have an Apple Watch, it will display your calendar alerts when your iPhone is locked. You can respond to invitations on the Apple Watch as well.

Track Your Commitments with Reminders

Your iPhone's Reminders app gives you an easy way to note your commitments and keep track of them. The Reminders app comes with a built-in list called Reminders, but you can create as many other lists as you need, giving each a distinctive color.

You can create a reminder with no due time or location or tie a reminder to a due time, arriving at or leaving a location, or both. Your iPhone can remind you of time- or location-based commitments at the appropriate time or place.

Track Your Commitments with Reminders

Open the Reminders App and Create Your Reminder Lists

1 Swipe up from the bottom of the screen.

The Home screen appears.

2 Tap **Reminders** (⦂).

The Reminders app opens, displaying the Lists screen.

Ⓐ If you have set up reminders or tasks on multiple accounts, such as iCloud and Exchange, a list appears for each account.

3 Tap **Add List** (➕).

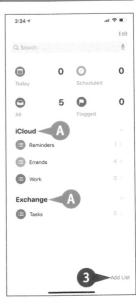

The Choose Account dialog opens.

Note: If you have only one Reminders account, the Choose Account dialog does not appear.

4 Tap the account in which you want to store the list.

The New List screen appears.

5 Type the name for the list.

6 Tap the color to use for the list.

7 Optionally, tap an icon for the list. If you do not choose an icon, the icon is a plain circle of the color you choose.

8 Tap **Done**.

The list appears.

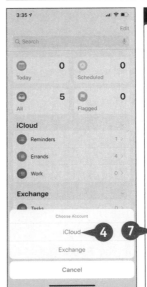

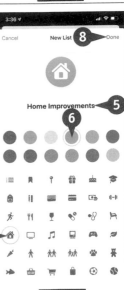

194

Create a New Reminder

1. To create a new reminder in this list, tap **New Reminder** (⊕). This icon's color matches the color you assigned to the list.

B You can tap **Lists** (<) to return to the Lists screen so you can switch to another list.

The keyboard appears.

2. Type the text for the reminder.

3. Tap **Information** (ⓘ).

The Details screen appears.

4. Optionally, tap **Notes** and type any notes.

5. To create a time-based reminder, set the **Remind me on a day** switch to On (changes to ⊙).

The Alarm button, the Remind Me at a Time switch, and the Repeat button appear.

6. Tap **Alarm**.

The date and time controls appear.

7. Set the date and time for the reminder.

8. Set the **Remind me at a time** switch to On (⊙) if you want to receive a reminder at the time you specified.

9. If you need to repeat the reminder, tap **Repeat**, choose the repeat interval on the Repeat screen, and then tap **Details** to return to the Details screen.

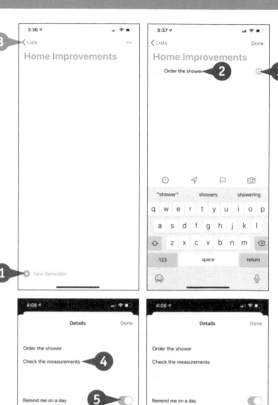

TIP

How do I sync my iPhone's reminders with my Mac's reminders?

You can sync your iPhone's reminders with your Mac's reminders via your iCloud account, via one or more Exchange accounts, or via both types of accounts.

Swipe up from the bottom of the screen to display the Home screen, and then tap **Settings** (⚙) to display the Settings screen. Tap **Apple ID** (the button that bears your Apple ID name) to display the Apple ID screen. Tap **iCloud** (☁) to display the iCloud screen, and then set the **Reminders** switch to On (⊙). On your Mac, click **Apple** () and **System Preferences** to open System Preferences. Click **iCloud** (☁) to display the iCloud pane, and then click **Reminders** (☐ changes to ☑).

continued ▶

You can assign different priorities to your reminders to give yourself a quick visual reference of their urgency. You can also add notes to a reminder to keep relevant information at hand. When you have completed a reminder, you can mark it as completed. You can view your list of scheduled reminders for quick reference, and you can choose whether to include your completed reminders in the list. If you no longer need a reminder, you can delete it from the list.

Track Your Commitments with Reminders (continued)

10 To create a location-based reminder, set the **Remind me at a location** switch to On (⬤).

Note: If Reminders prompts you to allow it to use your current location, tap **Allow**.

11 Tap **Location**.

The Location screen appears.

12 Start typing the location in the search box.

C You can tap **Current Location** to use your current location.

13 Tap the location in the list of results.

The Location screen displays a map of the location.

14 Tap **Arriving** or **Leaving**, as needed.

15 Tap **Details** (‹).

The Details screen appears again.

16 To assign a priority to the reminder, tap **Priority**, tap Low, Medium, High, or None; and then tap **Details** (‹).

D To assign the reminder to a different list than the current list, tap **List**. On the Change List screen, tap the list you want to use.

17 Tap **Done**.

The new reminder appears on your list of reminders.

18 Tap **New Reminder** (➕) to start creating a new reminder.

Ⓔ When you finish a task, tap its button (◯ changes to ◉) to mark the reminder as complete.

Note: To delete a reminder, tap **Edit** on the screen that contains it. Tap **Delete** (➖) to the left of the reminder, and then tap **Delete**.

19 Tap **Lists** (‹) to switch to another reminder list.

View a List of Your Scheduled Reminders

1 Tap **Scheduled** (◯).

The Scheduled list appears.

2 Tap the reminder you want to see.

Note: If you have many lists of reminders, you can arrange the lists in groups. To create a group, tap **Edit** on the Reminders screen, then tap **Add Group** in the lower-left corner. On the New Group screen, type the name for the group, then tap **Include**. On the Include screen, tap **Add** (➕) for each list you want to add to the new group.

TIP

How do I change the default list that Reminders puts my reminders in?

Swipe up from the bottom of the screen to display the Home screen, and then tap **Settings** (⚙) to display the Settings screen. Tap **Reminders** (⦂) to display the Reminders screen, tap **Default List** to display the Default List screen, and then tap the list you want to make the default.

Keep Essential Documents at Hand with Wallet

allet is an app for storing payment cards and electronic versions of essential documents, such as insurance cards, airline boarding passes, movie tickets, and hotel reservations. As explained in Chapter 1, the iPhone's setup routine walks you through adding a payment card for Apple Pay to Wallet; you can add other cards later, as needed.

You can add documents to Wallet from built-in apps such as Mail and Safari, as shown in this section, or by using custom apps for shopping, booking hotels, and booking flights.

Keep Essential Documents at Hand with Wallet

Add a Document to Wallet

1 In Mail, tap the message with the document attached.

The message opens.

2 Tap the document's button.

The document appears.

3 Tap **Add**.

Mail adds the document to Wallet.

The message appears again.

Note: In Safari, open the web page containing the document, and then tap **Add** to add the document to Wallet.

Open Wallet and Find the Documents You Need

1 Swipe up from the bottom of the screen.

The Home screen appears.

2 Tap **Wallet** ().

The Wallet app opens.

The documents you have added appear.

Note: Until you add one or more documents to Wallet, the app displays an information screen highlighting its uses.

3 Tap the document you want to view.

(A) The document appears above the other documents. You can then hold its barcode in front of a scanner to use the document.

(4) To see another document, tap the current top document and swipe down.

Wallet reshuffles the documents so you can see them all.

(B) You can also tap **Done** to return to the first Wallet screen, and then tap the document you want to view.

Choose Settings for a Document or Delete It

(1) Tap **Details** (⋯).

The Details screen appears.

(2) Set the **Automatic Updates** switch to On (◯) if you want to receive updates to this document.

(3) Set the **Allow Notifications** switch to On (◯) if you want to allow the document to raise notifications.

(4) Set the **Suggest on Lock Screen** switch to On (◯) if you want notifications about the document to appear on the lock screen.

(C) If you have no further need for the document, tap **Remove Pass** to remove it.

(5) Tap **Back** (〈).

(6) Tap **Done**.

TIP

What other actions can I take with documents in Wallet?

You can share a document with other people via e-mail, instant messaging, or AirDrop. To access these features, tap **Share** (⬆), and then tap **AirDrop**, **Mail**, or **Message** on the Share sheet that appears.

You can tap **Edit Passes** at the bottom of the main Wallet screen to display the Edit Passes screen. From here, you can scan QR codes to add passes, find apps that work with Apple Wallet, and delete all the passes of a particular type at once.

Find Your Location with Maps

Your iPhone's Maps app can pinpoint your location by using the Global Positioning System, known as GPS, or via triangulation using wireless networks. You can view your location on a road map, display a satellite picture with or without place labels, or view transit information. You can easily switch among map types to find the most useful one. To help you get your bearings, the Tracking feature in the Maps app can show you which direction you are facing.

Find Your Location with Maps

1. Swipe up from the bottom of the screen.

   The Home screen appears.

2. Tap **Maps** ( ).

   The Maps screen appears.

Ⓐ A blue dot shows your current location. The expanding circle around the blue dot shows that Maps is determining your location.

Note: It may take a minute for Maps to work out your location accurately. While Maps determines the location, the blue dot moves, even though the iPhone remains stationary.

3. Drag the gray handle down to collapse the Search pane.

4. Place your thumb and finger apart on the screen and pinch inward.

Note: To zoom in, place your thumb and finger on the screen and pinch apart.

   The map zooms out, showing a larger area.

5. Tap **Location** (changes to), turning on the Location service.

6. Tap **Location** (changes to).

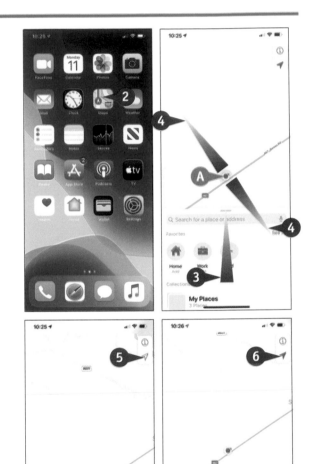

B The Compass icon appears (⬤). The red arrow indicates north.

C The map turns to show the direction the iPhone is facing, so that you can orient yourself.

7 When you need to restore the map orientation, tap **Compass** (⬤).

The map turns so that north is upward.

The Compass icon disappears.

8 Tap **Information** (ⓘ).

The Maps Settings dialog opens.

D You can tap **Transit** to display transit information for the area.

9 Tap **Satellite**.

The satellite map appears, showing photos with street and place names overlaid on them.

10 Set the **Traffic** switch to On (⬤) or Off ( ), as needed.

11 Set the **Labels** switch to On (⬤) to display labels.

12 Tap **Close** (✕).

The Maps Settings dialog closes.

Note: The satellite photos may be several years old and no longer accurate.

TIPS

How can I tell the scale of the map?

Place two fingers on the screen as if about to pinch outward or inward. Maps displays a scale in the upper-left corner of the screen.

How can I share my location?

Tap and hold the location you want to share. A Marked Location pin appears, and the Marked Location panel opens. Swipe up to open the Marked Location panel fully, and then tap **Share** (⬆) to display the Share sheet. You can then tap the means of sharing — such as AirDrop, Message, Mail, or Twitter — and follow the prompts to send or post your location.

Find Directions with Maps

Your iPhone's Maps app can give you directions to where you want to go. Maps can also show you current traffic congestion in some locales to help you identify the most viable route for a journey.

Maps displays driving directions by default, but you can make it display public transit directions and walking directions.

Find Directions with Maps

1 Swipe up from the bottom of the screen.

The Home screen appears.

2 Tap **Maps** (🗺️).

The Maps screen appears.

3 Tap **Search for a place or address**.

The Directions screen appears.

4 Start typing your destination.

A list of suggested matches appears.

5 Tap the correct match.

A map of the destination appears.

6 Tap **Directions**.

Note: If you want the directions to start from your current location, leave My Location in the From field. Go to step **10**.

7 Tap **My Location**.

CHAPTER
9
Keeping Your Life Organized

The Change Route dialog opens.

8 Tap **From** and start typing the start location for the directions.

9 Tap the correct match.

A You can tap **Switch Places** (⇅) to switch the start location and end location.

10 Tap **Route**.

A screen showing the driving directions appears.

B If multiple routes are available, tap a time button to view a different route. The time button changes to blue to indicate it is active.

C You can tap **Walk** (🚶) to see walking directions.

D You can tap **Transit** (🚆) to see transit directions.

E You can tap **Ride** (🚶) to see ride-sharing apps that are available.

11 Tap **Go**.

The first screen of directions appears.

12 Swipe left to display the next direction.

Note: When you start navigating the route, the directions change automatically to reflect your progress.

13 To finish using the directions, tap **End**.

The map appears again.

TIP

What else should I know about the directions for walking or public transit?

You should be aware that walking directions may be incomplete or inaccurate. Before walking the route, check that it does not send you across pedestrian-free bridges or through rail tunnels.

The Maps app provides transit information for only some routes. Even for these, it is advisable to double-check the information via online schedules, such as on the website or app of the transit company involved.

203

Explore with 3D Flyover

Maps is not only great for finding out where you are and for getting directions to places, but it can also show you 3D flyovers of the places on the map. Flyovers can be a useful way to explore a place virtually so that you can find your way around later in real life.

After switching on the 3D feature, you can zoom in and out, pan around, and move backward and forward.

Explore with 3D Flyover

1 Swipe up from the bottom of the screen.

The Home screen appears.

2 Tap **Maps** ().

The Maps screen appears.

3 Display the area of interest in the middle of the screen. For example, tap and drag the map, or search for the location you want.

4 Tap **Information** ().

The Maps Settings dialog opens.

5 Tap **Satellite**.

The map switches to Satellite view.

6 Tap **Close** ().

The Maps Settings dialog closes.

7 Tap **3D**.

Note: You can also swipe up the screen with two fingers to switch to 3D view.

The map switches to 3D view.

8 Place your thumb and finger on the screen and pinch outward.

The map zooms in.

Note: You can place your thumb and finger on the screen and pinch inward to zoom out.

Note: Tap and drag to scroll the map as needed.

9 Place two fingers on the screen and twist clockwise or counterclockwise to rotate the view.

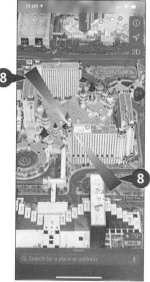

The rotated view appears.

A The Compass arrow (⊙) appears. You can tap it to restore the direction to north.

Note: Pan and zoom as needed to explore the area.

10 Tap and drag up with two fingers.

The viewing angle becomes shallower.

11 Tap **2D**.

The two-dimensional map reappears.

TIP

What does 3D do with the standard map?

When you swipe up the screen with two fingers to switch on Flyover with the standard map displayed, Maps tilts the map at an angle, as you might do with a paper map. In cities, building shapes appear when you zoom in on the map, enabling you to see the layout without using the full detail of the satellite photos.

Using Maps' Favorites and Contacts

When you want to return to a location easily in the Maps app, you can create a favorite for the location.

Similarly, you can add a location to your contacts, so that you can access it either from the Contacts app or from the Maps app. You can either create a new contact or add the location to an existing contact. You can also return quickly to locations you have visited recently but for which you have not created a favorite or contact.

Using Maps' Favorites and Contacts

Create a Favorite in Maps

1 Swipe up from the bottom of the screen.

The Home screen appears.

2 Tap **Maps** ( ).

The Maps screen appears.

3 Find the place for which you want to create a favorite. For example, tap and drag the map, or search for the location you want.

4 Tap and hold the place for which you want to create a favorite.

A The Maps app drops a pin on the place.

The Marked Location panel opens.

5 Swipe up.

The Marked Location panel opens further.

6 Tap **Add to Favorites** (★).

7 Tap **Close** (×).

The panel closes.

Create a Contact in Maps

1 Find the place for which you want to create a contact. For example, tap and drag the map, or search for the location you want.

2 Tap and hold the appropriate place.

The Maps app drops a pin on the place.

The Marked Location panel opens.

3 Swipe up.

The Marked Location panel opens further.

4 Tap **Create New Contact** (⦿).

B You can tap **Add to Existing Contact** (⦿) and then tap the contact to which you want to add the location instead.

The New Contact screen appears.

5 Type the first name for the contact record, as needed.

6 Type the last name for the contact record, as needed.

7 Add any other information the contact record requires.

8 Tap **Done**.

The Maps app creates the contact record for the location.

The Marked Location panel appears again.

9 Tap **Close** (×).

The Marked Location panel closes.

TIP

How do I go to a location for which I have created a favorite or a contact?

In the Maps app, tap **Where do you want to go?** to display the Search screen. Start typing the name of the favorite or contact, and then tap the appropriate search result.

Take Notes

Your iPhone is a great device for taking notes no matter where you happen to be. The Notes app enables you to create notes stored in an e-mail account — such as your iCloud account — or on your iPhone.

You can create straightforward notes in plain text for any account you add to Notes. For notes stored on Exchange, IMAP, or Google accounts, you can also add formatting. For notes stored in iCloud, you can add check boxes, photos, web links, and sketches.

Take Notes

1 Swipe up from the bottom of the screen.

The Home screen appears.

2 Tap **Notes** (—).

The Notes app opens.

Note: To change the account or folder in which you are working, tap **Back** (‹), and then tap the account or folder you want to use.

3 Tap **New** (✐).

A new note opens.

4 Type the title or first paragraph of the note.

5 Tap **More** (⊕).

The More bar appears.

6 Tap **Formatting** (Aa).

A You can tap **Table** (▦) to add a table.

B You can tap **Add Photo** (⌾) to add a new photo, an existing photo, or a scanned document to the note. This adds the photo or document as a separate item attached to the note.

C You can tap **Sketch** (Ⓐ) to draw a sketch in the note.

D You can tap **Close** (✕) when you no longer need the More bar displayed.

The Formatting pane appears.

7 Tap the style you want to apply to the paragraph.

The paragraph takes on the style.

8 Tap **Close** (×).

The Formatting pane closes.

9 Tap **return**.

The insertion point moves to a new paragraph.

10 Tap **Check box** (⊘).

E The Notes app inserts a check box on the current line.

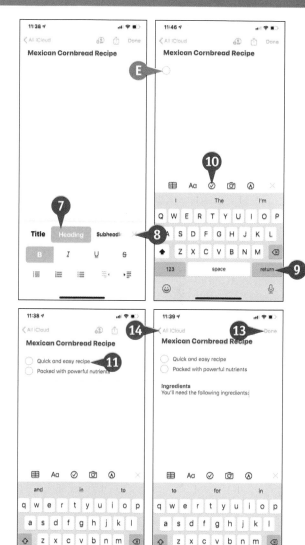

11 Type the text to accompany the check box.

12 Tap **return** twice.

The Notes app creates a new paragraph and discontinues the check boxes.

13 When you finish working on the note, tap **Done**.

The Notes app hides the keyboard.

14 Tap **Back** (‹) one or more times. The name varies depending on the folder you are using.

The Notes screen appears again, and you can work with other notes.

TIPS

How do I tell Siri the account for new notes?
Swipe up from the bottom of the screen to display the Home screen, tap **Settings** (⚙) to display the Settings screen, and then tap **Notes** (—). On the Notes screen, tap **Default Account** to display the Default Account screen, and then tap the appropriate account; or tap **On My iPhone** to store the notes only on your iPhone. The Notes widget in Today View also uses this default account.

What other settings can I configure for Notes?
You can choose the default style for the first line in each new note. Open the Notes screen in the Settings app as explained in the previous tip, tap **New Notes Start With**, and then tap the appropriate style — **Title**, **Heading**, or **Body** — on the New Notes Start With screen.

Using Stocks, Weather, and Clock

The iPhone includes several built-in apps that enable you to keep track of important information throughout the day. You can use the Stocks app to track stock prices so that you can take immediate action when it becomes necessary. You can use the Weather app to learn the current weather conditions and forecast for your current location and for as many cities as you need. And you can use the Clock app's World Clock, Alarm, Bedtime, Stopwatch, and Timer features to track and measure time.

Using the Stocks App

The Stocks app enables you to track a customized selection of stock prices.

Tap **Stocks** () on the Home screen to launch the Stocks app. The Stocks screen appears, showing the default selection of stocks. At the bottom is a news section that you can expand by swiping up. To view more information on a stock, tap it.

To change the stocks displayed, tap **Edit**. On the Stocks configuration screen that appears, tap **Add** (+) to display the Search screen. Type the name or stock symbol of the stock you want to add, tap the matching entry in the list to display the information panel, and then tap **Add to Watchlist**. You can tap stock handles (☰) and drag the stocks into your preferred order. Tap **Done** to return to the Stocks screen.

Using the Weather App

The Weather app lets you stay in touch with current weather conditions and forecasts for multiple locations.

Tap **Weather** () on the Home screen to launch the Weather app. You can then swipe left or right at the top of the screen, or tap the dots at the bottom of the screen, to display the city you want to see. Swipe the timeline left to see later hours. Swipe up to display further details, such as sunrise and sunset times, humidity, and wind.

To customize the locations, tap **Cities** (☰). You can then tap **Add** () to add a location, swipe a location left and tap **Delete** to delete it, or tap and hold and then drag to move a city up or down the list. When you finish customizing the list, tap the city whose weather you want to display.

Using the Clock App

The Clock app, which you can launch by tapping **Clock** (🕐) on the Home screen, has five main features: World Clock, Alarm, Bedtime, Stopwatch, and Timer. You tap the buttons at the bottom of the screen to select the feature you want to use.

The World Clock feature enables you to easily keep track of the time in different cities. From the list, you can remove a city by swiping its button left and then tapping **Delete**. To add cities, tap **Add** (🔳) and select the city on the Choose a City screen. To change the order of the list, tap **Edit** and drag cities up or down by their handles (☰); tap **Done** when you finish.

The Alarm feature lets you set as many alarms as you need, each with a different schedule and your choice of sound. Tap **Add** (🔳) to display the Add Alarm screen, set the details for a new alarm, and then tap **Save**. On the Alarm screen, you can set each alarm's switch to On (🔘) or Off (🔘), as needed.

The Bedtime feature encourages you to follow consistent times for going to bed and waking. It also provides sleep analysis.

The Stopwatch feature allows you to time events to the hundredth of a second. You can switch between the analog-look stopwatch and the digital-look stopwatch by swiping left or right. Tap **Start** to start the stopwatch, tap **Lap** to mark a lap time, and tap **Stop** to stop the stopwatch.

The Timer feature enables you to count down a set amount of time and play a sound when the timer ends. You can also use the Timer to play music or other media for a set amount of time. To do this, tap **When Timer Ends**, tap **Stop Playing** on the When Timer Ends screen, and then tap **Set**.

Using the Health App

The Health app integrates with third-party hardware and software to enable you to keep tabs on many different aspects of your health, ranging from your weight and blood pressure to your nutrition, activity levels, and body mass index. Swipe up from the bottom of the screen to display the Home screen, and then tap **Health** (♥) to launch the Health app.

Navigate the Health App's Screens

The Health app contains two main screens, the Summary screen and the Browse screen.

The Summary screen appears at first, showing the Favorites list, the Highlights list, the Get More from Health list, and the Apps list.

The Browse screen, which you can display by tapping **Browse** (▦ changes to ▦) at the bottom of the screen, contains the Health Categories list and the Health Records list.

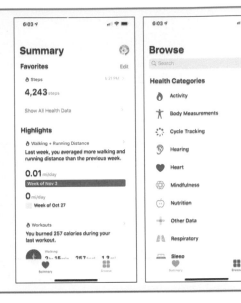

Set Up Your Health Profile and Medical ID

Tap **Account** (⊙ or your chosen photo) to display the Account screen. Here you can enter your medical details; connect to a provider to see your health records; specify privacy settings for apps, research studies, and devices; and export all your health data to share with medical professionals.

Start by tapping **Health Profile** and entering basic details, such as your date of birth and blood type, on the Health Profile screen. Then tap **Medical ID** to display the Medical ID screen. Here, you can enter your medical conditions, medical notes, allergies and reactions, medications, and emergency contact information. At the top of the screen, set the **Show When Locked** switch to On (◯) if you want to allow your Medical ID to be viewed from the iPhone's Power Off screen.

Set Up Your Favorites List

To put the items you will find most useful on your Favorites list, tap **Edit** to the right of Favorites. On the Edit Favorites screen, tap **Existing Data** to view the items that have data, or tap **All** to view all items. Tap **Favorite** (☆ changes to ★) to add an item to the Favorites list. Tap **Done** when you finish.

From the Favorites screen, you can tap an item to view its current data. For example, tap **Activity** to display the Activity screen, where you can examine your data for the Move, Exercise, and Stand targets.

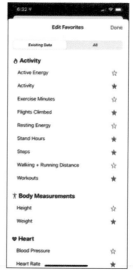
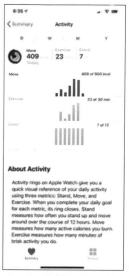

Add Data Points

The Health app can automatically accept data points from sources you approve, but you can also add data points manually. For example, if you weigh yourself on a manual scale or have your blood pressure taken, you can add your latest readings to the Health app so that you can track your weight and blood pressure over time.

Tap the appropriate button — for example, tap **Blood Pressure** — on the Favorites screen to display the Blood Pressure screen. Tap **Add Data** to display the data-entry screen, such as the Blood Pressure screen shown here, input the data, and then tap **Add**. If the values are abnormal, the Confirm Data dialog opens to prompt you to confirm the values; tap **Confirm** if they are correct.

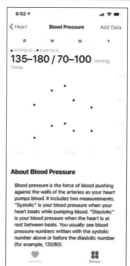

Manage Files with the Files App

The Files app enables you to work with files stored on your iPhone; files stored on network servers, such as macOS Server; and files stored on online storage services, such as iCloud Drive. You can quickly locate files by using the Recents screen, by using the Browse screen, or by searching by keyword. You can also recover recently deleted files by using the Recently Deleted Location. You navigate the Files app using similar techniques to those for navigating file-opening and file-saving features within apps.

Manage Files with the Files App

Open the Files App

1. Swipe up from the bottom of the screen.

   The Home screen appears.

2. Tap **Files** (▣).

   The Files app opens.

3. Tap **Browse** (▤ changes to ▥).

   The Browse screen appears.

Note: The Recently Deleted location contains files that you have deleted recently, somewhat like the Trash on macOS or the Recycle Bin on Windows. To retrieve a deleted file, tap **Recently Deleted**, tap and hold the file, and then tap **Recover** on the command bar that appears.

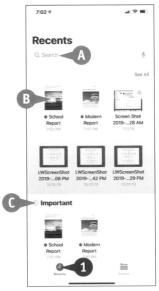

Browse Files and Open Files

1. Tap **Recents** (🕐 changes to 🕐).

   The Recents screen appears.

   Ⓐ You can search your recent files by tapping **Search** (🔍) and then typing a search term.

   Ⓑ Some of your most recent files appear at the top.

   Ⓒ Older files appear listed by their tags.

2. Tap **Browse** (▤ changes to ▥).

   The Browse screen appears.

   Ⓓ You can search all your files by tapping **Search** (🔍) and then typing a search term.

3. Tap the location you want to browse. This example uses iCloud Drive.

The screen for the location appears.

④ Swipe down from below the Search box and divider bar.

Additional commands appear.

Ⓔ You can tap **More** (⋯) to access more commands, including New Folder and Connect to Server.

Ⓕ You can change the sort order by tapping **Sorted by** and then tapping **Name**, **Date**, **Size**, **Kind**, or **Tags** in the Sort By dialog.

Ⓖ You can tap **List** (:≡) to display the files and folders as a list rather than as a grid.

⑤ Tap the folder you want to open.

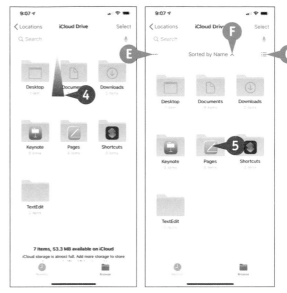

The folder opens.

⑥ Tap the file you want to open.

The file opens in the default app for the file type, assuming your iPhone has such an app.

The app appears, and you can work on the file.

Note: You can open only files for which your iPhone contains a suitable app. If there is no suitable app, Files displays the file for viewing if it has a suitable viewer, but you cannot change the file.

Ⓗ You can tap **Files** (◄) to return to the Files app.

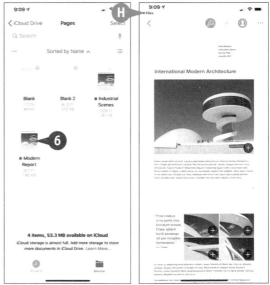

TIP

Can I move or delete multiple files at once?
Yes, you can take several actions with multiple files in the same folder. First, navigate to that folder, and then tap **Select** to switch to Selection Mode. Tap each item to select it (changes to ⊘). After selecting the items, tap the appropriate button at the bottom of the screen — **Duplicate**, **Move**, **Share**, or **Delete** — and then follow the prompts to complete the action.

continued ▶

As well as opening a file, the Files app enables you to take other actions with a file, such as renaming it, copying it and pasting a copy, duplicating it in the same location, or moving it to another location.

The Files app also enables you to use tags to group and sort your files. The Files app comes with default tags with color names, such as Red and Orange, but you can customize the names and create new tags as needed.

Manage Files with the Files App (continued)

Take Other Actions with a File

1 Tap and hold the file you want to affect.

The pop-up menu opens.

I Tap **Copy** (⎘) to copy the file. After copying the file, navigate to the location in which you want to paste the copy, tap and hold open space, and then tap **Paste** on the control bar.

J Tap **Duplicate** (⧉) to create a duplicate file in the same folder.

K Tap **Move** (🗀) to display a screen for moving the file. Tap the location, and then tap **Move**.

L Tap **Delete** (🗑) to delete the file.

M Tap **Info** (ⓘ) to display information about the file.

N Tap **Quick Look** (👁) to display a preview of the file.

O Tap **Rename** (✎) to display the Rename Document screen. Type the new name, and then tap **Done**.

P Tap **Share** (⬆) to open the Share sheet for sharing the file.

Q Tap **Compress** (🗜) to create a zip file containing the file.

2 Tap **Tags** (🏷).

The Tags screen appears.

3 Tap each tag you want to apply to the file. Also tap any applied tag that you want to remove.

4 Tap **Done**.

The Files app displays the folder from which you started.

Organize Your Locations and Tags

1 Tap **Browse** (📁 changes to 📂).

The Browse screen appears.

2 Tap **More** (...).

The menu opens.

3 Tap **Edit**.

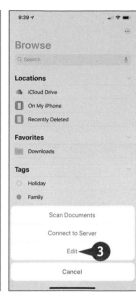

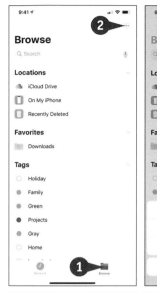

The Browse screen switches to Edit Mode.

4 In the Locations list, set a switch to Off (changes to) if you want to hide the location.

Note: If you have configured a compatible app, but it has not appeared in the Locations list, set its switch here to On ( ) to enable it.

5 Tap a handle and drag a location up or down, as needed.

6 In the Tags list, tap **Delete** (➖) and then tap **Delete** to delete a tag.

7 To change the tag order, tap the handle ( ) and drag the tag up or down the list.

8 When you finish editing the Browse screen, tap **Done**.

The Browse screen switches off Edit Mode.

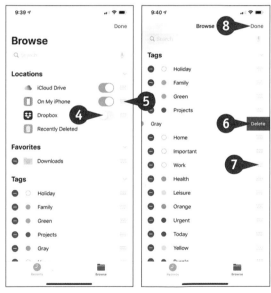

TIP

Can I create my own tags?

Yes, you can create your own tags when saving new files in the apps. For example, when you save a new document in Pages, you can create custom tags for it.

You cannot create new tags directly in the Files app, but you can rename the built-in tags. Tap **Browse** (📁 changes to 📂) to display the Browse screen, tap **More** (...) and then **Edit**, to switch to Edit Mode. You can then tap a tag, type a new name for it, and tap **Done** on the keyboard.

Understanding Shortcuts and Automation

Your iPhone includes the Shortcuts app, which gives you two ways of executing tasks quickly and effortlessly. The first way of executing tasks is using shortcuts, sequences of actions that run at the tap of a button. iOS comes with many prebuilt shortcuts, but you can also build your own custom shortcuts to take exactly the actions you want.

The second way of executing tasks is by using automations. Like a shortcut, an automation is a sequence of actions; the difference is that an automation runs automatically when an event occurs rather than when you tap a button.

Open the Shortcuts App and Navigate the Interface

To get started with shortcuts, swipe up from the bottom of the screen to display the Home screen, and then tap **Shortcuts** (). The Shortcuts app opens, displaying the My Shortcuts screen. At first, this screen may contain only the Create Shortcut button, which you can tap to start creating a new shortcut. You can add other shortcuts to this screen as needed. When you want to run a shortcut, you tap its button on the My Shortcuts screen.

On the Automation screen, the Create Personal Automation feature lets you configure the Shortcuts app to automatically trigger sequences of software tasks when certain conditions are met. You can also create automated tasks to be performed with HomeKit-compatible devices using the Home app's interface, again when certain conditions are met.

Explore Built-In Shortcuts in the Gallery

Before creating any shortcuts of your own, spend a few minutes exploring the prebuilt shortcuts. Tap **Gallery** (changes to) to display the Gallery screen.

At the top of this screen, you can search using keywords, or browse through highlighted collections.

In the Shortcuts from Your Apps section, you can tap any of the suggestions for custom shortcuts based on your recent iPhone usage. Below this are various categories of shortcuts. Scroll down to find a category of interest, and then scroll left to explore the shortcuts it contains; tap **See All** to display a screen showing the entire category.

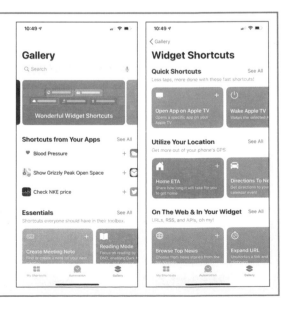

Add Shortcuts to the My Shortcuts Screen

When you find a shortcut you want to use on the Gallery screen, add it to the My Shortcuts screen. Tap the shortcut on the Gallery to display the information screen for the shortcut. Here, you can edit the shortcut's name in the When I Run text box as needed; for example, you might give the shortcut a snappier or more memorable name to help you identify it among many shortcuts. You can also tap the Do box to view the actions the shortcut will take. Then tap **Add Shortcut** to add the shortcut to the My Shortcuts screen.

From the Gallery screen, you can also add a shortcut to the My Shortcuts screen more quickly: Tap and hold the shortcut on the Gallery screen until the pop-up menu opens, and then tap **Add Shortcut** (**+**).

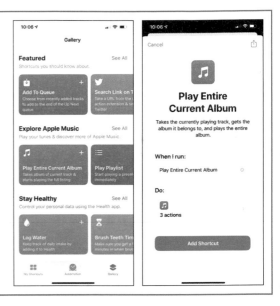

Configure or Modify a Shortcut

The Shortcuts app enables you to configure an existing shortcut or modify what it does. To start configuring or modifying a shortcut, tap **My Shortcuts** (■■ changes to ■■) to display the My Shortcuts screen. Then tap **Details** (•••) on the shortcut to open the shortcut in the shortcut editor.

You can then tap an item in an action to configure that item, or tap **Remove** (×) to remove an action.

To configure the shortcut, tap **Details** (•••) and work on the Details screen. Here, you can choose settings for the shortcut. For example, set the **Show in Widget** switch to On (◯) to add the shortcut to the widgets list. Tap **Done** when you finish configuring the shortcut, and then tap **Done** again to close the shortcut editor.

Create a Custom Shortcut

The Shortcuts app enables you to create custom shortcuts that perform exactly the actions you want. You can browse an extensive selection of actions, arrange the actions you need into the right order, and customize what the actions do. You can then assign your new shortcut a name and a *glyph* — an icon — with a colored background.

As with prebuilt shortcuts, you can run your custom shortcuts either from the My Shortcuts screen in the Shortcuts app or directly from the iPhone's Home screen.

Create a Custom Shortcut

1 Swipe up from the bottom of the screen to display the Home screen.

2 Tap **Shortcuts** (⬛) to open the Shortcuts app.

3 If the My Shortcuts screen does not appear at first, tap **My Shortcuts** (⬛⬛ changes to ⬛⬛) to display it.

4 Tap **Create Shortcut** (➕).

Note: You may need to scroll down to locate the Create Shortcut button.

A You can also tap **Create Shortcut** (➕).

The shortcut editor screen appears, showing a new shortcut with the default name New Shortcut.

5 Tap **Add Action** (➕).

The Action panel opens.

6 Locate the action you want to add to the shortcut.

B You can tap **Search** and enter a keyword to search for.

C You can tap a category, such as **Apps** (⬤) or **Media** (🎵), to view actions in that category.

D You can browse the Suggestions list to find an action based on your iPhone usage.

7 To follow this example, tap **Scripting** (x).

The contents of the Scripting category appear.

8 Tap the action you want to add.

The shortcut editor screen appears, with the action added to the shortcut.

9 Tap **Add Action** (⊕) and add other actions, as needed.

10 If an action has configurable items, tap the item you want to configure, and then choose options for it.

E For example, for the Show Result action, you can enter text to accompany the result returned by the previous action, such as the Get Battery Level action in the example.

11 Tap **Next**.

The screen for naming the shortcut appears.

12 Tap the default icon to display the icon screen, tap a color on the Color tab, tap **Glyph** and tap a glyph on the Glyph tab, and then tap **Done**.

13 Tap **Name** and type the name for the shortcut.

14 Tap **Done**.

The shortcut appears on the My Shortcuts screen.

15 Tap the new shortcut.

F The shortcut performs its actions — in this example, displaying a dialog that shows the battery level percentage.

TIP

How do I run a custom shortcut from the Home screen?

On the My Shortcuts screen, tap **More** (⋯) on the shortcut to display the screen for the shortcut. Tap **Details** (⋯) in the upper-right corner to display the Details screen. Tap **Add to Home Screen** to display the preview panel. Here, the Home Screen Name and Icon box shows the default icon and name for the shortcut. To change the icon, tap it; tap **Take Photo**, **Choose Photo**, or **Choose File**, as appropriate, and follow the prompts. To change the text, tap it, and then edit it as needed. When icon and text are satisfactory, tap **Add**. Tap **Done** to close the Details screen; also tap **Done** to close the shortcut's screen.

Get Your Bearings with Compass

When you need to get your bearings, use the Compass app that comes installed on your iPhone. With Compass, you can establish your relationship to the points of the compass and learn your precise GPS location. You can also determine your elevation and measure an angle between two points.

The Compass app can show either True North or Magnetic North. To switch, tap **Settings** (⚙) on the Home screen, tap **Compass** (◼), and then set the **Use True North** switch to On (⬤) or Off (◯), as needed.

Get Your Bearings with Compass

Open Compass and Get Your Bearings

1 Swipe up from the bottom of the screen to display the Home screen.

2 Tap **Utilities** (••) to open the Utilities folder.

3 Tap **Compass** (◼) to open the Compass app.

Note: If Compass displays a message prompting you to complete the circle to calibrate it, turn your iPhone this way and that until the circle is filled in. The compass then appears.

4 Point your iPhone in the direction whose bearing you want to take.

Ⓐ The readout shows the bearing.

Ⓑ You can tap the GPS location to switch to the Maps app and display the map for that location.

Ⓒ The readout shows the approximate elevation above sea level.

Measure an Angle

1 On the Compass screen, tap anywhere on the compass to fix the current bearing.

Ⓓ The bearing appears at the top of the compass.

2 Turn the iPhone toward the target point.

Ⓔ The red arc measures the difference between the two bearings.

3 Tap anywhere to release the compass.

Measure with the Measure App

The Measure app, which you can find in the Utilities folder, has two features. The Measure feature enables you to measure distances between points by using the iPhone's rear camera. The Level feature enables you to measure the current slant of an object, which can help you to level it precisely.

Measure with the Measure App

Open the Measure App and Measure Distances

1 Swipe up from the bottom of the screen to display the Home screen.

2 Tap **Utilities** (**⁙**) to open the Utilities folder.

3 Tap **Measure** (▤) to open the Measure app.

4 Point the dot in the center circle at the point where you want to start measuring.

5 Tap **Add** (⊕).

The Measure app starts measuring.

6 Move the dot to the end point for the measurement.

7 Tap **Add** (⊕) to lock the measurement.

8 To restart the measuring process, tap **Clear**.

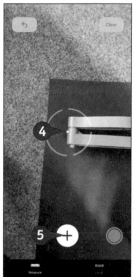

Using the Level Feature

1 In the Measure app, tap **Level** (▤ changes to ▦).

The Level screen appears.

Ⓐ The figure shows the angle of the object or surface.

2 Tilt your iPhone toward a level position to move the circles on top of each other.

Note: If the black-and-white color scheme is hard to see, tap anywhere on the screen to change the background color to red.

Ⓑ When you align the circles, the screen goes green.

CHAPTER 10

Enjoying Music, Videos, and Books

As well as being a phone and a powerful handheld computer, your iPhone is also a full-scale music and video player. To play music and listen to radio, you use the Music app; to play videos, you use the TV app. You can read digital books and PDF files using the Books app.

Navigate the Music App and Set Preferences

The Music app enables you to enjoy music you have loaded on your iPhone, music you have stored on Apple's iTunes Match service, and music on the Apple Music Radio service.

The Music app packs a wide range of functionality into its interface. The For You feature presents a selection of music customized to your tastes. The Browse feature gives you easy access to a wide variety of music online. The Radio feature allows you to listen to Apple Music Radio.

Navigate the Music App and Set Preferences

1 Swipe up from the bottom of the screen.

The Home screen appears.

2 Tap **Music** (♫).

The Music app opens.

3 If Library is not selected, tap **Library** (changes to).

The Library screen appears, showing your music library.

Ⓐ You can tap an item, such as Playlists or Artists, to browse the library.

Ⓑ The Recently Added section shows items added recently.

4 Tap **Edit**.

The Library screen opens for editing.

5 Tap an empty selection circle to select it (changes to ✓), adding that item to the Library list.

6 Tap a selected selection circle to deselect it (✓ changes to), removing that item from the Library list.

7 Drag a selection handle up or down to move an item in the list.

8 Tap **Done**.

The Library screen displays the customized list.

9 Tap **For You** (♥ changes to ♥).

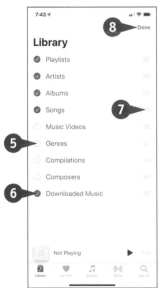

The For You screen appears, showing music suggestions for you.

Note: On the For You screen, you can scroll down to see different categories of items, such as Recently Updated and New Releases, intended to appeal to you. Scroll a category left to see more items in it.

Ⓒ You can tap **Account** (Ⓐ) to display the Account screen, on which you can edit your nickname for the account and set a photo to use.

🔟 Tap **Browse** (♫ changes to ♫).

The Browse screen appears, providing ways to browse music. Scroll down to browse the categories. Scroll a category left to view its contents.

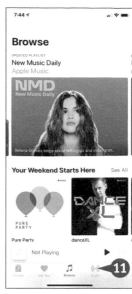

⑪ Tap **Radio** ((•)) changes to ((•))).

The Radio screen appears.

Ⓓ You can tap a station to start it playing.

Note: See the section "Listen to Apple Music Radio," later in this chapter, for more information on the Radio feature.

⑫ Tap **Search** (🔍 changes to 🔍).

The Search screen appears.

Ⓔ You can tap the Search box and type or dictate a search term.

Ⓕ You can tap a Trending search — terms other people are searching for — or one of your recent searches to repeat it.

TIP

How does the Search function work?

The Search function enables you to search both your own music and the Apple Music service. Tap **Search** (🔍 changes to 🔍) to display the Search screen, and then type your search terms in the box at the top of the screen. Tap the **Apple Music** tab button to see matching searches you can perform on Apple Music; you can then tap a search to perform it. Tap the **Your Library** tab button to see matching items in your music, broken down into categories such as Artists, Albums, or Songs. When you locate the item you want, tap the item to go to it.

Play Music Using the Music App

Y ou use the Music app to play back music from your iCloud Library or music you have loaded on your iPhone using iTunes. You can play music by song or by album, as described in this section. You can play songs in exactly the order you want by creating a custom playlist, as described in the later section, "Create a Music Playlist and Add Songs." You can also play by artist, genre, or composer.

Play Music Using the Music App

1 Swipe up from the bottom of the screen.

The Home screen appears.

2 Tap **Music** (♫) to open the Music app.

3 Tap **Library** (🎵 changes to 🎵).

The Library screen appears.

4 Tap the button for the means by which you want to browse your library. This example uses **Songs**, so the Songs screen appears.

A If the songs are sorted by artist or recent addition, tap **Sort** and then tap **Title** in the dialog that opens.

5 Tap the letter that starts the name of the item you want to play.

That section of the list appears.

Note: You can also swipe or drag your finger up the screen to scroll down.

Note: Tap above the letter A in the navigation letters to go back to the top of the screen.

6 Tap the song you want to play.

The song starts playing.

B The song appears on the Now Playing button.

C You can tap **Pause** (❚❚) to pause the song.

D You can tap **Next** (▶▶) to skip to the next song.

7 Tap **Now Playing**. You can tap either the song name or the album image.

The Now Playing panel opens.

8 Tap and drag the playhead to move through the song.

9 Tap and drag the volume control to change the volume. You can also press **Volume Up** or **Volume Down**, the iPhone's physical buttons.

10 Tap **More** (⋯).

The More panel opens. Its contents vary depending on how your library is configured and where the current song is stored.

E You can tap **Delete from Library** (🗑) to delete the song from your iPhone's library.

F You can tap **Add to a Playlist** (▣) to add the song to a new or existing playlist.

G You can tap **Love** (♡) or **Suggest Less Like This** (👎) to indicate your feeling toward the song.

11 Tap **Close** (×).

The More panel closes.

12 Tap **List** (▤ changes to ☰).

The List panel opens.

H You can tap **Shuffle** (⤭) to play songs in random order.

I You can tap **Repeat** (↻) to repeat the current song or current list.

J The Up Next section shows upcoming songs. You can tap a song to play it, or drag a handle (☰) to rearrange the list.

13 Tap **List** (▤ changes to ☰).

The Now Playing panel appears again.

Play Videos Using the TV App

To play videos — such as movies, TV shows, or music videos — you use the iPhone's TV app, which you can set up to use your existing TV provider. You can play a video on the iPhone's screen, which is handy when you are traveling; on a TV to which you connect the iPhone; or on a TV connected to an Apple TV box. Using a TV is great when you need to share a movie or other video with family, friends, or colleagues.

Play Videos Using the TV App

Set Up the TV App

1 Swipe up from the bottom of the screen.

The Home screen appears.

Note: You can also play videos included on web pages. To do so, swipe up to display the Home screen, tap **Safari**, navigate to the page, and then tap the video.

2 Tap **TV** (⬛).

The TV app opens.

Ⓐ You can tap **Account** (◉) to display the Account screen, from which you can manage your subscriptions.

3 Tap the video source. For this example, you would tap **Library** (⬛ changes to ⬛).

The Library screen appears.

4 Tap the video category, such as **Home Videos**.

The category screen appears.

5 Tap the video you want to view.

The details screen for the video appears.

6 Tap **Play** (▶).

The video starts playing.

Note: The playback controls appear for a few seconds, and then disappear automatically.

7 If the video is in landscape format, turn your iPhone sideways.

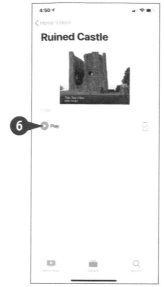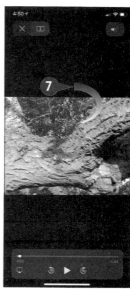

The video switches to landscape orientation.

8 When you need to control playback, tap the screen.

The playback controls appear.

Ⓑ Drag the playhead to move through the video.

Ⓒ Drag the volume control to change the volume.

Ⓓ Tap **Pause** (❚❚) to pause playback. Tap **Play** (▶) to resume playback.

Ⓔ Tap **Rewind** (🔄) to rewind the video.

Ⓕ Tap **Fast-Forward** (🔄) to fast-forward the video.

9 Tap **Close** (✕) when you want to return to the details screen for the video.

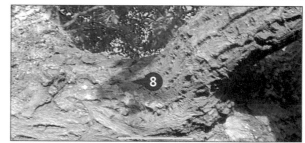

TIPS

How do I play videos on my television from my iPhone?

If you have an Apple TV or AirPlay-compatible device, use AirPlay, as explained in the next section, "Play Music and Videos Using AirPlay." Otherwise, use the Apple Lightning Digital AV Adapter and an HDMI cable to connect your iPhone to a TV.

What other video content can I watch on my iPhone?

You can also use your iPhone to watch or listen to *podcasts*, which are video or audio programs released via the Internet. The Podcasts app enables you to access podcasts covering many different topics, and the iTunes U app is your gateway to podcasts containing educational content, some free and some paid.

Play Music and Videos Using AirPlay

Using the AirPlay feature, you can play music from your iPhone on remote speakers connected to an AirPlay-compatible device such as an AirPort Express or Apple TV. Similarly, you can play video from your iPhone on a TV or monitor connected to an Apple TV. Even better, you can use the iOS feature called *Screen Mirroring* to display an iPhone app on a TV or monitor. For example, you can display a web page in Safari on your TV screen.

Play Music and Videos Using AirPlay

Play Music on External Speakers or an Apple TV

1. Swipe up from the bottom of the screen.

   The Home screen appears.

2. Tap **Music** (♫).

   The Music app opens.

3. Navigate to the song you want to play. For example, tap **Library** (🔲 changes to 🔳), tap **Songs**, and then tap the song.

   The song starts playing and appears on the Now Playing button.

4. Tap **Now Playing**.

   The Now Playing screen appears.

5. Tap **AirPlay** (📡).

   The AirPlay dialog opens.

6. Tap the AirPlay device on which you want the music to play.

   Your iPhone starts playing music on the device via AirPlay.

Note: When you want to stop using AirPlay, tap **AirPlay** (🔍), and then tap **iPhone** (▮).

232

Play Video or an App on an Apple TV

1 Open the app you want to use. This example uses **Notes** ( ).

2 Swipe down from the upper-right corner of the screen.

Control Center opens.

3 Tap **Screen Mirroring** ( ).

The Screen Mirroring panel opens.

4 Tap the Apple TV you want to use.

The iPhone's screen appears on the screen connected to the Apple TV.

A The Stop Mirroring button appears.

5 Tap outside the Screen Mirroring panel.

The Screen Mirroring panel closes.

6 Tap in the app above Control Center.

Control Center closes, and the app appears full-screen.

Note: When you are ready to stop screen mirroring, open Control Center, tap **Screen Mirroring** ( ), and then tap **Stop Mirroring**.

TIP

Can AirPlay play music through multiple sets of speakers at the same time?
AirPlay on the Mac or PC can play music through two or more sets of speakers at the same time, enabling you to play music throughout your home. However, as of this writing, AirPlay on the iPhone can play only to a single device at a time.

Create a Music Playlist and Add Songs

Instead of playing individual songs or playing a CD's songs from start to finish, you can create a playlist that contains only the songs you want in your preferred order. Playlists are a great way to enjoy music on your iPhone.

To help identify a playlist, you can add a new photo or an existing photo. Alternatively, you can let the Music app create a thumbnail from the covers of the songs you add to the playlist.

Create a Music Playlist and Add Songs

1 Swipe up from the bottom of the screen.

The Home screen appears.

2 Tap **Music** (♫).

The Music screen appears.

3 Tap **Library** (🎵 changes to 🎵).

The Library screen appears.

4 Tap **Playlists**.

The Playlists screen appears.

5 Tap **New Playlist**.

The New Playlist screen opens.

6 Tap **Playlist Name** and type the name for the playlist.

7 Optionally, tap **Description** and type a description for the playlist.

8 Optionally, tap **Photo** (📷), tap **Take Photo** or **Choose Photo**, and follow the prompts to add a photo.

9 Tap **Add Music** (➕).

The first Add Songs screen appears.

Ⓐ You can search for music by tapping **Search** (🔍) and typing your search term.

⑩ Tap **Library** (🎵), **For You** (♥), or **Browse** (♫), as needed. This example uses Library (🎵).

The corresponding screen appears — in this case, the Library screen.

⑪ Tap the button for the means by which you want to browse your library. This example uses **Songs**.

The appropriate screen appears, such as the Songs screen.

⑫ Tap each song you want to add (⊕ changes to ✓).

⑬ Tap **Done**.

The New Playlist screen appears.

⑭ Rearrange the songs as needed by dragging each song up or down by its handle (☰).

Ⓑ You can remove a song by tapping **Remove** (⊖) and then tapping the textual Remove button that appears.

⑮ Tap **Done**.

The Playlists screen appears.

TIP

How can I add songs to an existing playlist?

Navigate to the song you want to add, and then tap and hold it. In the panel that opens, tap **Add to a Playlist** (⊕≡). The Add to a Playlist screen appears, showing your playlists. Tap the playlist to which you want to add the song. You can use the same technique to add a whole album to a playlist. Alternatively, you can tap **New Playlist** to start creating a new playlist.

Listen to Apple Music Radio

The Radio feature in the Music app enables you to listen to the Apple Music Radio service. Apple Music Radio has two main parts, one free and one paid. The free part comprises the Beats 1 global radio station and other live radio stations. The paid part is curated, on-demand radio stations and custom radio stations, which require a subscription to the Apple Music service. At the time of this writing, an individual subscription costs $9.99 per month; a family subscription, which covers up to six people, costs $14.99 per month.

Listen to Apple Music Radio

1 Swipe up from the bottom of the screen.

The Home screen appears.

2 Tap **Music** (🎵).

The Music app opens.

3 Tap **Radio** ((•)) changes to ((•))).

The Radio screen appears.

A You can swipe left on the thumbnail bar to display other major stations.

B The Recently Played list shows stations you played recently.

4 Swipe up to scroll down.

The Apple Music Radio section and the Radio by Genre section appear.

C You can tap a station to start it playing.

5 Tap the genre you want to browse.

The list of stations in that genre appears.

Note: To share a station, tap and hold the station and then tap **Share Station** (⬆️) on the panel that appears.

6 Tap the station you want to play.

The current song on that station starts playing.

The Now Playing screen appears.

D You can navigate by using the playback controls. For example, tap **Pause** (⏸) to pause playback, or drag the playhead to move through the song.

7 Tap **Lyrics** (💬).

The Lyrics pane appears.

E The current line appears in white font.

8 Tap **Close**.

The Lyrics panel closes.

9 Tap **List** (☰ changes to ▤).

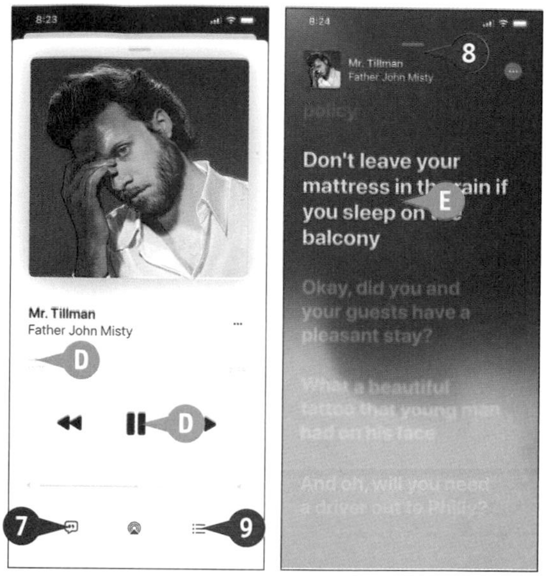

The List panel appears.

F The Up Next list shows the upcoming track or tracks.

10 Tap **More** (···).

Note: You can also tap **More** (···) on the Now Playing panel.

The More panel opens.

G You can take various actions, such as tapping **Copy** (⎘) to copy the song details, tapping **Share** (⇧) to share the song information, or tapping **Create Station** (⊙))) to create a station based on the song.

11 Tap **Close** (×).

The More panel closes.

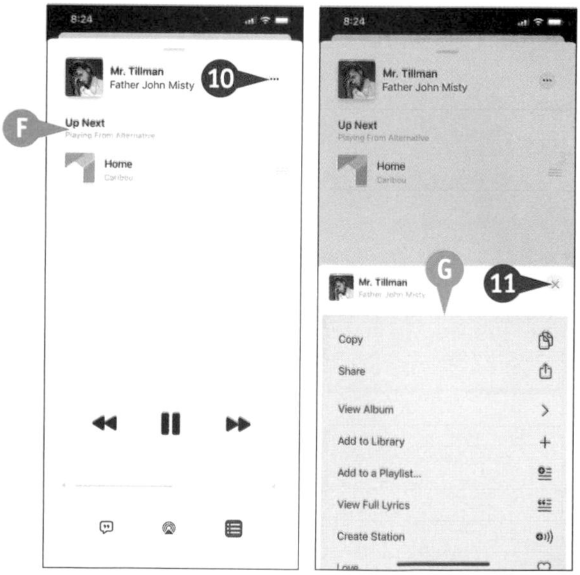

TIP

What do the Share Station and Share Song commands do?
The Share Station command enables you to share a link to a station on Apple Music Radio. Similarly, the Share Song command lets you share a link to a song on the iTunes Store. You can use various means of sharing, such as sending the link via Mail or Messages, posting it to Facebook or Twitter, or simply setting yourself a reminder to listen to — or avoid — the music.

Read Digital Books with the Books App

The Books app enables you to read e-books or PDF files that you load on the iPhone from your computer or sync via iCloud by enabling Books on your Mac and your iPhone to use iCloud. You can also read e-books and PDFs you download from online stores, download from web pages, or save from e-mail messages.

If you have already loaded some e-books, you can read them as described in this section. If Books contains no books, tap **Store** and browse the Book Store or sync books from your computer using iTunes.

Read Digital Books with the Books App

1 Swipe up from the bottom of the screen to display the Home screen.

2 Tap **Books** (📖).

Books opens, and the Reading Now screen appears.

Note: If the book you want to read appears on the Reading Now screen, tap the book to open it. Go to step **6**.

3 Tap **Library** (📚 changes to 📚).

The Library screen appears.

A To change the collection of books displayed, you can tap **Collections** (≡) and then tap the appropriate collection, such as **Books** (📖) or **PDFs** (📄).

4 To view the books as a list, tap **List** (:≡ changes to ▤) at the top of the screen.

B You can tap **Search** (🔍) and search to locate the book you want.

The list of books appears.

C You can tap **Sort** and then tap **Recent**, **Title**, **Author**, or **Manually** to sort the books differently.

5 Tap the book you want to open.

The book opens.

Note: When you open a book, Books displays your current page. When you open a book for the first time, Books displays the book's cover, first page, or default page.

D To change the font, tap **Font Settings** (ᴀA) and use the controls in the Font Settings dialog.

6 Tap anywhere on the screen to hide the reading controls.

The reading controls disappear.

Note: To display the reading controls again, tap anywhere on the screen.

7 Tap the right side of the page to display the next page.

Note: To display the previous page, tap the left side of the page. Alternatively, tap the left side of the page and drag to the right.

8 To look at the next page without fully revealing it, tap the right side and drag to the left. You can then either drag further to turn the page or release the page and let it fall closed.

9 To jump to another part of the book, tap **Table of Contents** (⋮☰).

Note: Alternatively, you can drag the slider at the bottom of the screen.

The table of contents appears.

10 Tap the part of the book you want to display.

11 To search in the book, tap **Search** (🔍).

The Search screen appears.

12 Type the search term.

The list of search results appears.

13 Tap the result you want to display.

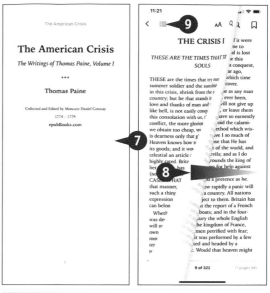

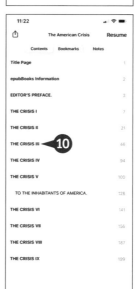

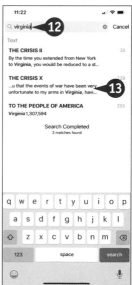

TIPS

How do I put my Mac's Books library on my iPhone manually?

Sync your books using Finder on macOS Catalina or iTunes on earlier versions of macOS. After connecting your iPhone to your Mac and displaying the iPhone control screens, click **Books** and then work with the controls on that screen.

Where can I find free e-books to read in Books?

On the Book Store, tap **Browse Sections** (☰) and then tap **Special Offers & Free** in the Book Store Sections list. Other sources of free e-books include ManyBooks.net (www.manybooks.net), Project Gutenberg (www.gutenberg.org), and the Baen Free Library (www.baen.com/library).

CHAPTER 11

Working with Photos and Video

Your iPhone's Camera app enables you to take high-quality still photos and videos. You can edit photos or apply filters to them, trim video clips down to length, and easily share both photos and videos.

Take Photos with the Camera App

Your iPhone includes a high-resolution rear camera and a lower-resolution screen-side camera. Both cameras can take photos and videos, and the screen-side camera works for video calls, too. To take photos using the camera, you use the Camera app. This app includes a digital zoom feature for zooming in and out; a flash that you can set to On, Off, or Auto; and a High Dynamic Range (HDR) feature that combines several photos into a single photo with adjusted color balance and intensity.

Take Photos with the Camera App

Open the Camera App

1. Swipe up from the bottom of the screen.

   The Home screen appears.

Note: From the lock screen, you can open the Camera app by swiping left.

2. Tap **Camera** (📷).

   The Camera app opens and displays whatever is in front of the lens.

Compose the Photo and Zoom if Necessary

1. Aim the iPhone so that your subject appears in the middle of the photo area. To focus on an item not in the center of the frame, tap that item to move the focus rectangle to it.

Note: If you need to take tightly composed photos, get a tripod mount for the iPhone. You can find various models on eBay and photography sites.

Ⓐ You can tap the zoom buttons to zoom to .5X, 1X, or 2X using different lenses. The iPhone 11 does not have 2X zoom.

2. If you need to zoom in, tap and hold the Zoom readout.

   The zoom track appears.

3. Drag along the zoom track to zoom.

Note: You can also zoom in by placing two fingers together on the screen and pinching outward. To zoom out, pinch inward.

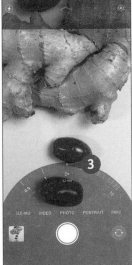

Choose Flash Settings

1 Tap **Show Controls** (━).

The Controls bar appears above the Shutter button.

2 Tap **Flash** (⚡, ⚡, or ⚡).

The Flash settings appear.

3 Tap **Flash On** to use the flash, **Auto** to use the flash if there is not enough light without it, or **Off** to turn the flash off.

4 Tap **Hide Controls** (━).

The Controls bar disappears.

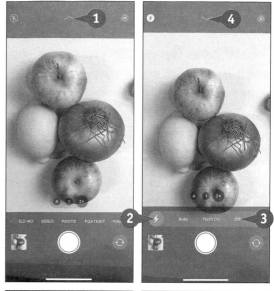

Take the Photo and View It

1 Tap **Take Photo** (◯).

Note: You can drag **Take Photo** (◯) left to take a burst of photos.

The Camera app takes the photo and displays a thumbnail.

2 Tap the thumbnail.

The photo appears.

Ⓑ From the photo screen, swipe or tap a thumbnail to display another photo. Tap **Delete** (🗑) to delete the current photo.

3 Tap **Back** (‹) when you want to go back to the Camera app.

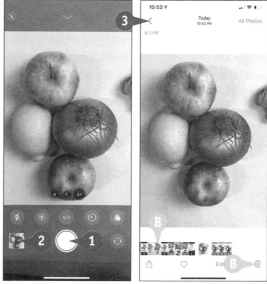

TIP

How do I switch to the front-facing camera?
Tap **Switch Cameras** (🔄) to switch from the rear-facing camera to the front-facing camera. The image that the front-facing camera is seeing appears on-screen, and you can take pictures as described in this section. HDR is available for the front-facing camera; flash is available only on some iPhone models. Tap **Switch Cameras** (🔄) again when you want to switch back to the rear-facing camera.

Take Live, Timed, and Different-Aspect Photos

The Camera app's Live Photo feature enables you to capture several seconds of video around a still photo. Live Photo is great for photographing moving subjects or setting the scene.

The self-timer feature lets you set the app to take a photo after a delay of 3 seconds or 10 seconds, which is good for group shots and for avoiding camera shake. You can also take photos in different-aspect ratios, such as square photos, and capture panoramas.

Take Live, Timed, Portrait, and Different-Aspect Photos

Open the Camera App, Take a Live Photo, and View It

1 Swipe up from the bottom of the screen.

The Home screen appears.

2 Tap **Camera** (📷).

The Camera app opens.

3 Tap **Live** (◎ changes to ◉).

Note: Live Photo starts recording video as soon as you enable the feature. Live Photo discards the video except for the segments before and after photos you shoot.

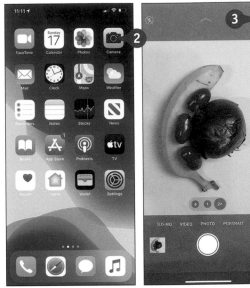

A The Live badge appears briefly.

4 Tap **Take Photo** (◯).

The Camera app captures the Live Photo.

5 Tap the photo's thumbnail.

The photo opens.

The Live Photo segment plays.

6 Tap and hold the photo to play the Live Photo segment again.

7 Tap **Back** (‹).

The Camera app appears again.

244

Take a Timed Photo

1 Tap **Show Controls** (▬).

The control bar appears.

2 Tap **Timer** (⏱).

The Timer settings appear.

3 Tap **3s** or **10s** to set the delay.

Ⓑ The delay appears at the top of the screen.

4 Tap **Take Photo** (◯).

Note: The Camera app displays an on-screen countdown, and the rear flash flashes to indicate the countdown to the subject.

When the countdown ends, the Camera app takes a photo.

Note: The timer remains set until you change it.

Take a Photo with a Different-Aspect Ratio

1 Tap **Show Controls** (▬).

The control bar appears.

2 Tap **Aspect Ratio**, the button that shows the current aspect ratio, such as 4:3.

The Aspect Ratio controls appear.

3 Tap the aspect ratio you want, such as **Square** or **16:9**.

Ⓒ The capture area takes on the aspect ratio you chose.

Ⓓ The Aspect Ratio button shows the aspect ratio. If you chose Square, the button shows 1:1.

4 Tap **Take Photo** (◯).

How do I take panorama photos?
Tap **Pano**. Holding the iPhone in portrait orientation, aim at the left end of the panorama. Tap **Take Photo** (◯); gradually move the iPhone to the right, keeping the white arrow on the horizontal line; and then tap **Stop** (◯).

How do I take time-lapse movies?
Tap **Time-Lapse**; if you cannot see Time-Lapse, drag the current setting to the right first. Set the iPhone up on a tripod or other steady holder, aim it at the subject, and then tap **Start** (◼). When you have captured enough, tap **Stop** (◼) to stop shooting.

Using Portrait Mode

The Camera app includes Portrait Mode, a mode optimized for taking portraits. After switching to Portrait Mode, you can apply special lighting presets to make the subject look the way you want. You can also edit or remove the Portrait Mode effect after taking a photo.

You can use Portrait Mode with either the main camera on the back of the iPhone or with the front-facing "selfie" camera.

Using Portrait Mode

1 Swipe up from the bottom of the screen.

The Home screen appears.

2 Tap **Camera** (📷).

The Camera app opens.

3 Tap **Portrait**.

The Camera app switches to Portrait Mode.

A On iPhone 11 Pro models, the Camera app switches to its 2X lens, making the subject appear larger. The 2X lens also gives better focus separation.

B The readout shows the current lighting effect.

4 Tap and hold **Lighting Effect**. The icon displayed varies depending on which effect is currently selected.

The Lighting Effect wheel appears.

5 Rotate the Lighting Effect wheel clockwise or counterclockwise.

Note: You can also tap **Lighting Effect** to display the wheel, and then tap an icon on it.

C The next lighting effect appears.

D The preview shows the lighting effect applied.

6 Release the Lighting Effect wheel when you find the effect you want.

7 Tap **Take Photo** (○).

8 Tap the photo thumbnail.

The photo opens.

E The Portrait readout appears.

9 Tap **Edit**.

The photo opens for editing.

10 Tap and hold **Lighting Effect**. As before, the icon varies, depicting the selected lighting effect.

The Lighting Effect Wheel appears.

11 Rotate the Lighting Effect wheel to change the effect.

12 To adjust the intensity of the effect, scroll the bar left or right.

13 Tap **Done**.

The photo closes.

How do I blur the background in a photo?

Tap **Portrait** to switch the Camera app to Portrait Mode. Tap **Aperture** (🄵 changes to 🄵) in the upper-right corner of the screen to display the Aperture controls, and then drag the slider left or right to adjust the effective aperture to control the amount of background separation from the subject. This simulates a "bokeh" effect, making the subject stand out from the background.

Apply Filters to Your Photos

You can use the Filter feature in the Camera app to change the look of a photo by applying a filter such as Vivid, Dramatic Warm, Mono, Silvertone, or Noir.

You can apply a filter either before taking the photo or after taking it. If you apply the filter before taking the photo, you can remove the filter afterward; the filter is an effect applied to the photo, not an integral part of the photo.

Apply Filters to Your Photos

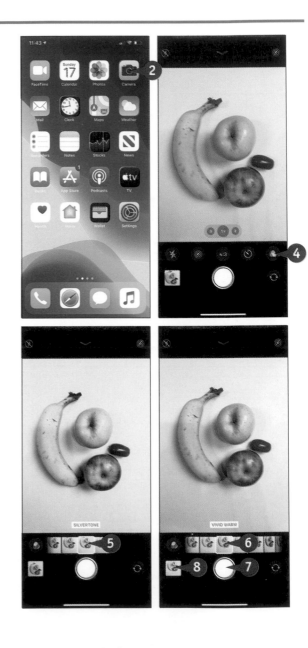

1 Swipe up from the bottom of the screen.

The Home screen appears.

2 Tap **Camera** ( ).

The Camera app opens.

3 Tap **Show Controls** ( ).

The control bar appears.

4 Tap **Filters** ( ).

The Filters screen appears.

5 Tap the filter you want to preview.

Camera applies the filter to the screen.

6 Tap the filter you want to apply.

7 Tap **Take Photo** ( ).

8 Tap the photo's thumbnail.

The photo appears.

9 Tap **Edit**.

The Edit Photo screen appears, showing the editing tools.

10 Tap **Filters** ().

The Choose Filter screen appears.

11 Tap the filter you want to apply.

Note: Tap **Original** if you want to remove filtering.

12 Tap **Done**.

iOS saves the change to the photo.

13 Tap **Back** (**<**) to return to the Camera app.

TIP

Is it better to apply a filter before taking a photo or after taking it?

This is up to you. Sometimes it is helpful to have the filter effect in place when composing a photo so that you can arrange the composition and lighting to complement the filtering. Other times, especially when you do not have time to experiment with filters, it is more practical to take the photos and then try applying filters afterward.

Edit Your Photos

To improve your photos, you can use the powerful but easy-to-use editing tools your iPhone includes. These tools include rotating a photo to a different orientation, straightening it by rotating it a little, and cropping off the parts you do not need.

You can access the editing tools either through the Recently Added album in the Photos app or through the Photos app. To start editing a photo, you open the photo by tapping it, and then tap **Edit**.

Edit Your Photos

Open a Photo for Editing

1 Swipe up from the bottom of the screen.

The Home screen appears.

2 Tap **Photos** (🌸).

The Photos app opens.

3 Navigate to the photo you want to edit.

A If the photo is part of a burst, the Burst readout appears. You can tap **Select** to select another photo from the burst instead of the default photo.

4 Tap **Edit**.

The Editing controls appear.

Crop, Rotate, and Straighten a Photo

1 Tap **Crop** (▣).

The tools for cropping, straightening, and rotating appear.

B You can tap **Rotate** (◻) to rotate the photo 90 degrees clockwise.

2 Tap and hold the degree bar.

C The grid appears.

3 Drag the degree dial left or right to straighten the photo.

D You can tap **Reset** to reset the photo.

④ Tap and hold an edge or corner of the crop box.

Ⓔ The nine-square grid appears. This is to help you compose the cropped photo.

⑤ Drag the edge or corner of the crop box to select only the area you want to keep.

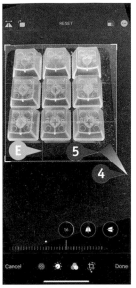 

Enhance the Colors in a Photo

① Tap **Auto-Enhance** (🪄 changes to 🪄).

iOS calculates a suitable enhancement and applies it.

Note: Tap **Auto-Enhance** again (🪄 changes to 🪄) if you want to remove the enhancement.

② Optionally, drag the slider left or right to adjust the degree of enhancement.

continued ▶

TIP

What does the three-squares button on the cropping screen do?

The button with three squares (▥) is the Aspect button. Tap **Aspect** (▥) when you need to crop to a specific aspect ratio, such as a square or the 16:9 widescreen aspect ratio. In the Aspect dialog that opens, tap the constraint you want to use. iOS adjusts the current cropping to match the aspect ratio. You may then need to move the portion of the photo shown to get the composition you want. If you adjust the cropping, tap **Aspect** (▥) again and reapply the aspect ratio.

The Red-Eye Reduction feature enables you to restore unwanted red eyes to normality. The Enhance feature enables you to adjust a photo's color balance and lighting quickly using default algorithms that analyze the photo and try to improve it. The Enhance feature often works well, but for greater control, you can use the Light settings and the Color settings to tweak the exposure, highlights, shadows, brightness, black point, contrast, vibrancy, and other settings manually.

Edit Your Photos (continued)

Remove Red Eye from a Photo

Note: You may need to zoom in on the photo in order to touch the red-eye patches accurately.

1 Tap **Red-Eye Reduction** (👁).

iOS prompts you to tap each eye.

2 Tap each red eye.

iOS removes the red eye.

3 Tap **Red-Eye Reduction** (👁).

iOS turns off the Red-Eye Reduction tool.

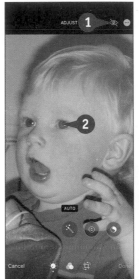

Fine-Tune a Photo

1 Tap **Adjust** (⬡).

The Adjust controls appear.

Note: You may want to try tapping **Auto-Enhance** and then adjusting the automatic enhancements manually. This section demonstrates making the changes from scratch.

2 Swipe left on the Adjust controls to bring the control you want to adjust to the middle of the screen, at which point it becomes active.

F The name of the active control appears, such as **Exposure**.

3 Drag the slider left or right to adjust the intensity of the active effect. For example, if the photo is too dark, you might increase the exposure to lighten it, as in this example.

4 Scroll the Adjust controls farther left to display more controls.

5 Tap the active control to enable or disable its effect.

Note: Photos remembers the setting for a disabled effect, so when you re-enable an effect, it has the same value as before you disabled it.

G The white dot indicates the zero point, at which the effect is disabled.

Note: A partial white ring () indicates a negative value for the setting; a partial yellow ring () indicates a positive value; a gray ring indicates the effect has a zero value or is disabled.

6 Adjust other settings as needed to make the photo look the way you want.

H You can tap **Sharpness** () to adjust the level of manufactured additional detail in the photo. This will not fix a blurry image but will accentuate existing detail.

I You can tap **Noise Reduction** () to reduce "noise," artifacts caused by taking photos in inadequate lighting. Reducing noise may also remove detail you want to keep.

7 Tap **Done**.

Photos displays the photo with the edits you have applied.

Photos preserves the original photo, and you can revert to it if you want.

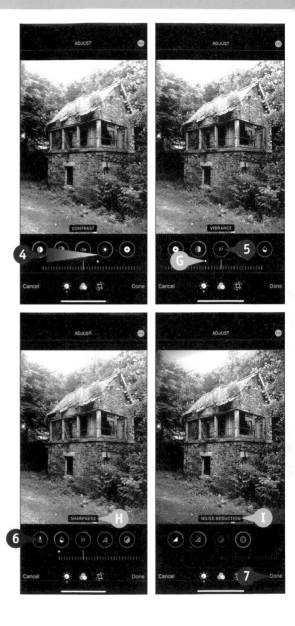

TIP

How do I get rid of changes I have made to a photo?
Tap **Cancel**, and then tap **Discard Changes** in the confirmation dialog that opens.

Capture Video

As well as capturing still photos, the Camera app can capture high-quality, full-motion video in either portrait orientation or landscape orientation. You launch the Camera app as usual, and then switch it to Video Mode for regular-speed shooting or to Slo-Mo Mode to shoot slow-motion footage. You can use flash, but it is effective only at close range for video. After taking the video, you can edit the clip by trimming off any unwanted frames at the beginning and end.

Capture Video

1 Swipe up from the bottom of the screen.

The Home screen appears.

2 Tap **Camera** (📷).

The Camera screen appears, showing the image the lens is seeing.

Ⓐ Tap **Slo-Mo** if you want to shoot slow-motion footage.

Note: You can start shooting video quickly by tapping and holding **Take Photo** (◯). When you have time, it is better to tap **Video** to switch to the video view first, as the video camera has a different field of view than the still camera.

3 Tap **Video**.

The video image and video controls appear.

4 Aim the camera at your subject.

Ⓑ If you need to use the flash for the video, tap **Flash** (⚡, ⚡, or ✕), and then tap **Auto** or **On**.

Note: To focus on a particular area of the screen, tap that area.

5 Tap **Record** (◯).

Ⓒ The camera starts recording, and the time readout shows the time that has elapsed.

6 To zoom in, tap and hold the Zoom readout, and then drag along the zoom track.

Note: You can also zoom by placing your thumb and forefinger on the screen and pinching apart or pinching together.

D To take a still photo while shooting video, tap **Take Photo** (◯).

7 To finish recording, tap **Stop** (◉).

The Camera app stops recording and displays a thumbnail of the video's first frame.

8 Tap the thumbnail.

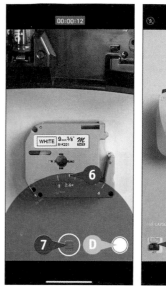

The video appears and starts playing automatically.

9 Tap anywhere on the screen to display the video controls. These disappear automatically after a few seconds of not being used.

Note: To trim the clip down to only the section you need, tap **Edit**. Tap and hold the left trim handle (❮) so that its background turns yellow, and then drag it to the starting frame. Drag the right trim handle (❯) to the ending frame. Tap **Done**, and then tap **Save as New Clip**.

10 When you finish viewing the video, tap **Back** (❮).

The Camera app appears again.

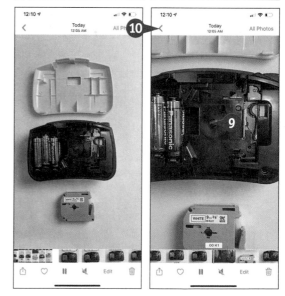

TIPS

How can I pause shooting a video?
As of this writing, you cannot pause while shooting in the Camera app. Either shoot separate video clips or trim out unwanted footage afterward. Alternatively, use a third-party camera app that offers this capability instead.

What does the bar of miniature pictures at the bottom of the video playback screen do?
The navigation bar gives you a quick way of moving forward and backward through the video. Tap the thumbnails and drag them left or right until the part of the video you want to view is at the vertical blue playhead bar. You can use the navigation bar either when the video is playing or when it is paused.

Browse Photos Using Years, Months, and Day

You can use the Photos app to browse the photos you have taken with your iPhone's camera, photos you have synced using iTunes or via iCloud's Shared Albums feature, and images you save from e-mail messages, instant messages, or web pages.

You can browse your photos by dates and locations using the smart groupings that Photos creates. Each Year grouping contains Months, which contain Days, which contain your photos. Alternatively, you can browse by albums, as explained in the section "Browse Photos Using Albums," later in this chapter.

Browse Photos Using Years, Collections, and Moments

1 Swipe up from the bottom of the screen.

The Home screen appears.

2 Tap **Photos** (🏵).

The Photos app opens.

3 Tap **Photos** (🖼 changes to 🖼).

The Photos screen appears, showing the Years list.

4 Tap the year you want to open.

The Months screen for the year appears.

5 Tap the month you want to open.

Note: Scroll up or down as needed to see other months.

The Days screen for the month appears.

6 Tap the photo you want to view.

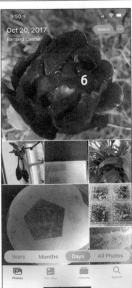

The photo opens.

A You can tap **Edit** to edit the photo, as explained earlier in this chapter.

B You can tap **Share** (⬆️) to share the photo, as explained later in this chapter.

C You can tap **Favorite** (♡ changes to ❤) to make the photo a favorite.

D You can tap **Trash** (🗑️) to delete the photo.

Note: The Trash icon does not appear for photos you cannot delete, such as photos in a shared photo stream.

7 In the thumbnail bar, tap the photo you want to view.

Note: You can also swipe left or right to display other photos.

The photo appears.

8 Tap **Back** (<).

The Days screen appears.

Note: You can scroll up or down to display other days.

9 Tap **Months** (<).

The Months screen appears.

Note: You can scroll up or down to display other months.

10 Tap **Years** (<).

The Years screen appears, and you can navigate to another year.

TIP

How can I move a photo to a different year?

To move a photo to a different year, you need to change the date set in the photo's metadata. You cannot do this with the Photos app, but you can change the date with a third-party app such as Pixelgarde, which is free from the App Store as of this writing. Alternatively, if you sync the photos from your computer, you can change the date in the photo on your computer. For example, in Photos on the Mac, select the photo, click **Image** on the menu bar, and then click **Adjust Date and Time**.

Browse Photos Using Memories

The Memories feature in the Photos app presents a movie of photos from a particular period of time, such as a given year or a trip to a certain geographical location.

You can customize the settings for a memory. You can either customize them quickly by choosing roughly how long a memory should be and what atmosphere it should have, or you can take complete control and specify exactly which items to include and which music to play.

Browse Photos Using Memories

1 Swipe up from the bottom of the screen to display the Home screen.

2 Tap **Photos** (✹) to open the Photos app.

3 Tap **For You** (▣ changes to ▣).

The For You screen appears.

4 Tap the memory you want to view.

Ⓐ You can tap **See All** to display the Memories screen, which contains the full list of memories.

The screen for the memory opens.

Ⓑ You can tap **Show More** to show more photos.

Ⓒ You can tap **Select** to select the photos you want to include.

5 Tap **Play** (▶).

The memory starts playing.

6 Tap the screen.

The customization controls appear.

7 Tap the desired mood, such as **Happy** or **Gentle**.

8 Tap **Short**, **Medium**, or **Long**, as needed.

9 For greater control, tap **Edit** to display the Edit screen. Here, you can choose settings for Title, Title Image, Music, Duration, and Photos & Videos. Tap **Done** when you finish.

10 Tap **Play** (▶).

The memory resumes playing, using the settings you chose.

Browse Photos Using the Map

The Camera app automatically stores location information — the longitude, the latitude, and the direction the camera was facing — in each photo and video you take, enabling the Photos app to sort your photos and videos by their locations. Starting from any photo, you can display other nearby photos, identifying them by their locations on the map. You can then browse the photos taken in a particular location.

Browse Photos Using the Map

1 In the Photos app, navigate to the photo from which you want to start browsing.

2 Swipe up.

The Places section for the photo appears.

A The map in the Places section shows the area in which the photo was taken.

3 Tap **Show Nearby Photos**.

The Map screen appears, showing nearby photos.

Note: Zoom in or out on the map as needed by placing your thumb and finger on the screen and moving them apart or pinching them together.

B You can tap **Grid** to display the places as a list.

4 Tap the place you want to view.

The photos in the place appear.

C You can tap **Show All** to display all the photos in a group.

5 Tap the photo you want to view.

The photo opens.

Browse Photos Using Shared Albums

Your iPhone's Photos app includes a feature called Shared Albums that enables you to share photos easily with others via iCloud and enjoy the photos they are sharing. You can add other people's shared albums to the Photos app on your iPhone by accepting invitations. You can then browse the photos those people are sharing.

The section "Share Your Shared Albums," later in this chapter, shows you how to share your own photos via Shared Albums.

Browse Photos Using Shared Albums

Accept an Invitation to a Shared Album

1 When you receive an invitation to subscribe to shared photos, open the e-mail message in Mail.

2 Tap **Subscribe**.

The Photos app becomes active.

The Shared screen appears.

3 Tap the shared album.

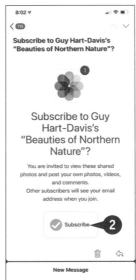

The album opens.

Ⓐ You can tap **People** to view the list of people with whom the album is shared.

4 Tap the thumbnail for the photo you want to view.

The photo opens.

Ⓑ You can tap **Share** (⬆️) to share the photo with others.

Ⓒ You can tap **Add a comment** if you want to add a comment on the photo.

Ⓓ You can tap **Like** to like the photo.

Note: Swipe left or right to display other photos.

5 Tap **Back** (‹).

The album's screen appears again.

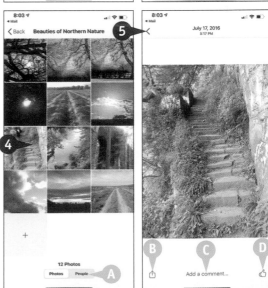

Browse the Latest Activity on Shared Albums

① In the Photos app, tap **For You** (📑 changes to 📑).

The For You screen appears.

② In the Shared Album Activity section, tap **See All**.

Note: The Activity item shows new activity on your shared albums. When you add a shared album, the Activity thumbnail shows the new album's thumbnail.

The Activity screen appears.

③ Swipe up to scroll down.

Other items appear.

④ Tap a photo.

The photo opens.

⑤ Tap **Activity** (‹).

The Activity screen appears.

⑥ When you finish browsing the latest activity, tap **For You** (‹).

The For You screen appears.

TIP

How do I remove a shared album?

In the Photos app, tap **For You** (📑 changes to 📑) to display the For You screen, and then navigate to the shared album. Tap **People** to display the People screen, and then tap **Unsubscribe**. In the confirmation dialog that opens, tap **Unsubscribe** again.

Browse Photos Using Albums

A long with browsing by collections and browsing shared albums, you can browse your photos by albums. The Camera app automatically stores each conventional photo you take in the All Photos album, each burst photo in an album called Bursts, and each video in an album called Videos. You can also create other albums manually from your photos or sync existing albums from your computer.

Browse Photos Using Albums

Open the Photos App and Browse an Album

1 Swipe up from the bottom of the screen.

The Home screen appears.

2 Tap **Photos** (🌼).

The Photos app opens.

3 Tap **Albums** (📁 changes to 📂).

The Albums screen appears.

4 Tap the album you want to browse. This example uses the Fall of Summer album.

Note: The All Photos album contains all the photos you take; photos you save from web pages, e-mail messages, instant messages, and social media apps; and photos you edit from other people's streams.

The album appears.

Note: The People album contains faces identified in photos. You can browse the photos in which a particular person appears.

5 Tap the photo you want to view.

The photo opens.

Note: Swipe left to display the next photo or right to display the previous photo.

6 Tap **Back** (<).

The album appears.

7 Tap **Albums** (<).

The Albums screen appears.

Create an Album

1 In the Photos app, tap **Albums** (📖 changes to 📖).

The Albums screen appears.

2 Tap **New** (+).

A dialog opens, giving you the choice between creating a regular album and a shared album.

3 Tap **New Album** or **New Shared Album**, as appropriate. This example uses New Album.

The New Album dialog opens.

4 Type the name to give the album.

5 Tap **Save**.

The screen for adding photos appears.

6 Tap the source of the photos. For example, tap **Albums**, and then tap the album.

7 Tap each photo to add to the collection, placing ✓ on each.

8 Tap **Done**.

Ⓐ The album appears on the Albums screen.

TIPS

How can I move through a long list of photos more quickly?

You can move through the photos more quickly by using momentum scrolling. Tap and flick up with your finger to set the photos scrolling. As the momentum drops, you can tap and flick up again to scroll further. Tap and drag your finger in the opposite direction to stop the scrolling.

How can I recover photos I deleted by mistake?

Tap **Albums**, and then tap **Recently Deleted**. In the Recently Deleted album, tap **Select**, tap the photos, and then tap **Recover**. Alternatively, tap **Recover All** to recover all the photos without selecting any.

Share Photos Using iCloud Photos

If you have an iCloud account, you can use the iCloud Photos feature to upload your photos to iCloud, making them available to all your iOS devices, your computer, and your Apple TV devices.

After you turn on iCloud Photos on your iPhone, other iOS devices, and your Macs or PCs, Photos automatically syncs your 1,000 most recent photos among your devices and your computers.

Share Photos Using iCloud Photos

Turn On My Photo Stream on Your iPhone

1 Swipe up from the bottom of the screen.

The Home screen appears.

2 Tap **Settings** (⚙️).

The Settings screen appears.

3 Tap **Apple ID**, the button bearing your Apple ID name.

The Apple ID screen appears.

4 Tap **iCloud** (☁️).

The iCloud screen appears.

5 Tap **Photos** (✳️).

The Photos screen appears.

Ⓐ You can set the **iCloud Photos** switch to On (🔘) to store your photo library in iCloud. You do not need to do this to use My Photo Stream.

6 Set the **Upload to My Photo Stream** switch to On (🔘).

Ⓑ You can set the **Upload Burst Photos** switch to On (🔘) to upload all bursts of photos instead of only favorite bursts.

7 If you also want to share your iCloud photo streams with others, set the **Shared Albums** switch to On (🔘). See the next section, "Share Your Shared Albums," for more information.

8 Tap **iCloud** (‹).

The iCloud screen appears.

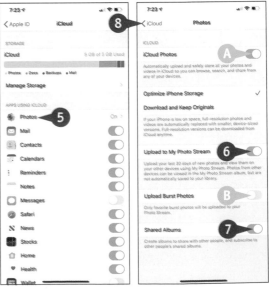

264

Set Your Mac to Upload Photos to Your Photo Stream

1 Click **Photos** ( ).

The Photos app opens.

2 Click **Photos** on the menu bar.

3 Click **Preferences**.

The Preferences window opens.

4 Tap **iCloud** ( ).

5 Click **iCloud Photos** (changes to) to enable the iCloud Photos feature.

6 Click **Shared Albums** (changes to) to enable the Shared Albums feature.

7 Click **Close** ( ).

The Preferences window closes.

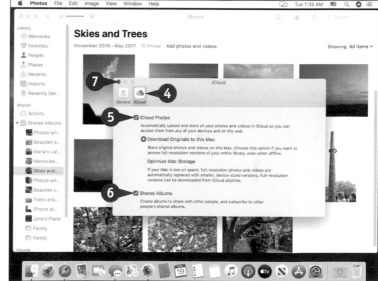

TIP

How do I use Photo Stream in Windows?

On Windows, you must install Apple's iCloud for Windows software, which you can download from www.apple.com/icloud/setup/pc.html. Then click **Start**, click **All Apps**, and then click **iCloud Photos**.

In the iCloud Photos window, click **Open iCloud**. Type your Apple ID and password and then click **Sign in**. Click **Photos** (changes to). Click **Options** to display the Photos Options dialog. Click **My Photo Stream** (changes to) and **Shared Albums** (changes to). Click **Change** and select the folder for photos, if necessary. Click **OK** and then click **Apply**.

Share Your Shared Albums

After turning on Shared Albums as described in the previous section, you can create shared photo albums, invite people to subscribe to them, and add photos.

You can also control whether subscribers can post photos and videos to your shared photo album, decide whether to make the album publicly available, and choose whether to receive notifications when subscribers comment on your photos or post their own.

Share Your Shared Albums

① Swipe up from the bottom of the screen.

The Home screen appears.

② Tap **Photos** (🌸).

The Photos app opens.

③ Tap **Albums** (🗂 changes to 🗂)

The Shared screen appears.

④ Tap **New** (+).

A dialog opens.

⑤ Tap **New Shared Album**.

The iCloud dialog opens.

⑥ Type the name for the album.

⑦ Tap **Next**.

Another iCloud dialog opens.

⑧ Tap **Add Contact** (⊕) to display the Contacts screen, and then tap the contact to add.

⑨ Repeat step **7** to add other contacts as needed. You can also type contact names or tap names that the list automatically suggests.

⑩ Tap **Create**.

The Shared screen appears.

⑪ Tap the new album.

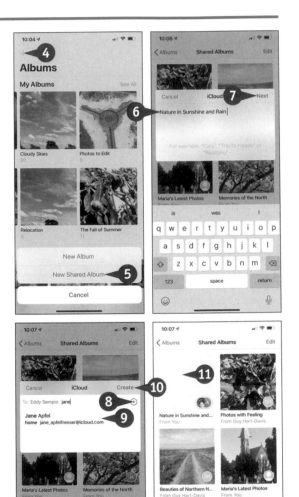

The album's screen appears.

12 Tap **Add** ($+$).

The Photos screen appears, with the selection controls displayed.

13 Navigate to another album if necessary. For example, tap **Albums** (📁 changes to 📂).

14 Tap each photo you want to add.

15 Tap **Done**.

Another iCloud dialog opens.

16 Type the text you want to post with the photos.

17 Tap **Post**.

The album's screen appears.

18 Tap **People**.

The People screen appears.

A To invite others to the album, tap **Invite People**.

19 Set the **Subscribers Can Post** switch to On (🔘) or Off ( ), as needed.

20 Set the **Public Website** switch to On (🔘) or Off ( ) to control whether to make the album publicly accessible on the iCloud.com website.

21 Set the **Notifications** switch to On (🔘) or Off ( ), as needed.

22 Tap **Back** (‹).

The Albums screen appears.

TIP

If I make a photo album public, how do people find the website?
When you set the **Public Website** switch on the People screen for a photo album to On (🔘), a Share Link button appears. Tap **Share Link** to display the Share sheet, and then tap the means of sharing you want to use — for example, Messages, Mail, Twitter, or Facebook.

Share and Use Your Photos and Videos

After taking photos and videos with your iPhone's camera, or after loading photos and videos on the iPhone using iTunes, you can share them with other people.

This section explains how to tweet photos to your Twitter account, assign photos to contacts, use photos as wallpaper, and print photos. Chapter 6 explains how to share items via the AirDrop feature.

Share and Use Your Photos and Videos

Select the Photo or Video to Share

1 Swipe up from the bottom of the screen.

The Home screen appears.

2 Tap **Photos** (🌸).

3 On the Photos screen, tap the item that contains the photo or video you want to share. For example, tap **Albums** (📁 changes to 📁), and then tap **Favorites**.

4 Tap the photo or video you want to share.

5 Tap **Share** (📤) to display the Share sheet.

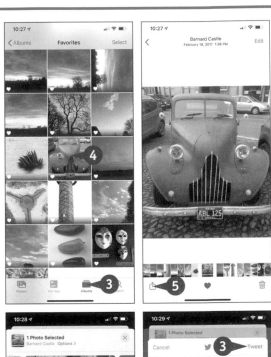

Share a Photo on Twitter

A You can tap the selection button (changes to ✓) to include another item in the sharing.

1 On the Share sheet, tap **Twitter** (🐦).

The Twitter dialog opens.

2 Type the text of the tweet.

3 Tap **Tweet**.

Your iPhone posts the tweet to Twitter.

Assign a Photo to a Contact

1 On the Share sheet, scroll down and tap **Assign to Contact** (⊚).

The list of contacts appears.

2 Tap the contact to which you want to assign the photo.

The Move and Scale screen appears.

3 If necessary, move the photo so that the relevant part appears centrally.

4 If necessary, pinch in to shrink the photo or pinch out to enlarge it.

5 Tap **Choose**.

Set a Photo as Wallpaper

1 On the Share sheet, tap **Use as Wallpaper** (▢).

The Move and Scale screen appears.

2 Move the photo to display the part you want.

3 If necessary, pinch in to shrink the photo or pinch out to enlarge it.

4 Tap **Perspective** (▣ or ▨) to turn Perspective on (▣) or off (▨).

5 Tap **Set**.

The Set Wallpaper dialog appears.

6 Tap **Set Lock Screen**, **Set Home Screen**, or **Set Both**, as needed.

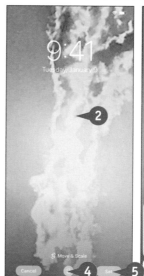

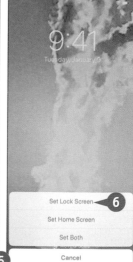

TIP

How do I print a photo?

Display the photo you want to print, and then tap **Share** (↥) to display the Share sheet. Tap **Print** (🖶) to display the Printer Options screen. If the Printer readout does not show the correct printer, tap **Select Printer** and then tap the printer. Back on the Printer Options screen, tap **Print** to print the photo.

Play Slide Shows of Photos

Your iPhone can not only display your photos, but also play a sequence of photos as a slide show. You can choose which theme to use, which music to play, and whether to repeat the slide show when it reaches the end. You can adjust the running speed of the slide show as a whole, but you cannot adjust individual slides.

Play Slide Shows of Photos

1 Swipe up from the bottom of the screen.

The Home screen appears.

Note: To play your photos on a bigger screen, either use AirPlay to play a TV connected to an Apple TV or use the Apple Lightning Digital AV Adapter and an HDMI cable to connect your iPhone to a TV or monitor with an HDMI input.

2 Tap **Photos** (✿).

The Photos app opens.

3 Navigate to the photo with which you want to start the slide show. For example, tap **Photos** (▣ changes to ▣) and then tap **All Photos**.

The photo collection you tapped opens.

4 Tap **Select**.

Photos switches to Selection Mode.

The photo opens.

5 Tap **Share** (⬆).

The Share sheet appears.

6 Tap **Slideshow** (▶).

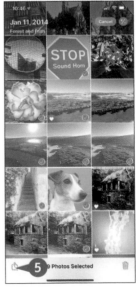

The slide show starts playing, using the default theme and music.

7 Tap the screen.

The controls appear.

8 Tap **Options**.

The Slideshow Options screen appears.

9 Tap **Theme**.

The Themes screen appears.

10 Tap the theme you want.

The Slideshow Options screen appears.

11 Tap **Music** and choose the music to play.

12 Set the **Repeat** switch to On (⬤) if you want the slide show to repeat.

13 Drag the **Speed** slider as needed to change the speed.

14 Tap **Done**.

The slide show resumes, using the settings you chose.

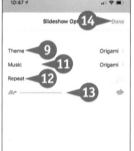

TIP

How do I choose music for a slide show?

First, choose the theme for the slide show, as explained in the main text. When you choose the theme, Photos automatically selects the theme's default music as the music for the slide show.

Next, tap **Music** on the Slideshow Options screen to display the Music screen. Here, you can either tap a different theme's music in the Theme Music list or tap **iTunes Music** to select music from your iTunes Music library.

CHAPTER 12

Advanced Features and Troubleshooting

You can connect your iPhone to VPNs and Exchange Server, troubleshoot problems, and locate it when it goes missing. You can also manage your Apple ID.

Take Screenshots or Screen Recordings

iOS enables you to capture screenshots and screen recordings. A screenshot is a still image that shows whatever appears on the screen and is great for capturing and sharing information easily. A screen recording is a video of what happens on screen and is useful for demonstrating how to take particular actions.

The screenshot functionality uses a keypress and is enabled by default. The screen recording functionality requires you to add the Screen Recording control to Control Center, from which you can then start a screen recording.

Take a Screenshot

To take a screenshot of what is currently displayed on the screen, press **Side** and **Volume Up** at the same time. A miniature version of the screen appears in the lower-left corner of the screen for a few seconds, and then disappears.

If you want to mark up the screenshot immediately, or share it, tap this miniature to open the screenshot for editing. To mark up the screenshot, use the icons at the bottom of the screen. At the top, tap **Undo** () to undo your last action, tap **Redo** () to redo the last action you undid, tap **Delete** (🗑) to delete the screenshot, or tap **Share** (📤) to share it.

Add the Screen Recording Control to Control Center

First, you need to add the Screen Recording control to Control Center so that you can access it. This control is not one of the default items in Control Center.

Swipe up to display the Home screen, and then tap **Settings** (⚙) to display the Settings screen. Tap **Control Center** (🎛) to display the Control Center screen, and then tap **Customize Controls** to display the Customize screen.

In the More Controls section, tap **Add** (➕) to the left of Screen Recording. The Screen Recording icon appears in the Include list at the top of the Customize screen.

Start a Screen Recording

Swipe down from the upper-right corner of the screen to display Control Center. Tap **Screen Recording** (). A 3-second countdown timer starts. Swipe up from the bottom of the screen to close Control Center unless you want to record it. A red Stop button (⬤) appears briefly in the upper-left corner of the screen in place of the clock readout. The red button then displays the clock readout.

Perform the actions you want to record. When you finish, tap the clock readout (11:56) to open the Screen Recording dialog, and then tap **Stop**.

Watch a Screen Recording

After you end a screen recording, a banner appears telling you that iOS has saved the screen recording. You can tap this banner to display the screen recording in the Photos app.

To open the screen recording later, swipe up to display the Home screen, and tap **Photos** (🌸). In the Photos app, tap **Albums** (⬛ changes to ⬛), and then tap **Screen Recording** (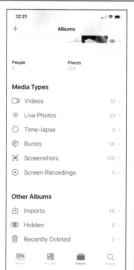) to display the screen recordings.

Tap the screen recording you want to play back.

Connect to a Network via VPN

Virtual private networking, or VPN, enables you to connect your iPhone securely to a network across the Internet. For example, you can connect to a network at your workplace.

You can use VPN on your iPhone in two ways. First, you can create a VPN connection in the Settings app, as shown on these pages. Second, you can use a dedicated app supplied by a commercial VPN provider.

Connect to a Network via VPN

Set Up the VPN Connection on the iPhone

1 Swipe up from the bottom of the screen.

The Home screen appears.

2 Tap **Settings** (⚙️).

The Settings screen appears.

Note: After you have set up a VPN configuration, the VPN switch appears in the top section of the Settings screen. You can connect to the currently selected virtual private network by setting the switch to On (changes to).

3 Tap **General** (⚙️).

The General screen appears.

4 Toward the bottom of the screen, tap **VPN**.

The VPN screen appears.

5 Tap **Add VPN Configuration**.

Note: If your iPhone already has a VPN configuration you want to use, tap it, and then go to step **1** of the next set of steps, "Connect to the Virtual Private Network."

The Add Configuration screen appears.

6 Tap **Type**.

The Type screen appears.

7 Tap the VPN type: **IKEv2**, **IPSec**, or **L2TP**.

8 Tap **Add Configuration** (<).

The Add Configuration screen appears again.

9 Fill in the details of the virtual private network.

Note: Set the **Send All Traffic** switch to On (◉) if you want your iPhone to send all Internet traffic across the virtual private network after you connect.

10 Tap **Done**.

The VPN configuration appears on the VPN screen.

Connect to the Virtual Private Network

1 On the VPN screen, set the **Status** switch to On (changes to ◉).

The iPhone connects to the virtual private network.

2 Work across the network connection as if you were connected directly to the network.

3 To see how long your iPhone has been connected, or to learn its IP address, tap **Information** (ⓘ).

4 Tap **VPN** (<) to return to the VPN screen.

5 When you are ready to disconnect from the virtual private network, set the **Status** switch to Off (◉ changes to).

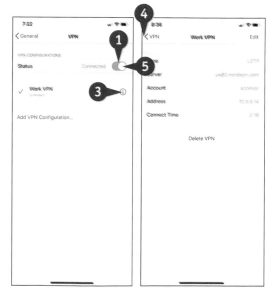

TIPS

Is there an easier way to set up a VPN connection?
Yes. An administrator can provide the VPN details in a configuration profile. This is a settings file that the administrator either installs directly on your iPhone or shares via e-mail or a website so that you can install it. Installing the profile adds its settings, such as the VPN details or the settings needed to connect to an Exchange Server system, to your iPhone. You can then connect to the virtual private network.

What can I do if my iPhone cannot connect to my company's VPN type?
Look in the App Store for an app for that VPN type.

Connect Your iPhone to Exchange Server

You can set up your iPhone to connect to Exchange Server or Office 365 for e-mail, contacts, calendaring, reminders, and notes. You can use either the built-in Mail app, as shown here, or Microsoft's Outlook app.

Ask an administrator for the Exchange connection details you need: your e-mail address, your password, the server name if required, and the domain name if required. You may be able to set up the account using only the e-mail address and password, but often you need the server name and domain as well.

Connect Your iPhone to Exchange Server

1 Swipe up from the bottom of the screen.

The Home screen appears.

2 Tap **Settings** (⚙).

The Settings screen appears.

Note: If you have not yet set up an e-mail account on the iPhone, you can also open the Add Account screen by tapping **Mail** (✉) on the iPhone's Home screen.

3 Tap **Passwords & Accounts** (🔑).

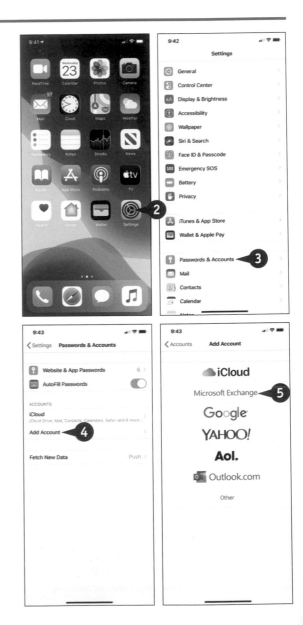

The Passwords & Accounts screen appears.

4 Tap **Add Account**.

The Add Account screen appears.

5 Tap **Microsoft Exchange**.

Note: You can also set up an Exchange account using a configuration profile file that an administrator provides.

The Exchange screen appears.

⑥ Type your e-mail address. As usual, you can tap and hold the period key to enter frequently used domains, such as .com and .org.

⑦ Type a descriptive name for the account field. The default name is *Exchange*.

⑧ Tap **Next**.

The Sign In to Your Exchange Account Using Microsoft? dialog opens.

⑨ Tap **Sign In**.

A password screen appears.

⑩ Enter your password.

⑪ Tap **Sign In**.

The Permissions Requested screen appears.

⑫ Read the permissions, and then tap **Accept** if you want to proceed.

Note: Tap **Consent on Behalf of Your Organization** (✅ changes to ◯) only if you are an administrator.

The Exchange screen appears.

⑬ Set the **Mail** switch to On (◯) or Off ( ).

⑭ Set the **Contacts** switch to On (◯) or Off ( ).

⑮ Set the **Calendars** switch to On (◯) or Off ( ).

⑯ Set the **Reminders** switch to On (◯) or Off ( ).

⑰ Set the **Notes** switch to On (◯) or Off ( ).

⑱ Tap **Save**.

The new account appears on the Mail screen.

TIPS

How do I know whether to enter a domain name when setting up my Exchange account?
You need to ask an administrator, because some Exchange implementations require you to enter a domain, whereas others do not.

How do I set up an Office 365 e-mail account?
Use the method explained in this section. You may not need the server address; if you do, use outlook. office365.com. Your username is typically your full e-mail address; if in doubt, ask an administrator.

Update Your iPhone's Software

Apple frequently releases new versions of the iPhone's software to fix problems, improve performance, and add new features. To keep your iPhone running quickly and smoothly, and to add any new features, update its software when a new version becomes available.

The easiest way to update your iPhone's software is directly on the iPhone. If you use your computer to manage your iPhone, you can also perform the update using your computer.

Update Your iPhone's Software

Update Your iPhone's Software on the iPhone

1 Swipe up from the bottom of the screen.

The Home screen appears.

A The badge on the Settings icon indicates that a Settings notification is waiting for you. Often, this means an update is available.

2 Tap **Settings** (⚙).

The Settings screen appears.

3 Tap **General** (⚙).

The General screen appears.

4 Tap **Software Update**.

The Software Update screen appears.

5 If Automatic Updates is set to Off, tap **Automatic Updates**.

If Automatic Updates is set to On, go to step **8**.

The Automatic Updates screen appears.

6 Set the **Automatic Updates** switch to On (⬤).

7 Tap **Back** (<).

The Software Update screen appears again.

8 Tap **Install Now**.

The installation of the update begins.

After iOS verifies the update and installs the files, your iPhone restarts.

B A Software Update banner confirms that your iPhone has been updated.

9 Swipe up from the bottom of the screen to unlock the iPhone.

You will need to enter your passcode to sign in following the restart.

TIP

How do I update my iPhone's software using my computer?

Connect your iPhone to your computer via the USB cable. On macOS Catalina, click **iPhone** (📱) under Locations in the Sidebar in a Finder window; the General screen appears. On earlier macOS versions or Windows, click **iPhone** (📱) on the navigation bar in iTunes; the Summary screen appears. Click **Check for Update** in the upper area. If the dialog that opens tells you that a new software version is available for the iPhone, click **Update** to download and install the update; verify that the update has completed before you disconnect the iPhone from the computer. If the dialog says your iPhone is up to date, click **OK**.

Extend Your iPhone's Runtime on the Battery

To extend your iPhone's runtime on the battery, you can reduce the power usage by dimming the screen; turning off Wi-Fi, Bluetooth, and cellular data when you do not need them; and setting your iPhone to go to sleep quickly. When the battery reaches 20 percent power, your iPhone prompts you to turn on Low Power Mode, which disables background app refreshing, slows down the processor, and turns off some demanding graphical features. You can also enable Low Power Mode manually anytime you want.

Extend Your iPhone's Runtime on the Battery

Dim the Screen

1. Swipe up from the bottom of the screen.

   The Home screen appears.

2. Swipe down from the upper-right corner of the screen.

   Control Center opens.

3. Swipe down the **Brightness** control.

   The screen brightness decreases.

4. Tap the bar at the bottom of the screen.

   Control Center closes.

Turn Off Wi-Fi, Bluetooth, and Cellular Data

1. Swipe up from the bottom of the screen.

   The Home screen appears.

2. Swipe down from the upper-right corner of the screen.

   Control Center opens.

A. You can turn off all communications by tapping **Airplane Mode** (changes to).

3. To turn off Wi-Fi, tap **Wi-Fi** (changes to).

4. To turn off Bluetooth, tap **Bluetooth** (changes to).

5. To turn off cellular data, tap **Cellular Data** (changes to).

6. Tap the bar at the bottom of the screen.

   Control Center closes.

Turn On Low Power Mode Manually

1 Swipe up from the bottom of the screen.

The Home screen appears.

2 Tap **Settings** (⚙️).

The Settings screen appears.

3 Tap **Battery** (🔋).

The Battery screen appears.

4 Set the **Low Power Mode** switch to On
(changes to ⚪).

The first time you set the Low Power Mode switch to On, the Low Power Mode dialog opens.

5 Tap **Continue**.

Your iPhone enables Low Power Mode.

Ⓑ The battery icon appears yellow to indicate that the iPhone is using Low Power Mode.

Note: For quick access to Low Power Mode, add its icon to Control Center. From the Home screen, tap **Settings** (⚙️), tap **Control Center** (🎛️), and then tap **Customize Controls**. On the Customize screen, tap **Add** (➕) to the left of Low Power Mode.

TIP

What else can I do to save power?

If you do not need your iPhone to track your location, you can turn off the GPS feature. On the Home screen, tap **Settings** (⚙️), and then tap **Privacy** (✋) to display the Privacy screen. Tap **Location Services** (📍) to display the Location Services screen, and then set the **Location Services** switch to Off (   ).

You can also set a short time for Auto-Lock. Press **Home**, tap **Settings** (⚙️), tap **Display & Brightness** (🔆), and then tap **Auto-Lock**. Tap a short interval — for example, **1 Minute**.

Back Up and Restore Using Your Computer

When you sync your iPhone with your computer, Finder or iTunes automatically backs up the iPhone's data and settings, unless you have chosen to back up your iPhone to iCloud instead. You can also run a backup manually as explained here.

If your iPhone suffers a software or hardware failure, you can use Finder or iTunes to restore the data and settings to your iPhone or to a new iPhone, an iPad, or an iPod touch. You must turn off the Find My iPhone feature before restoring your iPhone.

Back Up and Restore Using Your Computer

Back Up Your iPhone

① Connect your iPhone to your computer via the USB cable or via Wi-Fi.

The iPhone appears in the Sidebar in Finder on macOS Catalina or on the navigation bar in iTunes on earlier macOS versions of Windows.

② Click **iPhone** (⬚) in the Sidebar or on the navigation bar.

The iPhone's management screens appear.

③ On macOS Catalina, click **General** to display the General screen. On earlier macOS or Windows, click **Summary** to display the Summary screen.

④ Click **Back Up Now**.

iTunes backs up your iPhone.

Turn Off the Find My iPhone Feature on Your iPhone

① Swipe up from the bottom of the screen.

The Home screen appears.

② Tap **Settings** (⚙).

The Settings screen appears.

③ Tap **Apple ID**, the button bearing your Apple ID name.

The Apple ID screen appears.

④ Tap **Find My** (◉) to display the Find My screen.

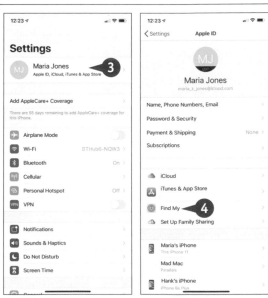

5 Tap **Find My iPhone** ( ).

The Find My iPhone screen appears.

6 Set the **Find My iPhone** switch to Off (changes to).

The Apple ID Password dialog opens.

7 Type the password for your Apple ID.

8 Tap **Turn Off**.

The iPhone turns off the Find My iPhone feature.

Restore Your iPhone

1 On the General screen in Finder or the Summary screen in iTunes, click **Restore iPhone**.

A dialog asks you to confirm that you want to restore the iPhone to its factory settings.

2 Click **Restore** or **Restore and Update**, depending on which button appears.

Finder or iTunes backs up the iPhone's data, restores the software on the iPhone, and returns the iPhone to its factory settings.

Note: Do not disconnect the iPhone during the restore process. Doing so can leave the iPhone in an unusable state.

3 On the Welcome to Your New Phone screen, click **Restore from this backup** (changes to).

4 Click and choose your iPhone by name.

5 Click **Continue**.

Finder or iTunes restores the data and settings to your iPhone.

Your iPhone restarts, appears in Finder or iTunes, and then syncs.

6 Disconnect the iPhone.

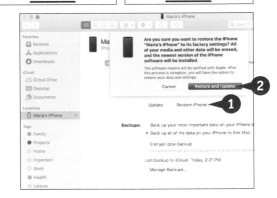

TIP

How can I protect confidential information in my iPhone's backups?
On the General screen in Finder or the Summary screen in iTunes, click **Encrypt local backup** (changes to). In the dialog that opens, type the password, and then click **Set Password**. iTunes then encrypts your backups using strong encryption.

Apart from protecting your confidential information, encrypting your iPhone also saves your passwords during backup and restores them to the iPhone when you restore the device.

Back Up and Restore Using iCloud

Instead of backing up your iPhone to your computer, you can back it up to iCloud, preferably via Wi-Fi, but optionally — if you have a generous data plan — via the cellular network. If your iPhone suffers a software or hardware failure, you can restore its data and settings from backup.

You can choose which items to back up to iCloud. You do not need to back up apps, media files, or games you have bought from the iTunes Store, because you can download them again.

Back Up and Restore Using iCloud

1 Swipe up from the bottom of the screen.

The Home screen appears.

2 Tap **Settings** (⚙).

The Settings screen appears.

3 Tap **Apple ID**, the button bearing your Apple ID name.

The Apple ID screen appears.

4 Tap **iCloud** (☁).

Note: The 5GB of storage in a standard free iCloud account is enough space to store your iPhone's settings and your most important data and files.

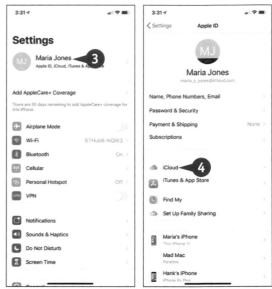

The iCloud screen appears.

5 Tap **Photos**.

The Photos screen appears.

6 Set the **iCloud Photos** switch to On (⬤) if you want to store all your photos in iCloud.

7 If you enable iCloud Photos, tap **Optimize iPhone Storage** or **Download and Keep Originals**, as needed.

8 Set the **Upload to My Photo Stream** switch to On (⬤) if you want to upload all your new photos.

9 Set the **Shared Albums** switch to On (⬤) if you want to share albums with others via iCloud.

10 Tap **iCloud** (‹).

The iCloud screen appears again.

A If you need more storage space, tap **Manage Storage** to display the iCloud Storage screen, and then tap **Change Storage Plan**.

11 In the Apps Using iCloud section, set each app's switch to On (○) or Off (○), as needed.

12 In the nameless lower sections, set each app's switch to On (○) or Off (○), as needed.

13 Set the **iCloud Drive** switch to On (○).

14 At the bottom of the Apps Using iCloud section, tap **iCloud Backup** (○).

The Backup screen appears.

15 Set the **iCloud Backup** switch to On (○).

16 If you want to back up your iPhone now, tap **Back Up Now**.

Your iPhone begins backing up its contents to iCloud.

TIP

How do I restore my iPhone from its iCloud backup?

First, reset the iPhone to factory settings. Press **Home**, tap **Settings** (⚙), tap **General** (⚙), tap **Reset**, and then tap **Erase All Content and Settings**. Tap **Erase iPhone** in both the first and the second confirmation dialogs. When the iPhone restarts and displays its setup screens, choose your language and country. On the Set Up iPhone screen, tap **Restore from iCloud Backup**, and then tap **Next**. On the Apple ID screen, enter your Apple ID, and then tap **Next**. On the Choose Backup screen, tap the backup you want to use — normally, the most recent backup — and then tap **Restore**.

Reset Your iPhone's Settings

If your iPhone malfunctions, you can reset its network settings, reset the Home screen's icons, reset your keyboard dictionary, reset your location and privacy settings, or reset all settings to eliminate tricky configuration issues. If your iPhone has intractable problems, you can back it up, erase all content and settings, and then set it up from scratch. You can also erase your iPhone before selling or giving it to someone else; you must turn off Find My iPhone first.

Reset Your iPhone's Settings

Display the Reset Screen

1 Swipe up from the bottom of the screen.

The Home screen appears.

2 Tap **Settings** (⚙).

The Settings screen appears.

Note: If your iPhone is not responding to the Home button or your taps, press and hold the **Sleep/Wake** button and **Home** for about 15 seconds to reset the iPhone.

3 Tap **General** (⚙).

The General screen appears.

4 Tap **Reset**.

The Reset screen appears.

You can then tap the appropriate button: **Reset All Settings**, **Erase All Content and Settings**, **Reset Network Settings**, **Reset Keyboard Dictionary**, **Reset Home Screen Layout**, or **Reset Location & Privacy**.

Reset Your Network Settings

1 On the Reset screen, tap **Reset Network Settings**.

Note: If your iPhone prompts you to enter your passcode at this point, do so.

A dialog opens, warning you that this action will delete all network settings and return them to their factory defaults.

2 Tap **Reset Network Settings**.

iOS resets your iPhone's network settings.

Restore Your iPhone to Factory Settings

Note: If you intend to sell or give away your iPhone, turn off Find My iPhone before restoring your iPhone to factory settings. See the second tip.

1 On the Reset screen, tap **Erase All Content and Settings**.

Note: Enter your passcode if prompted to do so.

Note: If iOS prompts you to update your iCloud backup before erasing, tap **Backup Then Erase**. If you have backed up just now, tap **Erase Now** instead.

2 Tap **Erase iPhone**.

3 Tap **Erase iPhone**.

iOS wipes your media and data and restores your iPhone to factory settings.

TIPS

Does the Reset All Settings command delete my data and my music files?

No. When you reset all the iPhone's settings, the settings go back to their defaults, but your data remains in place. But you need to set the iPhone's settings again, either by restoring them using iTunes or by setting them manually, in order to get your iPhone working the way you prefer.

How do I turn off the Find My iPhone feature?

Press **Home**, tap **Apple ID** — the button bearing your Apple ID name — and then tap **iCloud** (). Tap **Find My iPhone** (), and then set the **Find My iPhone** switch to Off (changes to).

Troubleshoot Wi-Fi Connections

To avoid exceeding your data plan, use Wi-Fi networks whenever they are available instead of using your cellular connection.

Normally, the iPhone automatically reconnects to Wi-Fi networks to which you have previously connected it and maintains those connections without problems. But you may sometimes need to request your iPhone's network address again, a process called *renewing the lease* on the IP address. You may also need to tell your iPhone to forget a network, and then rejoin the network manually, providing the password again.

Troubleshoot Wi-Fi Connections

Renew the Lease on Your iPhone's IP Address

1 Swipe up from the bottom of the screen.

The Home screen appears.

Note: You can sometimes resolve a Wi-Fi problem by turning Wi-Fi off and back on. Swipe diagonally down from the upper-right corner of the screen to open Control Center, tap **Wi-Fi** (changes to), and then tap **Wi-Fi** again (changes to).

2 Tap **Settings** ( ).

The Settings screen appears.

3 Tap **Wi-Fi** ( ).

The Wi-Fi screen appears.

4 Tap **Information** ( ) to the right of the network for which you want to renew the lease.

The network's screen appears.

5 Tap **Renew Lease**.

The Renew Lease dialog opens.

6 Tap **Renew Lease**.

7 Tap **Wi-Fi** ( ).

The Wi-Fi screen appears.

Forget a Network and Then Rejoin It

1 On the Wi-Fi screen, tap **Information** (ⓘ) to the right of the network.

The network's screen appears.

2 Tap **Forget This Network**.

Note: If turning Wi-Fi off and then back on does not resolve a Wi-Fi problem, try turning Airplane Mode on briefly and then turning it off again. Swipe down from the upper-right corner of the screen to open Control Center, tap **Airplane Mode** (🛧 changes to ⊕), and then tap **Airplane Mode** again (⊕ changes to 🛧).

The Forget Wi-Fi Network dialog opens.

3 Tap **Forget**.

The iPhone removes the network's details.

4 Tap **Wi-Fi** (<).

The Wi-Fi screen appears.

5 Tap the network's name.

The Enter Password screen appears.

6 Type the password for the network.

7 Tap **Join**.

The iPhone joins the network.

TIP

What else can I do to reestablish my Wi-Fi network connections?

If you are unable to fix your Wi-Fi network connections by renewing the IP address lease or by forgetting and rejoining the network, as described in this section, try restarting your iPhone. If that does not work, reset your network settings, as described earlier in this chapter, and then set up each connection again manually.

Locate Your iPhone with Find My iPhone

If you have an iCloud account, you can use the Find My iPhone feature to locate your iPhone if it has been lost or stolen. You can also display a message on the iPhone — for example, to tell the finder how to contact you — or remotely wipe the data on the iPhone.

To use Find My iPhone, you must first set up your iCloud account on your iPhone, and then enable the Find My iPhone feature. Normally, you perform both actions while first setting up your iPhone.

Locate Your iPhone with Find My iPhone

Turn On the Find My iPhone Feature

1 Set up your iCloud account on your iPhone as discussed in "Set Up and Activate Your iPhone" in Chapter 1.

Note: You may have turned on the Find My iPhone feature when setting up your iCloud account.

2 Swipe up from the bottom of the screen.

The Home screen appears.

3 Tap **Settings** (⚙).

The Settings screen appears.

4 Tap **Apple ID**, the button that bears your Apple ID name.

The Apple ID screen appears.

5 Tap **Find My** (◉).

The Find My screen appears.

6 Tap **Find My iPhone** (◉).

The Find My iPhone screen appears.

7 Set the **Find My iPhone** switch to On (◯).

8 Set the **Enable Offline Finding** switch to On (◯).

9 Set the **Send Last Location** switch to On (◯) if you want your iPhone to send Apple its location when the battery runs critically low.

Locate Your iPhone Using Find My iPhone

1 On a computer, open a web browser, such as Microsoft Edge, Internet Explorer, Chrome, or Safari.

Note: On an iOS device, use the Find My app to locate a missing iPhone. You cannot use an Android device.

2 Click the Address box.

3 Type www.icloud.com and press Enter in Windows or Return on a Mac.

The Sign in to iCloud web page appears.

4 Type your username.

5 Type your password.

6 Click **Sign In** (→).

The iCloud site appears, displaying either the Home page or the page you last used.

Note: If you have set up two-step verification on your Apple ID, the Verify Your Identity screen may appear. Click the device to use for verification, and then enter the code sent to the device on the Enter Verification Code screen. In the Trust This Browser? dialog that opens, click **Trust** or **Don't Trust**, as appropriate.

Note: If iCloud displays a page other than the Home page, click **iCloud** and then click **Find My iPhone** ( ) on the pop-up panel. Go to step **8**.

7 Click **Find iPhone** ( ).

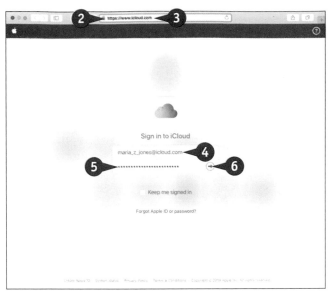

TIP

Is it worth displaying a message on my iPhone, or should I simply wipe it?
Almost always, it is definitely worth displaying a message on your iPhone. If you have lost your iPhone and someone has found it, that person may be trying to return it to you. The chances are good that the finder is honest, even if he has not discovered that you have locked the iPhone with a passcode. That said, if you are certain someone has stolen your iPhone, you may prefer simply to wipe it, using the technique explained next.

continued ▶

Find My iPhone is a powerful feature you can use when your iPhone goes missing.

If Find My iPhone reveals someone has taken your iPhone, you can wipe its contents to prevent anyone from hacking into your data. However, know that wiping your iPhone prevents you from locating the iPhone again — ever — except by chance. Wipe your iPhone only when you have lost it, you have no hope of recovering it, and you must destroy the data on it.

Locate Your iPhone with Find My iPhone (continued)

The iCloud Find My iPhone screen appears.

8 Click the pop-up menu at the top. Normally, this shows All Devices at first.

The My Devices pop-up panel appears.

9 Click your iPhone.

A Your iPhone's location appears.

The Info dialog appears, showing when the iPhone was last located.

10 If you want to play a sound on the iPhone, click **Play Sound** (🔊). This feature is primarily helpful for locating your iPhone if you have mislaid it somewhere nearby.

B A message indicates that the iPhone has played the sound.

Lock the iPhone with a Passcode

1 Click **Lost Mode** (◎) in the Info dialog.

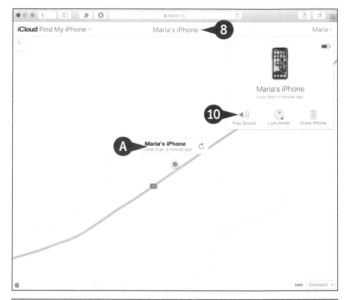

The Lost Mode dialog appears, prompting you to enter a phone number where you can be reached.

2 Optionally, click **Number** and type the number.

3 Click **Next**.

The Lost Mode dialog prompts you to enter a message.

4 Type a message to whoever finds your iPhone.

5 Click **Done**.

iCloud sends the lock request to the iPhone, which locks itself.

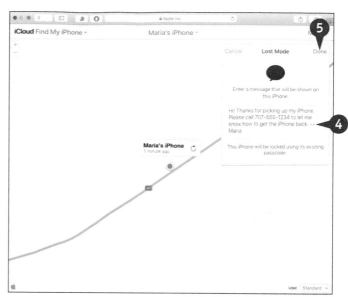

Remotely Erase Your iPhone

1 Click **Erase iPhone** (🗑) in the Info dialog.

The Erase This iPhone? dialog opens.

Note: If this iPhone is the last trusted device for your Apple ID, the Erase Last Trusted Device? dialog opens instead of the Erase This iPhone? dialog. Read the warning about having to use your Recovery Key to access your Apple ID. If you are sure you want to erase the iPhone, click **Erase**.

2 Click **Erase**.

iCloud sends the erase request to the iPhone, which erases its data.

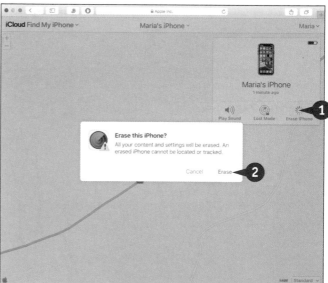

TIP

Can I remotely wipe the data on my iPhone if I do not have an iCloud account?

No, not remotely, but you can make the iPhone wipe itself. Set a passcode for the iPhone, as discussed in the section "Secure Your iPhone with Face ID and a Passcode" in Chapter 2, and then set the **Erase Data** switch on the Face ID & Passcode screen to On (⬤). This setting makes the iPhone automatically erase its data after ten successive failed attempts to enter the passcode. After five failed attempts, the iPhone enforces a delay before the next attempt; further failures increase the delay.

Manage Your Apple ID

Your iPhone uses your Apple ID for authentication and authorization. Using the Apple ID screen in the Settings app, you can review your Apple ID information and change it if necessary. For example, you may need to change your display name, add a payment method or shipping address, or verify that two-factor authentication is enabled for security. You can also edit the phone numbers and e-mail addresses at which you are reachable via iMessage and FaceTime.

Manage Your Apple ID

1 Swipe up from the bottom of the screen to display the Home screen.

2 Tap **Settings** (⚙) to display the Settings screen.

3 Tap **Apple ID**, the button that shows your Apple ID name, to display the Apple ID screen.

A To add a photo or update an existing photo, tap the account icon. In the Photo dialog that opens, tap **Take Photo** or **Choose Photo**, as appropriate, and then follow the prompts.

Note: At the bottom of the Apple ID screen is a Sign Out button that you can tap to sign out of your account.

4 Tap **Name, Phone Numbers, Email**.

Note: If the Sign In to iCloud dialog opens, type your password and then tap **OK**.

The Name, Phone Numbers, Email screen appears.

B You can tap **Name** and edit your name.

C You can add phone numbers and e-mail addresses to the Reachable At list by tapping **Edit** and then tapping **Add Email or Phone Number**.

5 In the Subscriptions section, set the switches to On (⬤) or Off (◯) to control which messages you receive.

6 Tap **Back** (‹).

The Apple ID screen appears again.

7 Tap **Password & Security**.

The Password & Security screen appears.

D You can tap **Change Password** and follow the prompts to change your Apple ID password.

8 Verify that the Two-Factor Authentication button shows On. If not, follow the prompts to enable two-factor authentication.

E You can tap **Edit** and then change your trusted phone numbers.

F You can tap **Get Verification Code** to get a code for signing in on another device or at iCloud.com.

9 Tap **Apple ID** (<).

The Apple ID screen appears.

10 Tap **Payment & Shipping**.

The Payment & Shipping screen appears.

G You can tap **Add Payment Method** to add a payment method.

H You can tap **Add Shipping Address** to add a shipping address.

11 Tap **Apple ID** (<).

The Apple ID screen appears.

12 Tap the button for your iPhone.

The Device Info screen appears.

13 Verify that the Find My iPhone button shows On. If not, tap **Find My iPhone** and set the **Find My iPhone** switch to On ( ).

I You can view your phone's details.

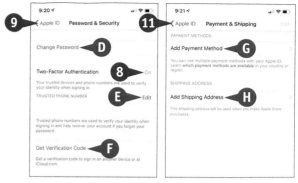

14 Tap **Apple ID** (<).

The Apple ID screen appears.

15 Tap **iTunes & App Stores**.

The iTunes & App Stores screen appears.

16 In the Automatic Downloads area, set each switch to On ( ) or Off ( ), as needed.

TIPS

How do I use a different Apple ID for the iTunes and App Store?

On the iTunes & App Stores screen, tap **Apple ID**. In the Apple ID dialog that opens, tap **Sign Out**. Tap **Apple ID** again to open the Apple ID Sign-in Requested dialog. Type the Apple ID and password you want to use, and then tap **Sign In**.

What does the Offload Unused Apps switch control?

Set the **Offload Unused Apps** switch to On ( ) if you want iOS to delete apps you have not used for a while. iOS keeps any documents you created in the app.

Index

Index